LONGER POEMS

OLD AND NEW

Selected and Edited by

A. S. CAIRNCROSS

M.A., D.LITT.

D1389680

MACMILLAN AND CO., LIMITED
ST. MARTIN'S STREET, LONDON
1947

B. MacLean IV

B. MacLean

Fiona Shiell V

BILLY MacLEAN Class IV

Billy MacLean Class IV 1958-59

Lila MacDonald VITA
1957-58

Fiona Shiell IV

Fiona Shiell IV
Session 1958-59

Fiona Shiell V. 1959-60.

Gair McKay IV 1960-61

Gair McKay IV 1960-61

Sheena IV

Sheena Shiell IV - 1961-62.

Margaret MacLean IV 1962-63

John McFarlane IV 1970-71

THE SCHOLAR'S LIBRARY
General Editor :—Guy Boas, M.A.

LONGER POEMS OLD AND NEW

ACKNOWLEDGMENTS

THE compiler wishes to express his indebtedness to the following, who have kindly given him permission to reprint the copyright poems included in this volume : Professor Lascelles Abercrombie and Messrs. John Lane, The Bodley Head Limited, for " Indignation : An Ode ", from *Interludes and Poems* ; Mr. Roy Campbell, for " Tristan da Cunha " ; Mr. G. K. Chesterton and Messrs. Burns, Oates and Washbourne, Ltd., for " Lepanto," from the author's *Collected Poems* ; the Clarendon Press, for " Elegy," from *Shorter Poems*, by Robert Bridges ; the Executors of the late Thomas Hardy, for " The Sacrilege," from the author's *Collected Poems* ; Messrs. William Heinemann, Ltd., for the Choruses from *Atalanta in Calydon*, by A. C. Swinburne ; Mr. Ralph Hodgson, for " The Song of Honour " from his *Poems* ; Mr. Aldous Huxley, for " Theatre of Varieties " ; and Mr. Wilfrid Meynell and Messrs. Burns, Oates & Washbourne, Ltd., for " The Hound of Heaven," by Francis Thompson.

PREFACE

THE long poem is to the short what a symphony of Beethoven is to a prelude of Chopin. The difference is not only of length : it is of range and complexity. The shorter form gives a moment's life to some fragment of experience—a casual emotion, a graceful fancy, the merest thread of incident : the longer demands some great argument, seen complete against the background of the universe. The lyric poem is a statement, like the prelude, of one primary simple theme : the long poem, like the symphony, introduces together themes as various and as wide as experience itself. Here the poet scans affairs, social and political, as do Mr. Huxley and Professor Abercrombie ; he soars into metaphysics, like Francis Thompson, and from that height plumbs the depths of the heart ; he criticises ecclesiastical administration like Milton, studies history like Matthew Arnold, or psychology like Browning. Taking the universe thus for his province, the poet transmutes it successfully into poetry when he has himself risen to view the wide prospect steadily and as a whole.

So to bring the universe together at one point calls for a knowledge, judgment, and character, not normally required for a short poem. Milton, with *Paradise Lost* in view, considered it necessary to add to many other requisites " industrious and select reading, steady observation, insight into all seemly and generous arts and affairs," and wrote, as the conclusion of the whole matter, " He who would not be frustrate of his hope to write well hereafter in laudable things, ought himself to be a true poem."

The range and complexity of the long poem make it relatively difficult to appreciate. The length, the frequent artificial treatment of the subject, and the intricate structure, are apt at first to puzzle and repel those to whom poetry in its simpler forms makes an immediate appeal. These difficulties must be faced by the lover of poetry as they are by the lover of music. The effort is repaid manyfold. The long poem is more generally and permanently satisfying. " A very short poem," says Edgar Allan Poe, " while now and then producing a brilliant and vivid, never produces a profound or enduring effect. There must be the steady pressing down of the stamp upon the wax." So, in music, George Eliot finally found supreme pleasure in " concerted music, which is the only music I care for much now." How many lyrics, for profound and enduring effect, will bear comparison with *Lycidas*, *The Rape of the Lock*, *Thyrsis*, or *Tintern Abbey* ? We return to the lyrics oftener, perhaps, for their very lightness and ease ; but for a deeper pleasure, inspiration, or consolation, it is to the longer poems that we must go.

A. S. C.

CONTENTS

CONTENTS

THE PARDONER'S TALE

In Flaundrès whilom was a compaignye
Of yongè folk, that haunteden folye,

. . .

They daunce and pleyen at dees, bothe day and nyght,
And eten also, and drynken over hir myght.

. . .

Thise riotourès thre, of which I telle,
Longe erst er primè rong of any belle,
Were set hem in a tavernè to drynke ;
And as they sat they herde a bellè clynke
Biforn a cors, was caried to his grave.
That oon of hem gan callen to his knave :   10
" Go bet," quod he, " and axè redily
What cors is this that passeth heer forby,
And lookè that thou reporte his namè weel."
    " Sire," quod this boy, " it nedeth never a deel ;
It was me toold er ye cam heere two houres ;
He was, *pardee*, an old felawe of youres,
And sodeynly he was y-slayn to-nyght ;
For-dronke, as he sat on his bench upright ;
Ther cam a privee theef men clepeth Deeth,
That in this contree al the peplè sleeth,   20
And with his spere he smoot his herte atwo,
And wente his wey withouten wordès mo.
He hath a thousand slayn this pestilence ;
And, maister, ere ye come in his presence,
Me thynketh that it werè necessarie

E   I

For to be war of swich an adversarie.
Beth redy for to meete hym everemoore ;
Thus taughté me my dame ; I sey na-moore."
   " By seinté Marié ! " seyde this taverner,
" The child seith sooth, for he hath slayn this yeer
Henne over a mile, withinne a greet village,
Bothe man and womman, child, and hyne, and page ;
I trowe his habitacioun be there ;
To been avyséd greet wysdom it were,
Er that he dide a man a dishonour."   10
   " Ye, Goddés armés ! " quod this riotour,
" Is it swich peril with hym for to meete ?
I shall hym seke by wey, and eek by strete
I make avow to Goddés digné bones !
Herkneth, felawés, we thre been al ones,
Lat ech of us holde up his hand til oother,
And ech of us bicomen otheres brother,
And we wol sleen this falsé traytour, Deeth ;
He shal be slayn, which that so manye sleeth,
By Goddés dignitee, er it be nyght ! "   20
   Togidres han thise thre hir trouthés plight
To lyve and dyen ech of hem for oother,
As though he were his owene y-born brother ;
And up they stirte, al dronken, in this rage,
And forth they goon towardés that village
Of which the taverner hadde spoke biforn.
And many a grisly ooth thanne han they sworn ;
And Cristés blessed body they to-rente,—
Deeth shal be deed, if that they may hym hente.
   Whan they han goon nat fully half a mile,   30
Right as they wolde han troden over a stile,
An oold man and a pouré with hem mette.
This oldé man ful mekély hem grette,
And seydé thus : " Now, lordés, God yow see ! "
   The proudest of thise riotourés three
Answerde agayn, " What, carl, with sory grace,
Why artow al for-wrappéd save thy face ?

Why lyvėstow so longe in so greet age ? "
  This oldė man gan looke in his visage,
And seydė thus : " For I ne kan nat fynde
A man, though that I walkėd into Ynde,
Neither in citee, nor in no village,
That woldė chaunge his youthė for myn age ;
And therfore moot I han myn agė stille,
As longė tyme as it is Goddės wille ;
Ne Deeth, allas ! ne wol nat han my lyf.
Thus walke I, lyk a restėlees kaityf.   10
And on the ground, which is my moodrės gate,
I knokkė with my staf, bothe erly and late,
And seyė, ' Leevė mooder, leet me in !
Lo, how I vanysshe, flessh and blood and skyn ;
Allas ! whan shul my bonės been at reste ?
Mooder, with yow wolde I chaungė my cheste
That in my chambrė longė tyme hath be,
Ye, for an heyrė-clowt to wrappė me ! '
But yet to me she wol nat do that grace,
For which ful pale and welkėd is my face.   20

  " But, sires, to yow it is no curteisye
To speken to an old man vileynye,
But he trespasse in word, or elles in dede.
In hooly writ ye may your self wel rede,
' Agayns an oold man, hoor upon his heed,
Ye sholde arise ' ; wherfore I yeve yow reed,
Ne dooth unto an oold man noon harm now,
Namoorė than that ye wolde men did to yow
In agė, if that ye so longe abyde.
And God be with yow, wher ye go or ryde ;   30
I moot go thider as I have to go."

  " Nay, oldė cherl, by God, thou shalt nat so ! "
Seydė this oother hasardour anon ;
" Thou partest nat so lightly, by seint John !
Thou spak right now of thilkė traytour, Deeth,
That in this contree alle oure freendės sleeth ;
Have heer my trouthe, as thou art his espye,

3

Telle where he is, or thou shalt it abye,
By God and by the hooly sacrement !
For soothly, thou art oon of his assent
To sleen us yongè folk, thou falsè theef ! "
  " Now, sires," quod he, " if that ye be so leef
To fyndè Deeth, turne up this croked wey,
For in that grove I lafte hym, by my fey,
Under a tree, and there he wole abyde ;
Noght for youre boost he wole him no thyng hyde.
Se ye that ook ?   Right there ye shal hym fynde.   10
God savè yow that boghte agayn mankynde,
And yow amende ! " thus seyde this oldè man ;
And evèrich of thise riotourès ran
Til he cam to that tree, and ther they founde,
Of floryns fyne, of gold y-coynèd rounde,
Wel ny an eightè busshels, as hem thoughte.
No lenger thannè after Deeth they soughte,
But ech of hem so glad was of that sighte,
For that the floryns been so faire and brighte,
That doun they sette hem by this precious hoord.   20
The worste of hem he spak the firstè word.
  " Bretheren," quod he, " taak kepè what I seye ;
My wit is greet, though that I bourde and pleye.
This tresor hath Fortúne unto us yeven
In myrthe and joliftee oure lyf to lyven ;
And lightly as it comth so wol we spende.
Ey, Goddès precious dignitee ! who wende
To-day, that we sholde han so fair a grace ?
But myghte this gold be caried fro this place
Hoom to myn hous, or ellès unto youres,—   30
For wel ye woot that al this gold is oures,—
Thanne werè we in heigh felicitee.
But trewèly, by daye it may nat bee ;
Men woldè seyn that we were thevès stronge,
And for oure owenè tresor doon us honge.
This tresor moste y-caried be by nyghte
As wisely and as slyly as it myghte.

4

Wherfore, I rede that cut among us alle
Be drawe, and lat se wher the cut wol falle ;
And he that hath the cut with hertè blithe
Shal rennè to the towne, and that ful swithe,
And brynge us breed and wyn ful privèly,
And two of us shul kepen subtilly
This tresor wel ; and if he wol nat tarie,
Whan it is nyght we wol this tresor carie,
By oon assent, where as us thynketh best."
That oon of hem the cut broghte in his fest,   10
And bad hem drawe and looke where it wol falle ;
And it fil on the yongeste of hem alle,
And forth toward the toun he wente anon ;
And al so soonè as that he was gon,
That oon of hem spak thus unto that oother :
" Thow knowest wel thou art my swornè brother ;
Thy profit wol I tellè thee anon ;
Thou woost wel that oure felawe is agon,
And heere is gold, and that ful greet plentee,
That shal departèd been among us thre ;   20
But nathèlees, if I kan shape it so
That it departed were among us two,
Hadde I nat doon a freendès torn to thee ? "
    That oother answerde, " I noot how that may be ;
He woot how that the gold is with us tweye ;
What shal we doon ? what shal we to hym seye ? "
    " Shal it be conseil ? " seyde the firstè shrewe,
" And I shal tellen in a wordès fewe
What we shal doon, and bryngen it wel aboute."
    " I grauntè," quod that oother, " out of doute,   30
That by my trouthe I shal thee nat biwreye."
" Now," quod the firste, " thou woost wel we be
        tweye,
And two of us shul strenger be than oon.
Looke whan that he is set, and right anoon
Arys, as though thou woldest with hym pleye,
And I shal ryve hym thurgh the sydès tweye,

Whil that thou strogelest with hym as in game,
And with thy daggere looke thou do the same ;
And thanne shal al this gold departed be,
My deerė freend, bitwixen me and thee.
Thanne may we bothe oure lustės all fulfille,
And pleye at dees right at oure owene wille."
And thus acorded been thise shrewės tweye,
To sleen the thridde, as ye han herd me seye.

This yongeste, which that wente unto the toun
Ful ofte in herte he rolleth up and doun   10
The beautee of thise floryns newe and brighte ;
" O Lord," quod he, " if so were that I myghte
Have al this tresor to my self allone,
Ther is no man that lyveth under the trone
Of God, that sholdė lyve so murye as I ! "
And attė laste the feend, oure enemy,
Putte in his thought that he sholde poyson beye,
With which he myghtė sleen hise felawes tweye ;
For-why the feend foond hym in swich lyvynge,
That he hadde levė hym to sorwė brynge,   20
For this was outrėly his fulle entente
To sleen hem bothe and never to repente.
And forth he gooth, no lenger wolde he tarie,
Into the toun, unto a pothecarie,
And preydė hym that he hym woldė selle
Som poysoun, that he myghte his rattės quelle ;
And eek ther was a polcat in his hawe,
That, as he seyde, hise capouns hadde y-slawe ;
And fayn he woldė wreke hym, if he myghte,
On vermyn, that destroyėd hym by nyghte.   30
The pothecarie answerdė, " And thou shalt have
A thyng that, al so God my soulė save !
In al this world ther is no creäture,
That eten or dronken hath of this confiture,
Noght but the montance of a corn of whete,
That he ne shal his lif anon forlete ;
Ye, sterve he shal, and that in lassė while

6

Than thou wolt goon a-paas nat but a mile ;
This poysoun is so strong and violent."
 This cursèd man hath in his hond y-hent
This poysoun in a box, and sith he ran
Into the nextè strete unto a man,
And borwèd hym largè botellès thre.
And in the two his poyson pourèd he ;
The thridde he kepte clene for his owenè drynke ;
For al the nyght he shoope hym for to swynke
In cariynge of the gold out of that place.   10
And whan this riotour with sory grace
Hadde filled with wyn his gretè botels thre,
To hise felawes agayn repaireth he.
 What nedeth it to sermone of it moore ?
For right as they hadde cast his deeth bifoore,
Right so they han hym slayn, and that anon,
And whan that this was doon thus spak that oon :
" Now lat us sitte and drynke, and make us merie,
And afterward we wol his body berie " ;
And with that word it happèd hym, *par cas*,   20
To take the botel ther the poysoun was,
And drank and yaf his felawe drynke also,
For which anon they storven bothè two.

GEOFFREY CHAUCER

LYCIDAS

[In this Monody the Author bewails a learned Friend, un-
fortunately drown'd in his Passage from Chester on the Irish Seas,
1637. And by occasion foretels the ruine of our corrupted
Clergy then in their height.]

YET once more, O ye Laurels, and once more
Ye Myrtles brown, with Ivy never-sear,
I com to pluck your Berries harsh and crude,
And with forc'd fingers rude,
Shatter your leaves before the mellowing year.

Bitter constraint, and sad occasion dear,
Compels me to disturb your season due :
For Lycidas is dead, dead ere his prime,
Young Lycidas, and hath not left his peer :
Who would not sing for Lycidas ? he knew
Himself to sing, and build the lofty rhyme.
He must not flote upon his watry bear
Unwept, and welter to the parching wind,
Without the meed of som melodious tear.

Begin then, Sisters of the sacred well,   10
That from beneath the seat of Jove doth spring,
Begin, and somwhat loudly sweep the string.
Hence with denial vain, and coy excuse,
So may som gentle Muse
With lucky words favour my destin'd Urn,
And as he passes turn,
And bid fair peace be to my sable shrowd.
For we were nurst upon the self-same hill,
Fed the same flock, by fountain, shade, and rill.
Together both, ere the high Lawns appear'd   20
Under the opening eye-lids of the morn,
We drove a field, and both together heard
What time the Gray-fly winds her sultry horn,
Batt'ning our flocks with the fresh dews of night,
Oft till the Star that rose, at Ev'ning, bright
Toward Heav'ns descent had slop'd his westering
        wheel.
Mean while the Rural ditties were not mute,
Temper'd to th'Oaten Flute ;
Rough Satyrs danc'd, and Fauns with clov'n heel,
From the glad sound would not be absent long,   30
And old Damoetas lov'd to hear our song.

But O the heavy change, now thou art gon,
Now thou art gon, and never must return !
Thee, Shepherd, thee the Woods, and desert Caves,
With wilde Thyme and the gadding Vine o'regrown,
And all their echoes mourn.

The Willows, and the Hazle Copses green,
Shall now no more be seen,
Fanning their joyous Leaves to thy soft layes.
As killing as the Canker to the Rose,
Or Taint-worm to the weanling Herds that graze,
Or Frost to Flowers, that their gay wardrop wear,
When first the White thorn blows ;
Such, Lycidas, thy loss to Shepherds ear.

   Where were ye Nymphs when the remorseless
     deep
Clos'd o're the head of your lov'd Lycidas ?   10
For neither were ye playing on the steep,
Where your old Bards, the famous Druids ly,
Nor on the shaggy top of Mona high,
Nor yet where Deva spreads her wisard stream :
Ay me, I fondly dream !
Had ye bin there—for what could that have don ?
What could the Muse her self that Orpheus bore,
The Muse her self, for her inchanting son
Whom Universal nature did lament,
When by the rout that made the hideous roar,   20
His goary visage down the stream was sent,
Down the swift Hebrus to the Lesbian shore.

   Alas ! What boots it with uncessant care
To tend the homely slighted Shepherds trade,
And strictly meditate the thankles Muse,
Were it not better don as others use,
To sport with Amaryllis in the shade,
Or with the tangles of Neaera's hair ?
Fame is the spur that the clear spirit doth raise
(That last infirmity of Noble mind)   30
To scorn delights, and live laborious dayes ;
But the fair Guerdon when we hope to find,
And think to burst out into sudden blaze,
Comes the blind Fury with th'abhorred shears,
And slits the thin spun life. But not the praise,
Phoebus repli'd, and touch'd my trembling ears ;

Fame is no plant that grows on mortal soil,
Nor in the glistering foil
Set off to th'world, nor in broad rumour lies,
But lives and spreds aloft by those pure eyes,
And perfet witnes of all judging Jove ;
As he pronounces lastly on each deed,
Of so much fame in Heav'n expect thy meed.

   O Fountain Arethuse, and thou honour'd floud,
Smooth-sliding Mincius, crown'd with vocall reeds,
That strain I heard was of a higher mood :   10
But now my Oate proceeds,
And listens to the Herald of the Sea
That came in Neptune's plea,
He ask'd the Waves, and ask'd the Fellon winds,
What hard mishap hath doom'd this gentle swain ?
And question'd every gust of rugged wings
That blows from off each beaked Promontory.
They knew not of his story,
And sage Hippotades their answer brings,
That not a blast was from his dungeon stray'd,   20
The Ayr was calm, and on the level brine,
Sleek Panope with all her sisters play'd.
It was that fatall and perfidious Bark
Built in th'eclipse, and rigg'd with curses dark,
That sunk so low that sacred head of thine.

   Next Camus, reverend Sire, went footing slow,
His Mantle hairy, and his Bonnet sedge,
Inwrought with figures dim, and on the edge
Like to that sanguine flower inscrib'd with woe.
Ah ; Who hath reft (quoth he) my dearest pledge? 30
Last came, and last did go,
The Pilot of the Galilean lake,
Two massy Keyes he bore of metals twain,
(The Golden opes, the Iron shuts amain)
He shook his Miter'd locks, and stern bespake,
How well could I have spar'd for thee, young swain,
Anow of such as for their bellies sake,

Creep and intrude, and climb into the fold ?
Of other care they little reck'ning make,
Then how to scramble at the shearers feast,
And shove away the worthy bidden guest.
Blind mouthes ! that scarce themselves know how to
    hold
A Sheep-hook, or have learn'd ought els the least
That to the faithfull Herdmans art belongs !
What recks it them ? What need they ? They are
    sped
And when they list, their lean and flashy songs
Grate on their scrannel Pipes of wretched straw, 10
The hungry Sheep look up, and are not fed,
But swoln with wind, and the rank mist they draw,
Rot inwardly, and foul contagion spread :
Besides what the grim Woolf with privy paw
Daily devours apace, and nothing sed,
But that two-handed engine at the door,
Stands ready to smite once, and smite no more.
    Return Alpheus, the dread voice is past,
That shrunk thy streams ; Return Sicilian Muse,
And call the Vales, and bid them hither cast 20
Their Bels, and Flourets of a thousand hues.
Ye valleys low where the milde whispers use,
Of shades and wanton winds, and gushing brooks,
On whose fresh lap the swart Star sparely looks,
Throw hither all your quaint enameld eyes,
That on the green terf suck the honied showres,
And purple all the ground with vernal flowres.
Bring the rathe Primrose that forsaken dies.
The tufted Crow-toe, and pale Gessamine,
The white Pink, and the Pansie freakt with jeat, 30
The glowing Violet,
The Musk-rose, and the well attir'd Woodbine,
With Cowslips wan that hang the pensive hed,
And every flower that sad embroidery wears :
Bid Amaranthus all his beauty shed,

And Daffadillies fill their cups with tears,
To strew the Laureat Herse where Lycid lies.
For so to interpose a little ease,
Let our frail thoughts dally with false surmise.
Ay me ! Whilst thee the shores, and sounding Seas
Wash far away, where ere thy bones are hurld,
Whether beyond the stormy Hebrides,
Where thou perhaps under the whelming tide
Visit'st the bottom of the monstrous world ;
Or whether thou to our moist vows deny'd,   10
Sleep'st by the fable of Bellerus old,
Where the great vision of the guarded Mount
Looks towards Namancos and Bayona's hold ;
Look homeward Angel now, and melt with ruth.
And, O ye Dolphins, waft the haples youth.
    Weep no more, woful Shepherds weep no more,
For Lycidas your sorrow is not dead,
Sunk though he be beneath the watry floar,
So sinks the day-star in the Ocean bed,
And yet anon repairs his drooping head,   20
And tricks his beams, and with new spangled Ore,
Flames in the forehead of the morning sky :
So Lycidas sunk low, but mounted high,
Through the dear might of him that walk'd the
    waves,
Where other groves, and other streams along,
With Nectar pure his oozy Lock's he laves,
And hears the unexpressive nuptiall Song,
In the blest Kingdoms meek of joy and love.
There entertain him all the Saints above,
In solemn troops, and sweet Societies   30
That sing, and singing in their glory move,
And wipe the tears for ever from his eyes.
Now Lycidas the Shepherds weep no more ;
Hence forth thou art the Genius of the shore,
In thy large recompense, and shalt be good
To all that wander in that perilous flood.

Thus sang the uncouth Swain to th'Okes and rills,
While the still morn went out with Sandals gray,
He touch'd the tender stops of various Quills,
With eager thought warbling his Dorick lay :
And now the Sun had stretch'd out all the hills,
And now was dropt into the Western bay ;
At last he rose, and twitch'd his Mantle blew :
To morrow to fresh Woods, and Pastures new.
                                        JOHN MILTON

CYMON AND IPHIGENIA

In that sweet isle, where Venus keeps her court,
And every grace, and all the loves, resort ;   10
Where either sex is formed of softer earth,
And takes the bent of pleasure from their birth ;
There lived a Cyprian lord, above the rest
Wise, wealthy, with a numerous issue blest.
But, as no gift of fortune is sincere,
Was only wanting in a worthy heir :
His eldest born, a goodly youth to view,
Excelled the rest in shape and outward shew,
Fair, tall, his limbs with due proportion joined,
But of a heavy, dull, degenerate mind.   20
His soul belied the features of his face ;
Beauty was there, but beauty in disgrace.
A clownish mien, a voice with rustic sound,
And stupid eyes that ever loved the ground,
He looked like Nature's error, as the mind
And body were not of a piece designed,
But made for two, and by mistake in one were joined.
The ruling rod, the father's forming care,
Were exercised in vain on wit's despair ;
The more informed, the less he understood,   30
And deeper sunk by floundering in the mud.
Now scorned of all, and grown the public shame,

13

The people from Galesus changed his name,
And Cymon called, which signifies a brute ;
So well his name did with his nature suit.

His father, when he found his labour lost,
And care employed that answered not the cost,
Chose an ungrateful object to remove,
And loathed to see what Nature made him love ;
So to his country-farm the fool confined ;
Rude work well suited with a rustic mind.
Thus to the wilds the sturdy Cymon went,   10
A squire among the swains, and pleased with banish-
      ment.

His corn and cattle were his only care,
And his supreme delight a country-fair.
  It happened on a summer's holiday,
That to the greenwood-shade he took his way ;
For Cymon shunned the church, and used not much
    to pray.
His quarter-staff, which he could ne'er forsake,
Hung half before and half behind his back.
He trudged along, unknowing what he sought,
And whistled as he went, for want of thought.   20

  By chance conducted, or by thirst constrained,
The deep recesses of the grove he gained ;
Where, in a plain defended by the wood,
Crept through the matted grass a crystal flood,
By which an alabaster fountain stood ;
And on the margin of the fount was laid,
Attended by her slaves, a sleeping maid ;
Like Dian and her nymphs, when, tired with sport,
To rest by cool Eurotas they resort.
The dame her self the goddess well expressed,   30
Not more distinguished by her purple vest
Than by the charming features of her face,
And, even in slumber, a superior grace :
Her comely limbs composed with decent care,
Her body shaded with a slight cymarr ;

Her bosom to the view was only bare :
Where two beginning paps were scarcely spied,
For yet their places were but signified :
The fanning wind upon her bosom blows,
To meet the fanning wind the bosom rose ;
The fanning wind and purling streams continue her
      repose.

  The fool of nature stood with stupid eyes,
And gaping mouth, that testified surprise,
Fixed on her face, nor could remove his sight,
New as he was to love, and novice in delight :   10
Long mute he stood, and leaning on his staff,
His wonder witnessed with an idiot laugh ;
Then would have spoke, but by his glimmering sense
First found his want of words, and feared offence :
Doubted for what he was he should be known,
By his clown-accent and his country-tone.

  Through the rude chaos thus the running light
Shot the first ray that pierced the native night :
Then day and darkness in the mass were mixed,
Till gathered in a globe the beams were fixed :   20
Last shone the sun, who, radiant in his sphere,
Illumined heaven and earth, and rolled around the
      year.
So reason in this brutal soul began :
Love made him first suspect he was a man ;
Love made him doubt his broad barbarian sound ;
By love his want of words and wit he found ;
That sense of want prepared the future way
To knowledge, and disclosed the promise of a day.

  What not his father's care nor tutor's art
Could plant with pains in his unpolished heart,   30
The best instructor, Love, at once inspired,
As barren grounds to fruitfulness are fired ;
Love taught him shame, and shame with love at strife
Soon taught the sweet civilities of life.
His gross material soul at once could find

Somewhat in her excelling all her kind ;
Exciting a desire till then unknown,
Somewhat unfound, or found in her alone.
This made the first impression in his mind,
Above, but just above, the brutal kind.
For beasts can like, but not distinguish too,
Nor their own liking by reflection know ;
Nor why they like or this or t'other face,
Or judge of this or that peculiar grace ;
But love in gross, and stupidly admire ;   10
As flies, allured by light, approach the fire.
Thus our man-beast, advancing by degrees,
First likes the whole, then separates what he sees ;
On several parts a several praise bestows,
The ruby lips, the well-proportioned nose,
The snowy skin, the raven-glossy hair,
The dimpled cheek, the forehead rising fair,
And even in sleep it self a smiling air.
From thence his eyes descending viewed the rest,
Her plump round arms, white hands, and heaving
        breast.   20
Long on the last he dwelt, though every part
A pointed arrow sped to pierce his heart.
   Thus in a trice a judge of beauty grown,
(A judge erected from a country clown,)
He longed to see her eyes in slumber hid,
And wished his own could pierce within the lid.
He would have waked her, but restrained his thought,
And love new-born the first good manners taught.
An awful fear his ardent wish withstood,
Nor durst disturb the goddess of the wood ;   30
For such she seemed by her celestial face,
Excelling all the rest of human race ;
And things divine, by common sense he knew,
Must be devoutly seen at distant view :
So checking his desire, with trembling heart
Gazing he stood, nor would nor could depart ;

Fixed as a pilgrim wildered in his way,
Who dares not stir by night, for fear to stray ;
But stands with awful eyes to watch the dawn of day.

At length awaking, Iphigene the fair
(So was the beauty called who caused his care)
Unclosed her eyes, and double day revealed,
While those of all her slaves in sleep were sealed.

The slavering cudden, propped upon his staff,
Stood ready gaping with a grinning laugh,
To welcome her awake, nor durst begin   10
To speak, but wisely kept the fool within.
Then she : " What make you, Cymon, here alone ? "
(For Cymon's name was round the country known,
Because descended of a noble race,
And for a soul ill sorted with his face.)

But still the sot stood silent with surprise,
With fixed regard on her new opened eyes,
And in his breast received the envenomed dart,
A tickling pain that pleased amid the smart.
But conscious of her form, with quick distrust   20
She saw his sparkling eyes, and feared his brutal lust.
This to prevent, she waked her sleepy crew,
And rising hasty took a short adieu.

Then Cymon first his rustic voice essayed,
With proffered service to the parting maid
To see her safe ; his hand she long denied,
But took at length, ashamed of such a guide.
So Cymon led her home, and leaving there,
No more would to his country clowns repair,
But sought his father's house, with better mind,   30
Refusing in the farm to be confined.

The father wondered at the son's return,
And knew not whether to rejoice or mourn ;
But doubtfully received, expecting still
To learn the secret causes of his altered will.
Nor was he long delayed : the first request
He made, was like his brothers to be dressed,

And, as his birth required, above the rest.
 With ease his suit was granted by his sire,
Distinguishing his heir by rich attire :
His body thus adorned, he next designed
With liberal arts to cultivate his mind ;
He sought a tutor of his own accord,
And studied lessons he before abhorred.
 Thus the man-child advanced, and learned so fast,
That in short time his equals he surpassed :
His brutal manners from his breast exiled,   10
His mien he fashioned, and his tongue he filed ;
In every exercise of all admired,
He seemed, nor only seemed, but was inspired :
Inspired by love, whose business is to please ;
He rode, he fenced, he moved with graceful ease,
More famed for sense, for courtly carriage more,
Than for his brutal folly known before.
 What then of altered Cymon shall we say,
But that the fire which choked in ashes lay,
A load too heavy for his soul to move,   20
Was upward blown below, and brushed away by love ?
Love made an active progress through his mind,
The dusky parts he cleared, the gross refined,
The drowsy waked ; and, as he went, impressed
The Maker's image on the human beast.
Thus was the man amended by desire,
And, though he loved perhaps with too much fire,
His father all his faults with reason scanned,
And liked an error of the better hand ;
Excused the excess of passion in his mind,   30
By flames too fierce, perhaps too much refined :
So Cymon, since his sire indulged his will,
Impetuous loved, and would be Cymon still ;
Galesus he disowned, and chose to bear
The name of fool, confirmed and bishoped by the fair.
 To Cipseus by his friends his suit he moved,
Cipseus the father of the fair he loved ;

But he was pre-engaged by former ties,
While Cymon was endeavouring to be wise ;
And Iphigene, obliged by former vows,
Had given her faith to wed a foreign spouse :
Her sire and she to Rhodian Pasimond,
Though both repenting, were by promise bound,
Nor could retract ; and thus, as Fate decreed,
Though better loved, he spoke too late to speed.
   The doom was past ; the ship already sent
Did all his tardy diligence prevent ;   10
Sighed to her self the fair unhappy maid,
While stormy Cymon thus in secret said :
" The time is come for Iphigene to find
" The miracle she wrought upon my mind ;
" Her charms have made me man, her ravished love
" In rank shall place me with the blessed above.
" For mine by love, by force she shall be mine,
" Or death, if force should fail, shall finish my design."
      Resolved he said ; and rigged with speedy care
A vessel strong, and well equipped for war.   20
The secret ship with chosen friends he stored,
And bent to die, or conquer, went aboard.
Ambushed he lay behind the Cyprian shore,
Waiting the sail that all his wishes bore ;
Nor long expected, for the following tide
Sent out the hostile ship and beauteous bride.
   To Rhodes the rival bark directly steered,
When Cymon sudden at her back appeared,
And stopped her flight : then standing on his prow,
In haughty terms he thus defied the foe :   30
" Or strike your sails at summons, or prepare
" To prove the last extremities of war."
Thus warned, the Rhodians for the fight provide ;
Already were the vessels side by side,
These obstinate to save, and those to seize the bride.
But Cymon soon his crooked grapples cast,
Which with tenacious hold his foes embraced,

And, armed with sword and shield, amid the press he
    passed.
Fierce was the fight, but hastening to his prey,
By force the furious lover freed his way ;
Him self alone dispersed the Rhodian crew,
The weak disdained, the valiant overthrew ;
Cheap conquest for his following friends remained,
He reaped the field, and they but only gleaned.

  His victory confessed, the foes retreat,
And cast their weapons at the victor's feet.
Whom thus he cheered: "O Rhodian youth, I fought 10
" For love alone, nor other booty sought ;
" Your lives are safe ; your vessel I resign,
" Yours be your own, restoring what is mine ;
" In Iphigene I claim my rightful due,
" Robbed by my rival, and detained by you :
" Your Pasimond a lawless bargain drove,
" The parent could not sell the daughter's love ;
" Or if he could, my love disdains the laws,
" And like a king by conquest gains his cause ;
" Where arms take place, all other pleas are vain; 20
" Love taught me force, and force shall love maintain.
" You, what by strength you could not keep, release,
" And at an easy ransom buy your peace."

    Fear on the conquered side soon signed the accord,
And Iphigene to Cymon was restored.
While to his arms the blushing bride he took,
To seeming sadness she composed her look ;
As if by force subjected to his will,
Though pleased, dissembling, and a woman still.
And, for she wept, he wiped her falling tears, 30
And prayed her to dismiss her empty fears ;
" For yours I am," he said, " and have deserved
" Your love much better, whom so long I served,
" Than he to whom your formal father tied
" Your vows, and sold a slave, not sent a bride."
Thus while he spoke, he seized the willing prey,

As Paris bore the Spartan spouse away.
Faintly she screamed, and even her eyes confessed
She rather would be thought, than was, distressed.
    Who now exults but Cymon in his mind?
Vain hopes and empty joys of human kind,
Proud of the present, to the future blind!
Secure of fate, while Cymon ploughs the sea,
And steers to Candy with his conquered prey,
Scarce the third glass of measured hours was run,
When like a fiery meteor sunk the sun,   10
The promise of a storm; the shifting gales
Forsake by fits and fill the flagging sails;
Hoarse murmurs of the main from far were heard,
And night came on, not by degrees prepared,
But all at once; at once the winds arise,
The thunders roll, the forky lightning flies.
In vain the master issues out commands,
In vain the trembling sailors ply their hands;
The tempest unforeseen prevents their care,
And from the first they labour in despair.   20
The giddy ship betwixt the winds and tides,
Forced back and forwards, in a circle rides,
Stunned with the different blows; then shoots amain,
Till counterbuffed she stops, and sleeps again.
Not more aghast the proud archangel fell,
Plunged from the height of heaven to deepest hell,
Than stood the lover of his love possessed,
Now cursed the more, the more he had been blessed;
More anxious for her danger than his own,
Death he defies, but would be lost alone.   30
    Sad Iphigene to womanish complaints
Adds pious prayers, and wearies all the saints;
Even if she could, her love she would repent,
But since she cannot, dreads the punishment:
Her forfeit faith and Pasimond betrayed
Are ever present, and her crime upbraid.
She blames her self, nor blames her lover less;

Augments her anger as her fears increase ;
From her own back the burden would remove,
And lays the load on his ungoverned love,
Which interposing durst, in Heaven's despite,
Invade and violate another's right :
The Powers incensed awhile deferred his pain,
And made him master of his vows in vain :
But soon they punished his presumptuous pride ;
That for his daring enterprise she died,
Who rather not resisted than complied.   10

Then, impotent of mind, with altered sense,
She hugged the offender, and forgave the offence,
Sex to the last. Mean time with sails declined
The wandering vessel drove before the wind,
Tossed and retossed, aloft, and then alow ;
Nor port they seek, nor certain course they know,
But every moment wait the coming blow.
Thus blindly driven, by breaking day they viewed
The land before them, and their fears renewed ;
The land was welcome, but the tempest bore   20
The threatened ship against a rocky shore.

A winding bay was near ; to this they bent,
And just escaped ; their force already spent.
Secure from storms, and panting from the sea,
The land unknown at leisure they survey ;
And saw (but soon their sickly sight withdrew)
The rising towers of Rhodes at distant view ;
And cursed the hostile shore of Pasimond,
Saved from the seas, and shipwrecked on the ground.

The frighted sailors tried their strength in vain   30
To turn the stern, and tempt the stormy main ;
But the stiff wind withstood the labouring oar,
And forced them forward on the fatal shore !
The crooked keel now bites the Rhodian strand,
And the ship moored constrains the crew to land :
Yet still they might be safe, because unknown ;
But as ill fortune seldom comes alone,

The vessel they dismissed was driven before,
Already sheltered on their native shore ;
Known each, they know, but each with change of
    cheer ;
The vanquished side exults ; the victors fear ;
Not them but theirs, made prisoners ere they fight,
Despairing conquest, and deprived of flight.

  The country rings around with loud alarms,
And raw in fields the rude militia swarms ;
Mouths without hands ; maintained at vast expense,
In peace a charge, in war a weak defence ;   10
Stout once a month they march, a blustering band,
And ever, but in times of need, at hand ;
This was the morn when, issuing on the guard,
Drawn up in rank and file they stood prepared
Of seeming arms to make a short essay,
Then hasten to be drunk, the business of the day.

  The cowards would have fled, but that they knew
Them selves so many, and their foes so few ;
But crowding on, the last the first impel,
Till overborne with weight the Cyprians fell.   20
Cymon enslaved, who first the war begun,
And Iphigene once more is lost and won.

  Deep in a dungeon was the captive cast,
Deprived of day, and held in fetters fast ;
His life was only spared at their request,
Whom taken he so nobly had released :
But Iphigenia was the ladies' care,
Each in their turn addressed to treat the fair ;
While Pasimond and his the nuptial feast prepare.

  Her secret soul to Cymon was inclined,   30
But she must suffer what her fates assigned ;
So passive is the church of womankind.
What worse to Cymon could his fortune deal,
Rolled to the lowest spoke of all her wheel ?
It rested to dismiss the downward weight,
Or raise him upward to his former height ;

The latter pleased ; and love (concerned the most)
Prepared the amends for what by love he lost.
   The sire of Pasimond had left a son,
Though younger, yet for courage early known,
Ormisda called, to whom, by promise tied,
A Rhodian beauty was the destined bride ;
Cassandra was her name, above the rest
Renowned for birth, with fortune amply blessed.
Lysimachus, who ruled the Rhodian state,
Was then by choice their annual magistrate :   10
He loved Cassandra too with equal fire,
But Fortune had not favoured his desire ;
Crossed by her friends, by her not disapproved,
Nor yet preferred, or like Ormisda loved :
So stood the affair : some little hope remained,
That, should his rival chance to lose, he gained.
   Meantime young Pasimond his marriage pressed,
Ordained the nuptial day, prepared the feast ;
And frugally resolved (the charge to shun,
Which would be double should he wed alone,)   20
To join his brother's bridal with his own.
   Lysimachus, oppressed with mortal grief,
Received the news, and studied quick relief :
The fatal day approached ; if force were used,
The magistrate his public trust abused ;
To justice liable, as law required,
For when his office ceased, his power expired :
While power remained, the means were in his hand
By force to seize, and then forsake the land :
Betwixt extremes he knew not how to move,   30
A slave to fame, but more a slave to love :
Restraining others, yet him self not free,
Made impotent by power, debased by dignity.
Both sides he weighed : but after much debate,
The man prevailed above the magistrate.
   Love never fails to master what he finds,
But works a different way in different minds,

The fool enlightens, and the wise he blinds.
This youth proposing to possess and scape,
Began in murder, to conclude in rape :
Unpraised by me, though Heaven sometime may bless
An impious act with undeserved success :
The great, it seems, are privileged alone,
To punish all injustice but their own.
But here I stop, not daring to proceed,
Yet blush to flatter an unrighteous deed ;
For crimes are but permitted, not decreed.   10
    Resolved on force, his wit the praetor bent
To find the means that might secure the event ;
Nor long he laboured, for his lucky thought
In captive Cymon found the friend he sought.
The example pleased : the cause and crime the same,
An injured lover and a ravished dame.
How much he durst he knew by what he dared,
The less he had to lose, the less he cared
To menage loathsome life when love was the reward.
    This pondered well, and fixed on his intent,   20
In depth of night he for the prisoner sent ;
In secret sent, the public view to shun,
Then with a sober smile he thus begun :
" The Powers above, who bounteously bestow
" Their gifts and graces on mankind below,
" Yet prove our merit first, nor blindly give
" To such as are not worthy to receive :
" For valour and for virtue they provide
" Their due reward, but first they must be tried :
" These fruitful seeds within your mind they sowed : 30
" 'Twas yours to improve the talent they bestowed ;
" They gave you to be born of noble kind,
" They gave you love to lighten up your mind
" And purge the grosser parts ; they gave you care
" To please, and courage to deserve the fair.
   " Thus far they tried you, and by proof they found
" The grain entrusted in a grateful ground :

" But still the great experiment remained,
" They suffered you to lose the prize you gained,
" That you might learn the gift was theirs alone,
" And, when restored, to them the blessing own.
" Restored it soon will be ; the means prepared,
" The difficulty smoothed, the danger shared :
" But be your self, the care to me resign,
" Then Iphigene is yours, Cassandra mine.
" Your rival Pasimond pursues your life,
" Impatient to revenge his ravished wife,   10
" But yet not his ; to-morrow is behind,
" And Love our fortunes in one band has joined :
" Two brothers are our foes, Ormisda mine
" As much declared as Pasimond is thine :
" To-morrow must their common vows be tied :
" With Love to friend, and Fortune for our guide,
" Let both resolve to die, or each redeem a bride.
    " Right I have none, nor hast thou much to plead ;
" 'Tis force, when done, must justify the deed :
" Our task performed, we next prepare for flight : 20
" And let the losers talk in vain of right :
" We with the fair will sail before the wind ;
" If they are grieved, I leave the laws behind.
" Speak thy resolves : if now thy courage droop,
" Despair in prison and abandon hope ;
" But if thou darest in arms thy love regain,
" (For liberty without thy love were vain :)
" Then second my design to seize the prey,
" Or lead to second rape, for well thou knowest the
        way."
    Said Cymon, overjoyed : " Do thou propose   30
" The means to fight, and only show the foes :
" For from the first, when love had fired my mind,
" Resolved, I left the care of life behind."
    To this the bold Lysimachus replied,
" Let Heaven be neuter and the sword decide :
" The spousals are prepared, already play

26

" The minstrels, and provoke the tardy day :
" By this the brides are waked, their grooms are
        dressed ;
" All Rhodes is summoned to the nuptial feast,
" All but my self, the sole unbidden guest.
" Unbidden though I am, I will be there,
" And, joined by thee, intend to joy the fair.
    " Now hear the rest ; when day resigns the light,
" And cheerful torches gild the jolly night,
" Be ready at my call ; my chosen few
" With arms administered shall aid thy crew.   10
" Then entering unexpected will we seize
" Our destined prey, from men dissolved in ease,
" By wine disabled, unprepared for fight,
" And hastening to the seas, suborn our flight :
" The seas are ours, for I command the fort,
" A ship well manned expects us in the port :
" If they, or if their friends, the prize contest,
" Death shall attend the man who dares resist."
    It pleased ; the prisoner to his hold retired,
His troop with equal emulation fired,   20
All fixed to fight, and all their wonted work required.
    The sun arose ; the streets were thronged around,
The palace opened, and the posts were crowned.
The double bridegroom at the door attends
The expected spouse, and entertains the friends :
They meet, they lead to church, the priests invoke
The Powers, and feed the flames with fragrant smoke.
This done, they feast, and at the close of night
By kindled torches vary their delight,
These lead the lively dance, and those the brimming
        bowls invite.   30
    Now, at the appointed place and hour assigned,
With souls resolved the ravishers were joined :
Three bands are formed ; the first is sent before
To favour the retreat and guard the shore ;
The second at the palace-gate is placed,

And up the lofty stairs ascend the last :
A peaceful troop they seem with shining vests,
But coats of mail beneath secure their breasts.
  Dauntless they enter, Cymon at their head,
And find the feast renewed, the table spread :
Sweet voices, mixed with instrumental sounds,
Ascend the vaulted roof, the vaulted roof rebounds.
When, like the harpies, rushing through the hall
The sudden troop appears, the tables fall,
Their smoking load is on the pavement thrown ;   10
Each ravisher prepares to seize his own :
The brides, invaded with a rude embrace,
Shriek out for aid, confusion fills the place.
Quick to redeem the prey their plighted lords
Advance, the palace gleams with shining swords.
  But late is all defence, and succour vain ;
The rape is made, the ravishers remain :
Two sturdy slaves were only sent before
To bear the purchased prize in safety to the shore.
The troop retires, the lovers close the rear,   20
With forward faces not confessing fear :
Backward they move, but scorn their pace to mend ;
Then seek the stairs, and with slow haste descend.
  Fierce Pasimond, their passage to prevent,
Thrust full on Cymon's back in his descent,
The blade returned unbathed, and to the handle bent.
Stout Cymon soon remounts, and cleft in two
His rival's head with one descending blow :
And as the next in rank Ormisda stood,
He turned the point ; the sword enured to blood   30
Bored his unguarded breast, which poured a purple
    flood.
  With vowed revenge the gathering crowd pursues,
The ravishers turn head, the fight renews ;
The hall is heaped with corps ; the sprinkled gore
Besmears the walls, and floats the marble floor.
Dispersed at length, the drunken squadron flies,

The victors to their vessel bear the prize,
And hear behind loud groans, and lamentable cries.
    The crew with merry shouts their anchors weigh,
Then ply their oars, and brush the buxom sea,
While troops of gathered Rhodians crowd the key.
What should the people do when left alone ?
The governor and government are gone ;
The public wealth to foreign parts conveyed ;
Some troops disbanded, and the rest unpaid.
Rhodes is the sovereign of the sea no more ;   10
Their ships unrigged, and spent their naval store ;
They neither could defend nor can pursue,
But grind their teeth, and cast a helpless view :
In vain with darts a distant war they try,
Short, and more short, the missive weapons fly.
Mean while the ravishers their crimes enjoy,
And flying sails and sweeping oars employ :
The cliffs of Rhodes in little space are lost ;
Jove's isle they seek, nor Jove denies his coast.
    In safety landed on the Candian shore,   20
With generous wines their spirits they restore ;
There Cymon with his Rhodian friend resides,
Both court and wed at once the willing brides.
A war ensues, the Cretans own their cause,
Stiff to defend their hospitable laws :
Both parties lose by turns, and neither wins,
Till peace, propounded by a truce, begins.
The kindred of the slain forgive the deed,
But a short exile must for show precede :
The term expired, from Candia they remove,   30
And happy each at home enjoys his love.

                              JOHN DRYDEN

THE RAPE OF THE LOCK

CANTO FIRST

WHAT dire offence from am'rous causes springs,
What mighty contests rise from trivial things,
I sing—This verse to CARYLL, Muse ! is due :
This, ev'n Belinda may vouchsafe to view :
Slight is the subject, but not so the praise,
If she inspire, and he approve my lays.

    Say what strange motive, goddess ! could compel
A well-bred lord t' assault a gentle belle ?
Oh, say what stranger cause, yet unexplored,
Could make a gentle belle reject a lord ?   10
In tasks so bold can little men engage,
And in soft bosoms dwells such mighty rage ?

    Sol through white curtains shot a tim'rous ray,
And oped those eyes that must eclipse the day :
Now lap-dogs give themselves the rousing shake,
And sleepless lovers, just at twelve, awake :
Thrice rung the bell, the slipper knock'd the ground,
And the press'd watch return'd a silver sound.
Belinda still her downy pillow prest,
Her guardian sylph prolong'd the balmy rest :   20
'Twas he had summon'd to her silent bed
The morning-dream that hover'd o'er her head ;
A youth more glitt'ring than a birth-night beau,
(That ev'n in slumber caused her cheek to glow)
Seem'd to her ear his winning lips to lay,
And thus in whispers said, or seem'd to say :

    " Fairest of mortals, thou distinguish'd care
Of thousand bright inhabitants of air !
If e'er one vision touch'd thy infant thought,
Of all the nurse and all the priest have taught ;   30
Of airy elves by moonlight shadows seen,
The silver token, and the circled green,

Or virgins visited by angel-powers
With golden crowns and wreaths of heavenly flowers ;
Hear and believe ! thy own importance know,
Nor bound thy narrow views to things below.
Some secret truths, from learned pride concealed,
To maids alone and children are revealed :
What though no credit doubting wits may give ?
The fair and innocent shall still believe.
Know, then, unnumber'd spirits round thee fly,
The light militia of the lower sky :   10
These, though unseen, are ever on the wing,
Hang o'er the box, and hover round the ring.
Think what an equipage thou hast in air,
And view with scorn two pages and a chair.
As now your own, our beings were of old,
And once inclosed in woman's beauteous mould ;
Thence, by a soft transition, we repair
From earthly vehicles to those of air.
Think not, when woman's transient breath is fled,
That all her vanities at once are dead ;   20
Succeeding vanities she still regards,
And though she plays no more, o'erlooks the cards.
Her joy in gilded chariots, when alive,
And love of ombre, after death survive.
For when the fair in all their pride expire,
To their first elements their souls retire :
The sprites of fiery termagants in flame
Mount up, and take a salamander's name.
Soft yielding minds to water glide away,
And sip, with nymphs, their elemental tea.   30
The graver prude sinks downward to a gnome,
In search of mischief still on earth to roam.
The light coquettes in sylphs aloft repair,
And sport and flutter in the fields of air.
  " Know further yet : whoever fair and chaste
Rejects mankind, is by some sylph embraced :
For spirits, freed from mortal laws, with ease

Assume what sexes and what shapes they please.
What guards the purity of melting maids,
In courtly balls, and midnight masquerades,
Safe from the treach'rous friend, the daring spark,
The glance by day, the whisper in the dark :
When kind occasion prompts their warm desires,
When music softens, and when dancing fires ?
'Tis but their sylph, the wise celestials know,
Tho' honour is the word with men below.

   " Some nymphs there are, too conscious of their face,
For life predestin'd to the gnomes' embrace.   11
These swell their prospects and exalt their pride,
When offers are disdain'd, and love denied :
Then gay ideas crowd the vacant brain,
While peers and dukes, and all their sweeping train,
And garters, stars, and coronets appear,
And in soft sounds, Your Grace salutes their ear.
'Tis these that early taint the female soul,
Instruct the eyes of young coquettes to roll,
Teach infant-cheeks a hidden blush to know,   20
And little hearts to flutter at a beau.

   " Oft, when the world imagine women stray,
The sylphs thro' mystic mazes guide their way,
Thro' all the giddy circle they pursue,
And old impertinence expel by new.
What tender maid but must a victim fall
To one man's treat, but for another's ball ?
When Florio speaks, what virgin could withstand,
If gentle Damon did not squeeze her hand ?
With varying vanities, from ev'ry part,   30
They shift the moving toyshop of their heart ;
Where wigs with wigs, with sword-knots sword-knots
      strive,
Beaux banish beaux, and coaches coaches drive.
This erring mortals levity may call,
Oh, blind to truth ! the sylphs contrive it all.

   " Of these am I, who thy protection claim,

A watchful sprite, and Ariel is my name.
Late, as I rang'd the crystal wilds of air,
In the clear mirror of thy ruling star
I saw, alas! some dread event impend,
Ere to the main this morning sun descend,
But Heaven reveals not what, or how, or where:
Warn'd by the sylph, oh, pious maid, beware!
This to disclose is all thy guardian can:
Beware of all, but most beware of man!"
  He said; when Shock, who thought she slept too
        long,   10
Leap'd up, and waked his mistress with his tongue.
'Twas then, Belinda, if report say true,
Thy eyes first open'd on a billet-doux;
Wounds, charms, and ardours, were no sooner read,
But all the vision vanish'd from thy head.
  And now, unveil'd, the toilet stands displayed,
Each silver vase in mystic order laid.
First, robed in white the nymph intent adores,
With head uncover'd, the cosmetic powers.
A heavenly image in the glass appears,   20
To that she bends, to that her eyes she rears;
Th' inferior priestess, at her altar's side,
Trembling begins the sacred rites of pride.
Unnumber'd treasures ope at once, and here
The various offerings of the world appear;
From each she nicely culls with curious toil,
And decks the goddess with the glittering spoil.
This casket India's glowing gems unlocks,
And all Arabia breathes from yonder box.
The tortoise here and elephant unite,   30
Transform'd to combs, the speckled and the white.
Here files of pins extend their shining rows,
Puffs, powders, patches, bibles, billets-doux.
Now awful beauty puts on all its arms;
The fair each moment rises in her charms,
Repairs her smiles, awakens every grace.

And calls forth all the wonders of her face ;
Sees by degrees a purer blush arise,
And keener lightnings quicken in her eyes.
The busy sylphs surround their darling care,
These set the head, and those divide the hair,
Some fold the sleeve, whilst others plait the gown ;
And Betty's praised for labours not her own.

CANTO SECOND

Not with more glories, in the ethereal plain,
The sun first rises o'er the purpled main,
Than, issuing forth, the rival of his beams   10
Launch'd on the bosom of the silver Thames.
Fair nymphs and well-dress'd youths around her
        shone,
But every eye was fix'd on her alone.
On her white breast a sparkling cross she wore,
Which Jews might kiss, and infidels adore.
Her lively looks a sprightly mind disclose,
Quick as her eyes, and as unfix'd as those :
Favours to none, to all she smiles extends ;
Oft she rejects, but never once offends.
Bright as the sun, her eyes the gazers strike,   20
And, like the sun, they shine on all alike,
Yet graceful ease, and sweetness void of pride,
Might hide her faults if belles had faults to hide :
If to her share some female errors fall,
Look on her face, and you'll forget 'em all.

   This nymph, to the destruction of mankind,
Nourished two locks, which graceful hung behind
In equal curls, and well conspired to deck
With shining ringlets the smooth ivory neck.
Love in these labyrinths his slaves detains,   30
And mighty hearts are held in slender chains.
With hairy springes we the birds betray,
Slight lines of hair surprise the finny prey.

Fair tresses man's imperial race ensnare,
And beauty draws us with a single hair.

    Th' advent'rous Baron the bright locks admired ;
He saw, he wish'd, and to the prize aspired.
Resolved to win, he meditates the way,
By force to ravish, or by fraud betray ;
For when success a lover's toil attends,
Few ask if fraud or force attain'd his ends.

    For this, ere Phoebus rose, he had implor'd
Propitious Heaven, and every power ador'd,   10
But chiefly Love—to Love an altar built,
Of twelve vast French romances, neatly gilt.
There lay three garters, half a pair of gloves,
And all the trophies of his former loves ;
With tender billets-doux he lights the pyre,
And breathes three am'rous sighs to raise the fire.
Then prostrate falls, and begs with ardent eyes
Soon to obtain, and long possess the prize :
The pow'rs gave ear and granted half his pray'r,
The rest the winds dispersed in empty air.   20

    But now secure the painted vessel glides,
The sunbeams trembling on the floating tides
While melting music steals upon the sky,
And soften'd sounds along the waters die :
Smooth flow the waves, the zephyrs gently play,
Belinda smiled, and all the world was gay.
All but the sylph ; with careful thoughts opprest,
Th' impending woe sat heavy on his breast.
He summons straight his denizens of air ;
The lucid squadrons round the sails repair :   30
Soft o'er the shrouds aërial whispers breathe,
That seem'd but zephyrs to the train beneath.
Some to the sun their insect-wings unfold,
Waft on the breeze, or sink in clouds of gold ;
Transparent forms, too fine for mortal sight,
Their fluid bodies half dissolved in light.
Loose to the wind their airy garments flew,

Thin glitt'ring textures of the filmy dew,
Dipt in the richest tincture of the skies,
Where light disports in ever-mingling dyes ;
While ev'ry beam new transient colours flings,
Colours that change whene'er they wave their wings.
Amid the circle, on the gilded mast,
Superior by the head, was Ariel plac'd ;
His purple pinions opening to the sun,
He raised his azure wand, and thus begun :

" Ye sylphs and sylphids, to your chief give ear, 10
Fays, fairies, genii, elves, and daemons, hear !
Ye know the spheres, and various tasks assigned
By laws eternal to th' aërial kind.
Some in the fields of purest ether play,
And bask and whiten in the blaze of day.
Some guide the course of wandering orbs on high,
Or roll the planets through the boundless sky.
Some, less refin'd, beneath the moon's pale light
Pursue the stars that shoot athwart the night,
Or suck the mists in grosser air below, 20
Or dip their pinions in the painted bow,
Or brew fierce tempests on the wintry main,
Or o'er the glebe distil the kindly rain.
Others on earth o'er human race preside,
Watch all their ways, and all their actions guide :
Of these the chief the care of nations own,
And guard with arms divine the British throne.

" Our humbler province is to tend the fair,
Not a less pleasing, tho' less glorious care ;
To save the powder from too rude a gale, 30
Nor let th' imprison'd essences exhale ;
To draw fresh colours from the vernal flow'rs ;
To steal from rainbows ere they drop in show'rs
A brighter wash ; to curl their waving hairs,
Assist their blushes, and inspire their airs ;
Nay oft, in dreams, invention we bestow,
To change a flounce, or add a furbelow.

36

" This day, black omens threat the brightest fair
That e'er deserved a watchful spirit's care ;
Some dire disaster, or by force, or slight ;
But what, or where, the fates have wrapt in night.
Whether the nymph shall break Diana's law,
Or some frail China jar receive a flaw ;
Or stain her honour, or her new brocade ;
Forget her pray'rs, or miss a masquerade ;
Or lose her heart, or necklace, at a ball ;
Or whether Heav'n has doom'd that Shock must fall.
Haste then, ye spirits ! to your charge repair :   11
The fluttering fan be Zephyretta's care ;
The drops to thee, Brillante, we consign ;
And, Momentilla, let the watch be thine ;
Do thou, Crispissa, tend her favourite lock ;
Ariel himself shall be the guard of Shock.
    " To fifty chosen sylphs, of special note,
We trust th' important charge, the petticoat :
Oft have we known that sevenfold fence to fail,
Though stiff with hoops and arm'd with ribs of whale ;
Form a strong line about the silver bound,   21
And guard the wide circumference around.
    " Whatever spirit, careless of his charge,
His post neglects, or leaves the fair at large,
Shall feel sharp vengeance soon o'ertake his sins,
Be stopp'd in vials, or transfix'd with pins ;
Or plung'd in lakes of bitter washes lie,
Or wedg'd whole ages in a bodkin's eye :
Gums and pomatums shall his flight restrain,
While clogg'd he beats his silken wings in vain ;   30
Or alum styptics, with contracting pow'r,
Shrink his thin essence like a rivelled flow'r :
Or, as Ixion fix'd, the wretch shall feel
The giddy motion of the whirling mill,
In fumes of burning chocolate shall glow,
And tremble at the sea that froths below ! "
    He spoke ; the spirits from the sails descend :

37

Some, orb in orb, around the nymph extend ;
Some thrid the mazy ringlets of her hair ;
Some hang upon the pendants of her ear ;
With beating hearts the dire event they wait,
Anxious, and trembling for the birth of fate.

CANTO THIRD

Close by those meads, for ever crown'd with flow'rs,
Where Thames with pride surveys his rising tow'rs,
There stands a structure of majestic frame,
Which from the neighb'ring Hampton takes its name.
Here Britain's statesmen oft the fall foredoom   10
Of foreign tyrants, and of nymphs at home ;
Here thou, great ANNA ! whom three realms obey,
Dost sometimes counsel take—and sometimes tea.
Hither the heroes and the nymphs resort,
To taste a while the pleasures of a court ;
In various talk th' instructive hours they pass'd,
Who gave the ball, or paid the visit last ;
One speaks the glory of the British Queen,
And one describes a charming Indian screen ;
A third interprets motions, looks, and eyes ;   20
At every word a reputation dies.
Snuff, or the fan, supply each pause of chat,
With singing, laughing, ogling, and all that.
    Meanwhile, declining from the noon of day,
The sun obliquely shoots his burning ray ;
The hungry judges soon the sentence sign,
And wretches hang that jurymen may dine ;
The merchant from th' Exchange returns in peace,
And the long labours of the toilet cease.
Belinda now, whom thirst of fame invites,   30
Burns to encounter two advent'rous knights,
At ombre singly to decide their doom ;
And swells her breast with conquests yet to come.
Straight the three bands prepare in arms to join,

Each band the number of the sacred nine.
Soon as she spreads her hand, th' aërial guard
Descend, and sit on each important card :
First Ariel perch'd upon a Matadore,
Then each according to the rank they bore ;
For sylphs, yet mindful of their ancient race,
Are, as when women, wondrous fond of place.

Behold, four kings, in majesty revered,
With hoary whiskers and a forky beard ;
And four fair queens whose hands sustain a flow'r,   10
The expressive emblem of their softer pow'r ;
Four knaves in garbs succinct, a trusty band,
Caps on their heads, and halberts in their hand ;
And parti-colour'd troops, a shining train,
Draw forth to combat on the velvet plain.

The skilful nymph reviews her force with care ;
Let spades be trumps ! she said, and trumps they
        were.

Now move to war her sable Matadores,
In show like leaders of the swarthy Moors.
Spadillio first, unconquerable lord !   20
Led off two captive trumps, and swept the board.
As many more Manillio forced to yield,
And march'd a victor from the verdant field.
Him Basto follow'd, but his fate more hard
Gain'd but one trump and one plebeian card.
With his broad sabre next, a chief in years,
The hoary majesty of Spades appears,
Puts forth one manly leg, to sight revealed,
The rest, his many-colour'd robe concealed.
The rebel knave, who dares his prince engage,   30
Proves the just victim of his royal rage.
Ev'n mighty Pam, that kings and queens o'erthrew,
And mow'd down armies in the fights of Loo,
Sad chance of war ! now destitute of aid,
Falls undistinguish'd by the victor spade !

Thus far both armies to Belinda yield ;

39

Now to the Baron fate inclines the field.
His warlike Amazon her host invades,
Th' imperial consort of the crown of Spades.
The Club's black tyrant first her victim died,
Spite of his haughty mien and barb'rous pride :
What boots the regal circle on his head,
His giant limbs, in state unwieldy spread ;
That long behind he trails his pompous robe,
And, of all monarchs, only grasps the globe ?
    The Baron now his Diamonds pours apace ;   10
Th' embroider'd King who shews but half his face,
And his refulgent Queen, with pow'rs combined,
Of broken troops an easy conquest find.
Clubs, Diamonds, Hearts, in wild disorder seen,
With throngs promiscuous strew the level green.
Thus when dispersed a routed army runs,
Of Asia's troops, and Afric's sable sons,
With like confusion different nations fly,
Of various habit, and of various dye ;
The pierc'd battalions disunited fall,   20
In heaps on heaps ; one fate o'erwhelms them all.
    The Knave of Diamonds tries his wily arts,
And wins (oh shameful chance !) the Queen of Hearts.
At this, the blood the virgin's cheek forsook,
A livid paleness spreads o'er all her look ;
She sees, and trembles at th' approaching ill,
Just in the jaws of ruin, and codille.
And now (as oft in some distemper'd state)
On one nice trick depends the general fate :
An Ace of Hearts steps forth : the King, unseen,   30
Lurk'd in her hand, and mourn'd his captive Queen:
He springs to vengeance with an eager pace,
And falls like thunder on the prostrate Ace.
The nymph exulting fills with shouts the sky ;
The walls, the woods, and long canals reply.
    Oh thoughtless mortals ! ever blind to fate,
Too soon dejected, and too soon elate.

Sudden these honours shall be snatch'd away,
And curs'd for ever this victorious day.
For lo ! the board with cups and spoons is crown'd,
The berries crackle, and the mill turns round ;
On shining altars of Japan they raise
The silver lamp ; the fiery spirits blaze :
From silver spouts the grateful liquors glide,
While China's earth receives the smoking tide :
At once they gratify their scent and taste,
And frequent cups prolong the rich repast. 10
Straight hover round the fair her airy band ;
Some, as she sipp'd, the fuming liquor fanned,
Some o'er her lap their careful plumes displayed,
Trembling, and conscious of the rich brocade.
Coffee (which makes the politician wise,
And see through all things with his half-shut eyes)
Sent up in vapours to the Baron's brain
New stratagems, the radiant lock to gain.
Ah cease, rash youth ! desist ere 'tis too late,
Fear the just gods, and think of Scylla's fate ! 20
Changed to a bird, and sent to flit in air,
She dearly pays for Nisus' injur'd hair !

But when to mischief mortals bend their will,
How soon they find fit instruments of ill !
Just then Clarissa drew, with tempting grace,
A two-edg'd weapon from her shining case :
So ladies in romance assist their knight,
Present the spear, and arm him for the fight.
He takes the gift with rev'rence, and extends
The little engine on his fingers' ends ; 30
This just behind Belinda's neck he spread,
As o'er the fragrant steams she bends her head.
Swift to the lock a thousand sprites repair,
A thousand wings, by turns, blow back the hair ;
And thrice they twitch'd the diamond in her ear ;
Thrice she look'd back, and thrice the foe drew near.
Just in that instant anxious Ariel sought

The close recesses of the virgin's thought :
As on the nosegay in her breast reclin'd,
He watch'd th' ideas rising in her mind,
Sudden he view'd, in spite of all her art,
An earthly lover lurking at her heart.
Amaz'd, confus'd, he found his power expired,
Resign'd to fate, and with a sigh retired.

The peer now spreads the glitt'ring forfex wide,
T' enclose the lock ; now joins it, to divide.
Even then, before the fatal engine closed,   10
A wretched sylph too fondly interposed ;
Fate urged the shears, and cut the sylph in twain,
(But airy substance soon unites again)
The meeting points the sacred hair dissever
From the fair head, for ever, and for ever !

Then flash'd the living lightning from her eyes,
And screams of horror rend the affrighted skies ;
Not louder shrieks to pitying Heav'n are cast,
When husbands, or when lapdogs, breathe their last ;
Or when rich China vessels fallen from high,   20
In glitt'ring dust, and painted fragments lie !

Let wreaths of triumph now my temples twine,
(The victor cried) the glorious prize is mine !
While fish in streams, or birds delight in air,
Or in a coach-and-six the British fair,
As long as Atalantis shall be read,
Or the small pillow grace a lady's bed,
While visits shall be paid on solemn days,
When num'rous wax-lights in bright order blaze,
While nymphs take treats, or assignations give,   30
So long my honour, name, and praise shall live !
What time would spare, from steel receives its date,
And monuments, like men, submit to fate !
Steel could the labour of the gods destroy,
And strike to dust th' imperial towers of Troy ;
Steel could the works of mortal pride confound,
And hew triumphal arches to the ground.

What wonder then, fair nymph ! thy hairs should feel
The conqu'ring force of unresisted steel ?

CANTO FOURTH

But anxious cares the pensive nymph opprest,
And secret passions labour'd in her breast.
Not youthful kings in battle seiz'd alive,
Not scornful virgins who their charms survive,
Not ardent lovers robb'd of all their bliss,
Not ancient ladies when refus'd a kiss,
Not tyrants fierce that unrepenting die,
Not Cynthia when her manteau's pinn'd awry,   10
E'er felt such rage, resentment, and despair,
As thou, sad virgin ! for thy ravish'd hair.

For, that sad moment, when the sylphs withdrew,
And Ariel weeping from Belinda flew,
Umbriel, a dusky, melancholy sprite,
As ever sullied the fair face of light,
Down to the central earth, his proper scene,
Repair'd to search the gloomy cave of Spleen.

Swift on his sooty pinions flits the gnome,
And in a vapour reach'd the dismal dome.   20
No cheerful breeze this sullen region knows,
The dreaded east is all the wind that blows.
Here in a grotto, shelter'd close from air,
And screen'd in shades from day's detested glare,
She sighs for ever on her pensive bed,
Pain at her side, and Megrim at her head.

Two handmaids wait the throne : alike in place,
But differing far in figure and in face.
Here stood Ill-nature like an ancient maid,
Her wrinkled form in black and white arrayed ;   30
With store of pray'rs, for mornings, nights, and noons,
Her hand is fill'd ; her bosom with lampoons.

There Affectation, with a sickly mien,
Shows in her cheek the roses of eighteen,

43

Practised to lisp, and hang the head aside,
Faints into airs, and languishes with pride,
On the rich quilt sinks with becoming woe,
Wrapt in a gown, for sickness, and for show.
The fair ones feel such maladies as these,
When each new night-dress gives a new disease.

    A constant vapour o'er the palace flies ;
Strange phantoms rising as the mists arise ;
Dreadful, as hermits' dreams in haunted shades,
Or bright, as visions of expiring maids.   10
Now glaring fiends, and snakes on rolling spires,
Pale spectres, gaping tombs, and purple fires :
Now lakes of liquid gold, Elysian scenes,
And crystal domes, and angels in machines.

    Unnumber'd throngs on every side are seen,
Of bodies changed to various forms by Spleen.
Here living tea-pots stand, one arm held out,
One bent ; the handle this, and that the spout :
A pipkin there, like Homer's tripod, walks ;
Here sighs a jar, and there a goose-pye talks ;   20
Men prove with child, as powerful fancy works,
And maids, turn'd bottles, call aloud for corks.

    Safe pass'd the gnome through this fantastic band,
A branch of healing spleenwort in his hand.
Then thus address'd the pow'r : " Hail, wayward
        queen !
Who rule the sex to fifty from fifteen :
Parent of vapours and of female wit,
Who give th' hysteric, or poetic fit,
On various tempers act by various ways,
Make some take physic, others scribble plays ;   30
Who cause the proud their visits to delay,
And send the godly in a pet to pray.
A nymph there is, that all thy power disdains,
And thousands more in equal mirth maintains.
But oh ! if e'er thy gnome could spoil a grace,
Or raise a pimple on a beauteous face,

Like citron-waters matrons' cheeks inflame,
Or change complexions at a losing game ;
Or caused suspicion when no soul was rude,
Or discompos'd the head-dress of a prude,
Or e'er to costive lapdog gave disease,
Which not the tears of brightest eyes could ease :
Hear me, and touch Belinda with chagrin,
That single act gives half the world the spleen."
　　The goddess, with a discontented air,
Seems to reject him, tho' she grants his prayer. 10
A wondrous bag with both her hands she binds,
Like that where once Ulysses held the winds ;
There she collects the force of female lungs,
Sighs, sobs, and passions, and the war of tongues.
A vial next she fills with fainting fears,
Soft sorrows, melting griefs, and flowing tears.
The gnome rejoicing bears her gifts away,
Spreads his black wings, and slowly mounts to day.
　　Sunk in Thalestris' arms the nymph he found,
Her eyes dejected, and her hair unbound. 20
Full o'er their heads the swelling bag he rent,
And all the Furies issued at the vent.
Belinda burns with more than mortal ire,
And fierce Thalestris fans the rising fire.
"O wretched maid!" she spread her hands, and cried,
(While Hampton's echoes, "Wretched maid!" replied)
"Was it for this you took such constant care
The bodkin, comb, and essence to prepare ?
For this your locks in paper durance bound ?
For this with torturing irons wreath'd around ? 30
For this with fillets strain'd your tender head
And bravely bore the double loads of lead ?
Gods ! shall the ravisher display your hair,
While the fops envy, and the ladies stare !
Honour forbid ! at whose unrivall'd shrine
Ease, pleasure, virtue, all our sex resign.
Methinks already I your tears survey,

Already hear the horrid things they say ;
Already see you a degraded toast,
And all your honour in a whisper lost !
How shall I, then, your hapless fame defend ?
'Twill then be infamy to seem your friend !
And shall this prize, th' inestimable prize,
Exposed through crystal to the gazing eyes,
And heighten'd by the diamond's circling rays,
On that rapacious hand for ever blaze ?
Sooner shall grass in Hyde Park Circus grow,   10
And wits take lodgings in the sound of Bow ;
Sooner let earth, air, sea, to chaos fall,
Men, monkeys, lapdogs, parrots, perish all ! "
    She said ; then raging to Sir Plume repairs,
And bids her beau demand the precious hairs :
(Sir Plume, of amber snuff-box justly vain,
And the nice conduct of a clouded cane)
With earnest eyes, and round, unthinking face,
He first the snuff-box open'd, then the case,
And thus broke out—" My lord, why, what the
        devil !   20
Zounds ! damn the lock ! 'fore Gad, you must be
        civil !
Plague on 't ! 'tis past a jest—nay, prithee, pox !
Give her the hair "—he spoke, and rapp'd his box.
    " It grieves me much " (replied the peer again)
" Who speaks so well should ever speak in vain.
But by this lock, this sacred lock, I swear,
(Which never more shall join its parted hair ;
Which never more its honours shall renew,
Clipp'd from the lovely head where late it grew)
That while my nostrils draw the vital air,   30
This hand, which won it, shall for ever wear."
He spoke, and speaking, in proud triumph spread
The long-contended honours of her head.
    But Umbriel, hateful gnome ! forbears not so ;
He breaks the vial whence the sorrows flow.

46

Then see ! the nymph in beauteous grief appears,
Her eyes half-languishing, half-drown'd in tears ;
On her heav'd bosom hung her drooping head,
Which with a sigh she rais'd ; and thus she said :
 " For ever curs'd be this detested day,
Which snatch'd my best, my favourite curl away !
Happy ! ah, ten times happy had I been,
If Hampton Court these eyes had never seen !
Yet am not I the first mistaken maid,
By love of courts to num'rous ills betrayed.   10
Oh, had I rather unadmir'd remained
In some lone isle, or distant northern land ;
Where the gilt chariot never marks the way,
Where none learn ombre, none e'er taste bohea !
There kept my charms conceal'd from mortal eye,
Like roses, that in deserts bloom and die.
What moved my mind with youthful lords to roam ?
Oh, had I stay'd, and said my prayers at home !
'Twas this the morning omens seem'd to tell,
Thrice from my trembling hand the patch-box fell ;
The tott'ring china shook without a wind,   21
Nay, Poll sat mute, and Shock was most unkind !
A sylph, too, warn'd me of the threats of fate,
In mystic visions, now believ'd too late !
See the poor remnants of these slighted hairs !
My hands shall rend what ev'n thy rapine spares :
These in two sable ringlets taught to break,
Once gave new beauties to the snowy neck ;
The sister-lock now sits uncouth, alone,
And in its fellow's fate foresees its own ;   30
Uncurl'd it hangs, the fatal shears demands,
And tempts, once more, thy sacrilegious hands.
Oh, hadst thou, cruel ! been content to seize
Hairs less in sight, or any hairs but these ! "

Canto Fifth

She said : the pitying audience melt in tears ;
But Fate and Jove had stopp'd the Baron's ears.
In vain Thalestris with reproach assails,
For who can move when fair Belinda fails ?
Not half so fix'd the Trojan could remain,
While Anna begg'd and Dido rag'd in vain.
Then grave Clarissa graceful wav'd her fan ;
Silence ensu'd, and thus the nymph began :
" Say, why are beauties prais'd and honour'd most,
The wise man's passion, and the vain man's toast?   10
Why deck'd with all that land and sea afford,
Why angels call'd, and angel-like adored ?
Why round our coaches crowd the white-glov'd
    beaux,
Why bows the side-box from its inmost rows ?
How vain are all these glories, all our pains,
Unless good sense preserve what beauty gains :
That men may say, when we the front-box grace,
' Behold the first in virtue as in face ! '
Oh ! if to dance all night, and dress all day,
Charm'd the small-pox, or chas'd old age away ;   20
Who would not scorn what housewife's cares produce,
Or who would learn one earthly thing of use ?
To patch, nay ogle, might become a saint,
Nor could it sure be such a sin to paint.
But since, alas ! frail beauty must decay,
Curl'd or uncurl'd, since locks will turn to gray ;
Since painted or not painted, all shall fade,
And she who scorns a man must die a maid ;
What then remains but well our pow'r to use,
And keep good-humour still, whate'er we lose ?   30
And trust me, dear ! good-humour can prevail,
When airs, and flights, and screams, and scolding fail ;
Beauties in vain their pretty eyes may roll ;
Charms strike the sight, but merit wins the soul."

So spoke the dame, but no applause ensu'd ;
Belinda frown'd, Thalestris call'd her prude.
" To arms, to arms ! " the fierce virago cries,
And swift as lightning to the combat flies.
All side in parties, and begin the attack ;
Fans clap, silks rustle, and tough whalebones crack ;
Heroes' and heroines' shouts confus'dly rise,
And bass and treble voices strike the skies.
No common weapons in their hands are found,
Like gods they fight, nor dread a mortal wound.   10

So when bold Homer makes the gods engage,
And heav'nly breasts with human passions rage ;
'Gainst Pallas, Mars ; Latona, Hermes arms ;
And all Olympus rings with loud alarms :
Jove's thunder roars, heav'n trembles all around,
Blue Neptune storms, the bellowing deeps resound :
Earth shakes her nodding tow'rs, the ground gives
            way,
And the pale ghosts start at the flash of day !

Triumphant Umbriel, on a sconce's height,
Clapp'd his glad wings, and sate to view the fight :   20
Propp'd on their bodkin spears, the sprites survey
The growing combat, or assist the fray.

While through the press enrag'd Thalestris flies,
And scatters death around from both her eyes,
A beau and witling perished in the throng,
One died in metaphor, and one in song.
" O cruel nymph ! a living death I bear ! "
Cried Dapperwit, and sunk beside his chair.
A mournful glance Sir Fopling upwards cast,
" Those eyes are made so killing ! "—was his last.   30
Thus on Maeander's flow'ry margin lies
Th' expiring swan, and as he sings he dies.

When bold Sir Plume had drawn Clarissa down,
Chloe stepp'd in and kill'd him with a frown :
She smil'd to see the doughty hero slain,
But, at her smile the beau reviv'd again.

Now Jove suspends his golden scales in air,
Weighs the man's wits against the lady's hair ;
The doubtful beam long nods from side to side ;
At length the wits mount up, the hairs subside.

See, fierce Belinda on the Baron flies,
With more than usual lightning in her eyes :
Nor fear'd the chief th' unequal fight to try,
Who sought no more than on his foe to die.
But this bold lord, with manly strength endu'd,
She with one finger and a thumb subdu'd :   10
Just where the breath of life his nostrils drew,
A charge of snuff the wily virgin threw ;
The gnomes direct, to every atom just,
The pungent grains of titillating dust.
Sudden with starting tears each eye o'erflows,
And the high dome re-echoes to his nose.

" Now meet thy fate ! " incens'd Belinda cried,
And drew a deadly bodkin from her side.
(The same, his ancient personage to deck,
Her great-great-grandsire wore about his neck,   20
In three seal-rings ; which after, melted down,
Form'd a vast buckle for his widow's gown :
Her infant grandame's whistle next it grew,
The bells she jingled, and the whistle blew ;
Then in a bodkin grac'd her mother's hairs,
Which long she wore, and now Belinda wears.)
" Boast not my fall," (he cried) " insulting foe !
Thou by some other shalt be laid as low.
Nor think, to die dejects my lofty mind ;
All that I dread is leaving you behind !   30
Rather than so, ah ! let me still survive,
And burn in Cupid's flames—but burn alive."

" Restore the Lock ! " she cries ; and all around,
" Restore the Lock ! " the vaulted roofs rebound.
Not fierce Othello in so loud a strain,
Roar'd for the handkerchief that caus'd his pain.
But see how oft ambitious aims are cross'd,

And chiefs contend till all the prize is lost !
The lock, obtain'd with guilt, and kept with pain,
In every place is sought, but sought in vain :
With such a prize no mortal must be blest,
So Heav'n decrees ! with Heav'n who can contest ?
  Some thought it mounted to the lunar sphere,
Since all things lost on earth are treasur'd there.
There heroes' wits are kept in pond'rous vases,
And beaux' in snuff-boxes and tweezer-cases.
There broken vows and death-bed alms are found,   10
And lovers' hearts with ends of riband bound,
The courtier's promises, and sick men's prayers,
The smiles of harlots, and the tears of heirs,
Cages for gnats, and chains to yoke a flea,
Dried butterflies, and tomes of casuistry.
  But trust the Muse—she saw it upward rise,
Though mark'd by none but quick, poetic eyes :
(So Rome's great founder to the heav'ns withdrew,
To Proculus alone confess'd in view)
A sudden star, it shot through liquid air,   20
And drew behind a radiant trail of hair.
Not Berenice's locks first rose so bright,
The heavens bespangling with dishevell'd light.
The sylphs behold it kindling as it flies,
And pleas'd pursue its progress through the skies.
  This the beau monde shall from the Mall survey,
And hail with music its propitious ray ;
This the blest lover shall for Venus take,
And send up vows from Rosamonda's lake ;
This Partridge soon shall view in cloudless skies,   30
When next he looks through Galileo's eyes ;
And hence th' egregious wizard shall foredoom
The fate of Louis, and the fall of Rome.
  Then cease, bright Nymph ! to mourn thy ravish'd
      hair,
Which adds new glory to the shining sphere !
Not all the tresses that fair head can boast,

Shall draw such envy as the lock you lost.
For after all the murders of your eye,
When, after millions slain, yourself shall die ;
When those fair suns shall set, as set they must,
And all those tresses shall be laid in dust,
This lock the Muse shall consecrate to fame,
And 'midst the stars inscribe Belinda's name.

ALEXANDER POPE

THE BARD

A PINDARIC ODE

I 1

" RUIN seize thee, ruthless King !
Confusion on thy banners wait,
Tho' fann'd by Conquest's crimson wing   10
They mock the air with idle state.
Helm, nor Hauberk's twisted mail,
Nor even thy virtues, Tyrant, shall avail
To save thy secret soul from nightly fears,
From Cambria's curse, from Cambria's tears ! "
Such were the sounds, that o'er the crested pride
Of the first Edward scatter'd wild dismay,
As down the steep of Snowdon's shaggy side
He wound with toilsome march his long array.
Stout Glo'ster stood aghast in speechless trance :   20
To arms ! cried Mortimer, and couch'd his quiv'ring
lance.

I 2

On a rock, whose haughty brow
Frowns o'er old Conway's foaming flood,
Robed in the sable garb of woe,
With haggard eyes the Poet stood ;
(Loose his beard, and hoary hair

Stream'd, like a meteor, to the troubled air)
And with a Master's hand, and Prophet's fire,
Struck the deep sorrows of his lyre.
" Hark, how each giant-oak, and desert cave,
Sighs to the torrent's aweful voice beneath !
O'er thee, oh King ! their hundred arms they wave,
Revenge on thee in hoarser murmurs breath ;
Vocal no more, since Cambria's fatal day,
To high-born Hoel's harp, or soft Llewellyn's lay.

I 3

   " Cold is Cadwallo's tongue,   10
That hush'd the stormy main :
Brave Urien sleeps upon his craggy bed :
Mountains, ye mourn in vain
Modred, whose magic song
Made huge Plinlimmon bow his cloud-top'd head.
On dreary Arvon's shore they lie,
Smear'd with gore, and ghastly pale :
Far, far aloof th' affrighted ravens sail ;
The famish'd Eagle screams, and passes by.
Dear lost companions of my tuneful art,   20
Dear, as the light that visits these sad eyes,
Dear, as the ruddy drops that warm my heart,
Ye died amidst your dying country's cries—
No more I weep.   They do not sleep.
On yonder cliffs, a griesly band,
I see them sit, they linger yet,
Avengers of their native land :
With me in dreadful harmony they join,
And weave with bloody hands the tissue of thy line."

II 1

   " Weave the warp, and weave the woof,   30
The winding-sheet of Edward's race.

Give ample room, and verge enough
The characters of hell to trace.
Mark the year, and mark the night,
When Severn shall re-eccho with affright
The shrieks of death, thro' Berkley's roofs that ring,
Shrieks of an agonizing King !
She-Wolf of France, with unrelenting fangs,
That tear'st the bowels of thy mangled Mate,
From thee be born, who o'er thy country hangs
The scourge of Heav'n. What Terrors round him
      wait !   10
Amazement in his van, with Flight combined,
And sorrow's faded form, and solitude behind.

II 2

  " Mighty Victor, mighty Lord,
Low on his funeral couch he lies !
No pitying heart, no eye, afford
A tear to grace his obsequies.
Is the sable Warriour fled ?
Thy son is gone.   He rests among the Dead.
The Swarm, that in thy noon-tide beam were born ?
Gone to salute the rising Morn.   20
Fair laughs the Morn, and soft the Zephyr blows,
While proudly riding o'er the azure realm
In gallant trim the gilded Vessel goes ;
Youth on the prow, and Pleasure at the helm ;
Regardless of the sweeping Whirlwind's sway,
That, hush'd in grim repose, expects his evening-prey.

II 3

  " Fill high the sparkling bowl,
The rich repast prepare,
Reft of a crown, he yet may share the feast :
Close by the regal chair   30

Fell Thirst and Famine scowl
A baleful smile upon their baffled Guest.
Heard ye the din of battle bray,
Lance to lance, and horse to horse ?
Long Years of havock urge their destined course,
And thro' the kindred squadrons mow their way.
Ye Towers of Julius, London's lasting shame,
With many a foul and midnight murther fed,
Revere his Consort's faith, his Father's fame,
And spare the meek Usurper's holy head.   10
Above, below, the rose of snow,
Twined with her blushing foe, we spread :
The bristled Boar in infant-gore
Wallows beneath the thorny shade.
Now, Brothers, bending o'er th' accursed loom,
Stamp we our vengeance deep, and ratify his doom.

III 1

  " Edward, lo ! to sudden fate
(Weave we the woof.   The thread is spun)
Half of thy heart we consecrate.
(The web is wove.   The work is done.) "   20
" Stay, oh stay ! nor thus forlorn
Leave me unbless'd, unpitied, here to mourn :
In yon bright track, that fires the western skies,
They melt, they vanish from my eyes.
But oh ! what solemn scenes on Snowdon's height
Descending slow their glitt'ring skirts unroll ?
Visions of glory, spare my aching sight,
Ye unborn Ages, crowd not on my soul !
No more our long-lost Arthur we bewail.
All-hail, ye genuine Kings, Britannia's Issue, hail !   30

III 2

  " Girt with many a Baron bold
Sublime their starry fronts they rear ;

And gorgeous Dames, and Statesmen old
In bearded majesty, appear.
In the midst a Form divine !
Her eye proclaims her of the Briton-Line ;
Her lyon-port, her awe-commanding face,
Attemper'd sweet to virgin-grace.
What strings symphonious tremble in the air,
What strains of vocal transport round her play !
Hear from the grave, great Taliessin, hear ;
They breathe a soul to animate thy clay.   10
Bright Rapture calls, and soaring, as she sings,
Waves in the eye of Heav'n her many-colour'd wings.

III 3

" The verse adorn again
Fierce War, and faithful Love,
And Truth severe, by fairy Fiction drest.
In buskin'd measures move
Pale Grief, and pleasing Pain,
With Horrour, Tyrant of the throbbing breast.
A Voice, as of the Cherub-Choir,
Gales from blooming Eden bear ;   20
And distant warblings lessen on my ear,
That lost in long futurity expire.
Fond impious Man, think'st thou, yon sanguine cloud,
Rais'd by thy breath, has quench'd the Orb of day ?
To-morrow he repairs the golden flood,
And warms the nations with redoubled ray.
Enough for me : With joy I see
The different doom our Fates assign.
Be thine Despair, and scept'red Care,
To triumph, and to die, are mine."   30
He spoke, and headlong from the mountain's height
Deep in the roaring tide he plung'd to endless night.

THOMAS GRAY

THE DESERTED VILLAGE

SWEET AUBURN ! loveliest village of the plain,
Where health and plenty cheer'd the labouring swain,
Where smiling spring its earliest visit paid,
And parting summer's ling'ring blooms delay'd :
Dear lovely bowers of innocence and ease,
Seats of my youth, when every sport could please,
How often have I loiter'd o'er thy green,
Where humble happiness endear'd each scene ;
How often have I paus'd on every charm,
The shelter'd cot, the cultivated farm.   10
The never-failing brook, the busy mill,
The decent church that topp'd the neighbouring hill,
The hawthorn bush, with seats beneath the shade,
For talking age and whisp'ring lovers made ;
How often have I bless'd the coming day,
When toil remitting lent its turn to play,
And all the village train, from labour free,
Led up their sports beneath the spreading tree ;
While many a pastime circled in the shade,
The young contending as the old survey'd ;   20
And many a gambol frolick'd o'er the ground,
And sleights of art and feats of strength went round ;
And still as each repeated pleasure tir'd,
Succeeding sports the mirthful band inspir'd ;
The dancing pair that simply sought renown,
By holding out to tire each other down ;
The swain mistrustless of his smutted face,
While secret laughter titter'd round the place ;
The bashful virgin's side-long looks of love,
The matron's glance that would those looks reprove: 30
These were thy charms, sweet village ; sports like
          these,
With sweet succession, taught e'en toil to please ;
These round thy bowers their cheerful influence shed,

These were thy charms—But all these charms are
    fled.

Sweet smiling village, loveliest of the lawn,
Thy sports are fled, and all thy charms withdrawn ;
Amidst thy bowers the tyrant's hand is seen,
And desolation saddens all thy green :
One only master grasps the whole domain,
And half a tillage stints thy smiling plain :
No more thy glassy brook reflects the day,
But chok'd with sedges, works its weedy way.
Along thy glades, a solitary guest,   10
The hollow-sounding bittern guards its nest ;
Amidst thy desert walks the lapwing flies,
And tires their echoes with unvaried cries.
Sunk are thy bowers in shapeless ruin all,
And the long grass o'ertops the mould'ring wall ;
And trembling, shrinking from the spoiler's hand,
Far, far away, thy children leave the land.

Ill fares the land, to hast'ning ills a prey,
Where wealth accumulates, and men decay :
Princes and lords may flourish, or may fade ;   20
A breath can make them, as a breath has made ;
But a bold peasantry, their country's pride,
When once destroy'd, can never be supplied.

A time there was, ere England's griefs began,
When every rood of ground maintain'd its man ;
For him light labour spread her wholesome store,
Just gave what life requir'd, but gave no more :
His best companions, innocence and health ;
And his best riches, ignorance of wealth.

But times are alter'd ; trade's unfeeling train   30
Usurp the land and dispossess the swain ;
Along the lawn, where scatter'd hamlets rose,
Unwieldy wealth, and cumbrous pomp repose ;

And every want to opulence allied,
And every pang that folly pays to pride.
Those gentle hours that plenty bade to bloom,
Those calm desires that ask'd but little room,
Those healthful sports that grac'd the peaceful scene,
Liv'd in each look, and brighten'd all the green ;
These, far departing, seek a kinder shore,
And rural mirth and manners are no more.

Sweet AUBURN ! parent of the blissful hour,
Thy glades forlorn confess the tyrant's power.   10
Here as I take my solitary rounds,
Amidst thy tangling walks, and ruin'd grounds,
And, many a year elaps'd, return to view
Where once the cottage stood, the hawthorn grew,
Remembrance wakes with all her busy train,
Swells at my breast, and turns the past to pain.

In all my wand'rings round this world of care,
In all my griefs—and GOD has given my share—
I still had hopes my latest hours to crown,
Amidst these humble bowers to lay me down ;   20
To husband out life's taper at the close,
And keep the flame from wasting by repose.
I still had hopes, for pride attends us still,
Amidst the swains to show my book-learn'd skill,
Around my fire an evening group to draw,
And tell of all I felt, and all I saw ;
And, as a hare, whom hounds and horns pursue,
Pants to the place from whence at first she flew,
I still had hopes, my long vexations pass'd,
Here to return—and die at home at last.   30

O blest retirement, friend to life's decline,
Retreats from care, that never must be mine,
How happy he who crowns in shades like these,
A youth of labour with an age of ease ;

Who quits a world where strong temptations try
And, since 'tis hard to combat, learns to fly !
For him no wretches, born to work and weep,
Explore the mine, or tempt the dangerous deep ;
No surly porter stands in guilty state
To spurn imploring famine from the gate ;
But on he moves to meet his latter end,
Angels around befriending Virtue's friend ;
Bends to the grave with unperceiv'd decay,
While Resignation gently slopes the way ;   10
And, all his prospects bright'ning to the last,
His Heaven commences ere the world be pass'd !

Sweet was the sound, when oft at evening's close
Up yonder hill the village murmur rose ;
There, as I pass'd with careless steps and slow,
The mingling notes came soften'd from below ;
The swain responsive as the milk-maid sung,
The sober herd that low'd to meet their young ;
The noisy geese that gabbled o'er the pool,
The playful children just let loose from school ;   20
The watchdog's voice that bay'd the whisp'ring wind,
And the loud laugh that spoke the vacant mind ;
These all in sweet confusion sought the shade,
And fill'd each pause the nightingale had made.
But now the sounds of population fail,
No cheerful murmurs fluctuate in the gale,
No busy steps the grass-grown foot-way tread,
For all the bloomy flush of life is fled.
All but yon widow'd, solitary thing
That feebly bends beside the plashy spring ;   30
She, wretched matron, forc'd, in age, for bread,
To strip the brook with mantling cresses spread,
To pick her wintry faggot from the thorn,
To seek her nightly shed, and weep till morn ;
She only left of all the harmless train,
The sad historian of the pensive plain.

Near yonder copse, where once the garden smil'd,
And still where many a garden flower grows wild ;
There, where a few torn shrubs the place disclose,
The village preacher's modest mansion rose.
A man he was to all the country dear,
And passing rich with forty pounds a year ;
Remote from towns he ran his godly race,
Nor e'er had chang'd, nor wished to change his
    place ;
Unpractis'd he to fawn, or seek for power,
By doctrines fashion'd to the varying hour ;   10
Far other aims his heart had learned to prize,
More skill'd to raise the wretched than to rise.
His house was known to all the vagrant train,
He chid their wand'rings, but reliev'd their pain ;
The long-remember'd beggar was his guest,
Whose beard descending swept his aged breast ;
The ruin'd spendthrift, now no longer proud,
Claim'd kindred there, and had his claims allow'd ;
The broken soldier, kindly bade to stay,
Sat by his fire, and talk'd the night away ;   20
Wept o'er his wounds, or tales of sorrow done,
Shoulder'd his crutch, and show'd how fields were
    won.
Pleas'd with his guests, the good man learn'd to glow,
And quite forgot their vices in their woe ;
Careless their merits, or their faults to scan,
His pity gave ere charity began.

Thus to relieve the wretched was his pride,
And e'en his failings lean'd to Virtue's side.
But in his duty prompt at every call,
He watch'd and wept, he pray'd and felt, for all ;   30
And, as a bird each fond endearment tries
To tempt its new-fledg'd offspring to the skies,
He tried each art, reprov'd each dull delay,
Allur'd to brighter worlds, and led the way.

Beside the bed where parting life was laid,
And sorrow, guilt, and pain, by turns dismay'd,
The reverend champion stood.   At his control,
Despair and Anguish fled the struggling soul ;
Comfort came down the trembling wretch to raise,
And his last falt'ring accents whisper'd praise.

At church, with meek and unaffected grace,
His looks adorn'd the venerable place ;
Truth from his lips prevail'd with double sway,
And fools, who came to scoff, remain'd to pray.   10
The service pass'd, around the pious man,
With steady zeal, each honest rustic ran ;
Even children follow'd with endearing wile,
And pluck'd his gown, to share the good man's smile.
His ready smile a parent's warmth express'd,
Their welfare pleas'd him, and their cares distress'd ;
To them his heart, his love, his griefs were given,
But all his serious thoughts had rest in Heaven.
As some tall cliff, that lifts its awful form,
Swells from the vale, and midway leaves the storm,   20
Though round its breast the rolling clouds are spread,
Eternal sunshine settles on its head.

Beside yon straggling fence that skirts the way,
With blossom'd furze unprofitably gay,
There, in his noisy mansion, skill'd to rule,
The village master taught his little school ;
A man severe he was, and stern to view ;
I knew him well, and every truant knew ;
Well had the boding tremblers learn'd to trace
The day's disasters in his morning face ;   30
Full well they laugh'd, with counterfeited glee,
At all his jokes, for many a joke had he ;
Full well the busy whisper, circling round,
Convey'd the dismal tidings when he frown'd ;
Yet he was kind ; or if severe in aught,

The love he bore to learning was in fault ;
The village all declar'd how much he knew ;
'Twas certain he could write, and cypher too ;
Lands he could measure, terms and tides presage,
And e'en the story ran that he could gauge.
In arguing too, the parson own'd his skill,
For e'en though vanquish'd, he could argue still ;
While words of learned length and thund'ring sound
Amazed the gazing rustics rang'd around,
And still they gaz'd, and still the wonder grew,   10
That one small head could carry all he knew.

But past is all his fame.   The very spot
Where many a time he triumph'd, is forgot.
Near yonder thorn, that lifts its head on high,
Where once the sign-post caught the passing eye,
Low lies that house where nut-brown draughts in-
        spir'd,
Where grey-beard mirth and smiling toil retir'd,
Where village statesmen talk'd with looks profound,
And news much older than their ale went round.
Imagination fondly stoops to trace   20
The parlour splendours of that festive place ;
The white-wash'd wall, the nicely sanded floor,
The varnish'd clock that click'd behind the door ;
The chest contriv'd a double debt to pay,
A bed by night, a chest of drawers by day ;
The pictures plac'd for ornament and use,
The twelve good rules, the royal game of goose ;
The hearth, except when winter chill'd the day,
With aspen boughs, and flowers, and fennel gay ;
While broken tea-cups, wisely kept for show,   30
Rang'd o'er the chimney, glisten'd in a row.

Vain, transitory splendours !   Could not all
Reprieve the tottering mansion from its fall !
Obscure it sinks, nor shall it more impart

An hour's importance to the poor man's heart ;
Thither no more the peasant shall repair
To sweet oblivion of his daily care ;
No more the farmer's news, the barber's tale,
No more the wood-man's ballad shall prevail ;
No more the smith his dusky brow shall clear,
Relax his pond'rous strength, and lean to hear ;
The host himself no longer shall be found
Careful to see the mantling bliss go round ;
Nor the coy maid, half willing to be press'd,　　　10
Shall kiss the cup to pass it to the rest.

Yes ! let the rich deride, the proud disdain,
These simple blessings of the lowly train ;
To me more dear, congenial to my heart,
One native charm, than all the gloss of art ;
Spontaneous joys, where Nature has its play,
The soul adopts, and owns their first-born sway ;
Lightly they frolic o'er the vacant mind,
Unenvied, unmolested, unconfin'd :
But the long pomp, the midnight masquerade,　　　20
With all the freaks of wanton wealth array'd,
In these, ere triflers half their wish obtain,
The toiling pleasure sickens into pain ;
And, e'en while fashion's brightest arts decoy,
The heart distrusting asks, if this be joy.

Ye friends to truth, ye statesmen, who survey
The rich man's joys increase, the poor's decay,
'Tis yours to judge, how wide the limits stand
Between a splendid and a happy land.
Proud swells the tide with loads of freighted ore,　　　30
And shouting Folly hails them from her shore ;
Hoards, e'en beyond the miser's wish abound,
And rich men flock from all the world around.
Yet count our gains. This wealth is but a name
That leaves our useful products still the same.

Not so the loss.   The man of wealth and pride
Takes up a space that many poor supplied ;
Space for his lake, his park's extended bounds,
Space for his horses, equipage, and hounds ;
The robe that wraps his limbs in silken sloth
Has robb'd the neighbouring fields of half their
        growth ;
His seat, where solitary sports are seen,
Indignant spurns the cottage from the green ;
Around the world each needful product flies,
For all the luxuries the world supplies :   10
While thus the land adorn'd for pleasure, all
In barren splendour feebly waits the fall.

  As some fair female unadorn'd and plain,
Secure to please while youth confirms her reign,
Slights every borrow'd charm that dress supplies,
Nor shares with art the triumph of her eyes :
But when those charms are pass'd, for charms are frail,
When time advances, and when lovers fail,
She then shines forth, solicitous to bless,
In all the glaring impotence of dress.   20
Thus fares the land, by luxury betray'd,
In nature's simplest charms at first array'd ;
But verging to decline, its splendours rise,
Its vistas strike, its palaces surprise ;
While scourg'd by famine from the smiling land,
The mournful peasant leads his humble band ;
And while he sinks, without one arm to save,
The country blooms—a garden, and a grave.

  Where then, ah ! where, shall poverty reside,
To 'scape the pressure of contiguous pride ?   30
If to some common's fenceless limits stray'd,
He drives his flock to pick the scanty blade,
Those fenceless fields the sons of wealth divide,
And e'en the bare-worn common is denied.

65

If to the city sped—What waits him there ?
To see profusion that he must not share ;
To see ten thousand baneful arts combin'd
To pamper luxury and thin mankind ;
To see those joys the sons of pleasure know
Extorted from his fellow creature's woe.
Here, while the courtier glitters in brocade,
There the pale artist plies the sickly trade ;
Here, while the proud their long-drawn pomps display,
There the black gibbet glooms beside the way.   10
The dome where Pleasure holds her midnight reign
Here, richly deck'd, admits the gorgeous train ;
Tumultuous grandeur crowds the blazing square,
The rattling chariots clash, the torches glare.
Sure scenes like these no troubles e'er annoy !
Sure these denote one universal joy !
Are these thy serious thoughts ?—Ah, turn thine eyes
Where the poor houseless shiv'ring female lies.
She once, perhaps, in village plenty bless'd,
Has wept at tales of innocence distress'd ;   20
Her modest looks the cottage might adorn,
Sweet as the primrose peeps beneath the thorn ;
Now lost to all, her friends, her virtue fled,
Near her betrayer's door she lays her head,
And, pinch'd with cold, and shrinking from the
            shower,
With heavy heart deplores that luckless hour,
When idly first, ambitious of the town,
She left her wheel and robes of country brown.

Do thine, sweet AUBURN, thine, the loveliest train,
Do thy fair tribes participate her pain ?   30
E'en now, perhaps, by cold and hunger led,
At proud men's doors they ask a little bread !

Ah, no.   To distant climes, a dreary scene,
Where half the convex world intrudes between,
Through torrid tracts with fainting steps they go,

Where wild Altama murmurs to their woe.
Far different there from all that charm'd before,
The various terrors of that horrid shore ;
Those blazing suns that dart a downward ray,
And fiercely shed intolerable day ;
Those matted woods where birds forget to sing.
But silent bats in drowsy clusters cling ;
Those pois'nous fields with rank luxuriance crown'd,
Where the dark scorpion gathers death around ;
Where at each step the stranger fears to wake   10
The rattling terrors of the vengeful snake ;
Where crouching tigers wait their hapless prey,
And savage men more murd'rous still than they ;
While oft in whirls the mad tornado flies,
Mingling the ravag'd landscape with the skies.
Far different these from every former scene,
The cooling brook, the grassy-vested green,
The breezy covert of the warbling grove,
That only shelter'd thefts of harmless love.

Good Heaven ! what sorrows gloom'd that parting
          day,   20
That call'd them from their native walks away ;
When the poor exiles, every pleasure pass'd,
Hung round their bowers, and fondly look'd their last,
And took a long farewell, and wish'd in vain
For seats like these beyond the western main ;
And shudd'ring still to face the distant deep,
Return'd and wept, and still return'd to weep.
The good old sire the first prepar'd to go
To new-found worlds, and wept for others' woe ;
But for himself, in conscious virtue brave,   30
He only wish'd for worlds beyond the grave.
His lovely daughter, lovelier in her tears,
The fond companion of his helpless years,
Silent went next, neglectful of her charms,
And left a lover's for a father's arms.

With louder plaints the mother spoke her woes,
And bless'd the cot where every pleasure rose,
And kiss'd her thoughtless babes with many a tear,
And clasp'd them close, in sorrow doubly dear ;
Whilst her fond husband strove to lend relief
In all the silent manliness of grief.

O Luxury ! thou curs'd by Heaven's decree,
How ill exchang'd are things like these for thee !
How do thy potions, with insidious joy
Diffuse their pleasures only to destroy !   10
Kingdoms by thee, to sickly greatness grown,
Boast of a florid vigour not their own ;
At every draught more large and large they grow,
A bloated mass of rank unwieldy woe ;
Till sapp'd their strength, and every part unsound,
Down, down they sink, and spread a ruin round.

E'en now the devastation is begun,
And half the business of destruction done ;
E'en now, methinks, as pond'ring here I stand,
I see the rural virtues leave the land :   20
Down where yon anchoring vessel spreads the sail,
That idly waiting flaps with ev'ry gale,
Downward they move, a melancholy band,
Pass from the shore, and darken all the strand.
Contented toil, and hospitable care,
And kind connubial tenderness, are there ;
And piety, with wishes plac'd above,
And steady loyalty, and faithful love.
And thou, sweet Poetry, thou loveliest maid,
Still first to fly where sensual joys invade ;   30
Unfit in these degenerate times of shame,
To catch the heart, or strike for honest fame ;
Dear charming nymph, neglected and decried,
My shame in crowds, my solitary pride ;
Thou source of all my bliss, and all my woe,

That found'st me poor at first, and keep'st me so ;
Thou guide by which the nobler arts excel,
Thou nurse of every virtue, fare thee well !
Farewell, and Oh ! where'er thy voice be tried,
On Torno's cliffs, or Pambamarca's side,
Whether where equinoctial fervours glow,
Or winter wraps the polar world in snow,
Still let thy voice, prevailing over time,
Redress the rigours of th' inclement clime ;
Aid slighted truth ; with thy persuasive strain   10
Teach erring man to spurn the rage of gain ;
Teach him, that states of native strength possess'd,
Though very poor, may still be very bless'd ;
That trade's proud empire hastes to swift decay,
As ocean sweeps the labour'd mole away ;
While self-dependent power can time defy,
As rocks resist the billows and the sky.

OLIVER GOLDSMITH

ON THE RECEIPT OF MY MOTHER'S PICTURE OUT OF NORFOLK

THE GIFT OF MY COUSIN ANN BODHAM

OH that those lips had language !   Life has pass'd
With me but roughly since I heard thee last.
Those lips are thine—thy own sweet smiles I see,   20
The same that oft in childhood solaced me ;
Voice only fails, else, how distinct they say,
" Grieve not, my child, chase all thy fears away ! "
The meek intelligence of those dear eyes
(Blest be the art that can immortalize,
The art that baffles Time's tyrannic claim
To quench it) here shines on me still the same.
  Faithful remembrancer of one so dear,
Oh welcome guest, though unexpected here !

Who bidd'st me honour with an artless song,
Affectionate, a mother lost so long,
I will obey, not willingly alone,
But gladly, as the precept were her own ;
And, while that face renews my filial grief,
Fancy shall weave a charm for my relief—
Shall steep me in Elysian reverie,
A momentary dream, that thou art she.

    My mother, when I learn'd that thou wast dead,
Say, wast thou conscious of the tears I shed ?   10
Hover'd thy spirit o'er thy sorrowing son,
Wretch even then, life's journey just begun ?
Perhaps thou gav'st me, though unseen, a kiss ;
Perhaps a tear, if souls can weep in bliss—
Ah that maternal smile ! it answers—Yes.
I heard the bell toll'd on thy burial day,
I saw the hearse that bore thee slow away,
And, turning from my nurs'ry window, drew
A long, long sigh, and wept a last adieu !
But was it such ?—It was.—Where thou art gone   20
Adieus and farewells are a sound unknown.
May I but meet thee on that peaceful shore,
The parting sound shall pass my lips no more !
Thy maidens griev'd themselves at my concern,
Oft gave me promise of a quick return.
What ardently I wish'd, I long believ'd,
And, disappointed still, was still deceiv'd ;
By disappointment every day beguil'd,
Dupe of *to-morrow* even from a child.
Thus many a sad to-morrow came and went,   30
Till, all my stock of infant sorrow spent,
I learn'd at last submission to my lot ;
But, though I less deplor'd thee, ne'er forgot.

    Where once we dwelt our name is heard no more,
Children not thine have trod my nurs'ry floor ;
And where the gard'ner Robin, day by day,
Drew me to school along the public way,

Delighted with my bauble coach, and wrapt
In scarlet mantle warm, and velvet capt,
'Tis now become a history little known,
That once we call'd the past'ral house our own.
Short-liv'd possession ! but the record fair
That mem'ry keeps of all thy kindness there,
Still outlives many a storm that has effac'd
A thousand other themes less deeply trac'd.
Thy nightly visits to my chamber made,
That thou might'st know me safe and warmly laid ; 10
Thy morning bounties ere I left my home,
The biscuit, or confectionary plum ;
The fragrant waters on my cheeks bestow'd
By thy own hand, till fresh they shone and glow'd ;
All this, and more endearing still than all,
Thy constant flow of love, that knew no fall,
Ne'er roughen'd by those cataracts and brakes
That humour interpos'd too often makes ;
All this still legible in mem'ry's page,
And still to be so, to my latest age, 20
Adds joy to duty, makes me glad to pay
Such honours to thee as my numbers may ;
Perhaps a frail memorial, but sincere,
Not scorn'd in heav'n, though little notic'd here.
　　Could Time, his flight revers'd, restore the hours,
When, playing with thy vesture's tissued flow'rs,
The violet, the pink, and jessamine,
I prick'd them into paper with a pin.
(And thou wast happier than myself the while,
Would'st softly speak, and stroke my head and smile), 30
Could those few pleasant hours again appear,
Might one wish bring them, would I wish them here ?
I would not trust my heart—the dear delight
Seems so to be desir'd, perhaps I might.—
But no—what here we call our life is such,
So little to be lov'd, and thou so much,
That I should ill requite thee to constrain

Thy unbound spirit into bonds again.
　　Thou, as a gallant bark from Albion's coast
(The storms all weather'd and the ocean cross'd)
Shoots into port at some well-haven'd isle,
Where spices breathe and brighter seasons smile,
There sits quiescent on the floods that show
Her beauteous form reflected clear below,
While airs impregnated with incense play
Around her, fanning light her streamers gay ;
So thou, with sails how swift ! hast reach'd the shore　10
" Where tempests never beat nor billows roar,"
And thy lov'd consort on the dang'rous tide
Of life, long since, has anchor'd at thy side.
But me, scarce hoping to attain that rest,
Always from port withheld, always distress'd—
Me howling winds drive devious, tempest toss'd,
Sails ript, seams op'ning wide, and compass lost,
And day by day some current's thwarting force
Sets me more distant from a prosp'rous course.
But oh the thought, that thou art safe, and he !　　20
That thought is joy, arrive what may to me.
My boast is not that I deduce my birth
From loins enthron'd, and rulers of the earth ;
But higher far my proud pretensions rise—
The son of parents pass'd into the skies.
And now, farewell—Time, unrevok'd, has run
His wonted course, yet what I wish'd is done.
By contemplation's help, not sought in vain,
I seem t' have liv'd my childhood o'er again ;
To have renew'd the joys that once were mine,　　30
Without the sin of violating thine :
And, while the wings of fancy still are free,
And I can view this mimic show of thee,
Time has but half succeeded in his theft—
Thyself remov'd, thy power to soothe me left.

WILLIAM COWPER

PETER GRIMES

OLD Peter Grimes made fishing his employ,
His wife he cabin'd with him and his boy,
And seem'd that life laborious to enjoy :
To town came quiet Peter with his fish,
And had of all a civil word and wish.
He left his trade upon the sabbath-day,
And took young Peter in his hand to pray :
But soon the stubborn boy from care broke loose,
At first refused, then added his abuse :
His father's love he scorn'd, his power defied,   10
But being drunk, wept sorely when he died.

Yes ! then he wept, and to his mind there came
Much of his conduct, and he felt the shame,—
How he had oft the good old man reviled,
And never paid the duty of a child ;
How, when the father in his Bible read,
He in contempt and anger left the shed :
" It is the word of life," the parent cried ;
—" This is the life itself," the boy replied ;
And while old Peter in amazement stood,   20
Gave the hot spirit to his boiling blood :—
How he, with oath and furious speech, began
To prove his freedom and assert the man ;
And when the parent check'd his impious rage,
How he had cursed the tyranny of age,—
Nay, once had dealt the sacrilegious blow
On his bare head, and laid his parent low ;
The father groan'd—" If thou art old," said he,
" And hast a son—thou wilt remember me :
Thy mother left me in a happy time,   30
Thou kill'dst not her—Heav'n spares the double
    crime."

On an inn-settle, in his maudlin grief,
This he revolved, and drank for his relief.

Now lived the youth in freedom, but debarr'd
From constant pleasure, and he thought it hard ;
Hard that he could not every wish obey,
But must awhile relinquish ale and play ;
Hard ! that he could not to his cards atte..d,
But must acquire the money he would spend.

With greedy eye he look'd on all he saw,
He knew not justice, and he laugh'd at law ;
On all he mark'd he stretch'd his ready hand ;
He fish'd by water, and he filch'd by land :   10
Oft in the night has Peter dropp'd his oar,
Fled from his boat and sought for prey on shore ;
Oft up the hedge-row glided, on his back
Bearing the orchard's produce in a sack,
Or farm-yard load, tugg'd fiercely from the stack ;
And as these wrongs to greater numbers rose,
The more he look'd on all men as his foes.

He built a mud-wall'd hovel, where he kept
His various wealth, and there he oft-times slept ;
But no success could please his cruel soul,   20
He wish'd for one to trouble and control ;
He wanted some obedient boy to stand
And bear the blow of his outrageous hand ;
And hoped to find in some propitious hour
A feeling creature subject to his power.

Peter had heard there were in London then,—
Still have they being !—workhouse-clearing men,
Who, undisturb'd by feelings just or kind,
Would parish-boys to needy tradesmen bind :
They in their want a trifling sum would take,   30
And toiling slaves of piteous orphans make.

Such Peter sought, and when a lad was found,
The sum was dealt him, and the slave was bound.
Some few in town observed in Peter's trap
A boy, with jacket blue and woollen cap ;
But none inquired how Peter used the rope,
Or what the bruise, that made the stripling stoop ;

None could the ridges on his back behold,
None sought him shiv'ring in the winter's cold ;
None put the question,—" Peter, dost thou give
The boy his food ?—What, man ! the lad must live :
Consider, Peter, let the child have bread,
He'll serve thee better if he's stroked and fed."
None reason'd thus—and some, on hearing cries,
Said calmly, "Grimes is at his exercise."

    Pinn'd, beaten, cold, pinch'd, threaten'd, and
        abused—
His efforts punish'd and his food refused,—   10
Awake tormented,—soon aroused from sleep,—
Struck if he wept, and yet compell'd to weep,
The trembling boy dropp'd down and strove to pray,
Received a blow, and trembling turn'd away,
Or sobb'd and hid his piteous face ;—while he,
The savage master, grinn'd in horrid glee :
He'd now the power he ever loved to show,
A feeling being subject to his blow.

    Thus lived the lad, in hunger, peril, pain,
His tears despised, his supplications vain :   20
Compell'd by fear to lie, by need to steal,
His bed uneasy and unbless'd his meal,
For three sad years the boy his tortures bore,
And then his pains and trials were no more.

    " How died he, Peter ? " when the people said,
He growl'd—" I found him lifeless in his bed ; "
Then tried for softer tone, and sigh'd, " Poor Sam is
        dead."
Yet murmurs were there, and some questions ask'd,—
How he was fed, how punish'd, and how task'd ?
Much they suspected, but they little proved,   30
And Peter pass'd untroubled and unmoved.

    Another boy with equal ease was found,
The money granted, and the victim bound ;
And what his fate ?—One night it chanced he fell
From the boat's mast and perish'd in her well,

Where fish were living kept, and where the boy
(So reason'd men) could not himself destroy :—
    " Yes ! so it was," said Peter, " in his play,
(For he was idle both by night and day,)
He climb'd the main-mast and then fell below ; "—
Then show'd his corpse and pointed to the blow :
" What said the jury ? "—they were long in doubt
But sturdy Peter faced the matter out :
So they dismiss'd him, saying at the time,
" Keep fast your hatchway when you've boys who
        climb."   10
This hit the conscience, and he colour'd more
Than for the closest questions put before.
    Thus all his fears the verdict set aside,
And at the slave-shop Peter still applied.
    Then came a boy, of manners soft and mild,—
Our seamen's wives with grief beheld the child ;
All thought (the poor themselves) that he was one
Of gentle blood, some noble sinner's son,
Who had, belike, deceived some humble maid,
Whom he had first seduced and then betray'd :—   20
However this, he seem'd a gracious lad,
In grief submissive and with patience sad.
    Passive he labour'd, till his slender frame
Bent with his loads, and he at length was lame :
Strange that a frame so weak could bear so long
The grossest insult and the foulest wrong ;
But there were causes—in the town they gave
Fire, food, and comfort, to the gentle slave ;
And though stern Peter, with a cruel hand,
And knotted rope, enforced the rude command,   30
Yet he consider'd what he'd lately felt,
And his vile blows with selfish pity dealt.
    One day such draughts the cruel fisher made,
He could not vend them in his borough-trade,
But sail'd for London-mart : the boy was ill,
But ever humbled to his master's will ;

And on the river, where they smoothly sail'd,
He strove with terror and awhile prevail'd ;
But new to danger on the angry sea,
He clung affrighten'd to his master's knee :
The boat grew leaky and the wind was strong,
Rough was the passage and the time was long ;
His liquor fail'd, and Peter's wrath arose,—
No more is known—the rest we must suppose,
Or learn of Peter ;—Peter says, he " spied
The stripling's danger and for harbour tried ;   10
Meantime the fish, and then th' apprentice died."

    The pitying women raised a clamour round,
And weeping said, "Thou hast thy 'prentice drown'd."

    Now the stern man was summon'd to the hall,
To tell his tale before the burghers all :
He gave th' account ; profess'd the lad he loved,
And kept his brazen features all unmoved.

    The mayor himself with tone severe replied,—
" Henceforth with thee shall never boy abide ;
Hire thee a freeman, whom thou durst not beat,   20
But who, in thy despite, will sleep and eat :
Free thou art now !—again shouldst thou appear,
Thou'lt find thy sentence, like thy soul, severe."

    Alas ! for Peter not a helping hand,
So was he hated, could he now command ;
Alone he row'd his boat, alone he cast
His nets beside, or made his anchor fast ;
To hold a rope or hear a curse was none,—
He toil'd and rail'd ; he groan'd and swore alone.

    Thus by himself compell'd to live each day,   30
To wait for certain hours the tide's delay ;
At the same times the same dull views to see,
The bounding marsh-bank and the blighted tree ;
The water only, when the tides were high,
When low, the mud half-cover'd and half-dry ;
The sun-burnt tar that blisters on the planks,
And bank-side stakes in their uneven ranks ;

Heaps of entangled weeds that slowly float,
As the tide rolls by the impeded boat.
　　When tides were neap, and, in the sultry day,
Through the tall bounding mud-banks made their
　　　　way,
Which on each side rose swelling, and below
The dark warm flood ran silently and slow ;
There anchoring, Peter chose from man to hide,
There hang his head, and view the lazy tide
In its hot slimy channel slowly glide ;
Where the small eels that left the deeper way　　10
For the warm shore, within the shallows play ;
Where gaping mussels, left upon the mud,
Slope their slow passage to the fallen flood ;—
Here dull and hopeless he'd lie down and trace
How sidelong crabs had scrawl'd their crooked race ;
Or sadly listen to the tuneless cry
Of fishing gull or clanging golden-eye ;
What time the sea-birds to the marsh would come,
And the loud bittern, from the bulrush home,
Gave from the salt-ditch side the bellowing boom :　20
He nursed the feelings these dull scenes produce,
And loved to stop beside the opening sluice ;
Where the small stream, confined in narrow bound,
Ran with a dull, unvaried, sadd'ning sound ;
Where all, presented to the eye or ear,
Oppress'd the soul with misery, grief, and fear.
　　Besides these objects, there were places three,
Which Peter seem'd with certain dread to see ;
When he drew near them he would turn from each,
And loudly whistle till he pass'd the reach.　　30
　　A change of scene to him brought no relief ;
In town, 'twas plain, men took him for a thief :
The sailors' wives would stop him in the street,
And say, " Now, Peter, thou'st no boy to beat : "
Infants at play, when they perceived him, ran,
Warning each other—" That's the wicked man : "

He growl'd an oath, and in an angry tone
Cursed the whole place and wish'd to be alone.
  Alone he was, the same dull scenes in view,
And still more gloomy in his sight they grew :
Though man he hated, yet employ'd alone
At bootless labour, he would swear and groan,
Cursing the shoals that glided by the spot,
And gulls that caught them when his arts could not.
  Cold nervous tremblings shook his sturdy frame,
And strange disease—he couldn't say the name ;   10
Wild were his dreams, and oft he rose in fright,
Waked by his view of horrors in the night,—
Horrors that would the sternest minds amaze,
Horrors that demons might be proud to raise :
And though he felt forsaken, grieved at heart,
To think he lived from all mankind apart ;
Yet, if a man approach'd, in terrors he would start.
  A winter pass'd since Peter saw the town,
And summer-lodgers were again come down ;
These, idly curious, with their glasses spied   20
The ships in bay as anchor'd for the tide,—
The river's craft,—the bustle of the quay,—
And sea-port views, which landmen love to see.
  One, up the river, had a man and boat
Seen day by day, now anchor'd, now afloat ;
Fisher he seem'd, yet used no net nor hook ;
Of sea-fowl swimming by no heed he took,
But on the gliding waves still fix'd his lazy look :
At certain stations he would view the stream,
As if he stood bewilder'd in a dream,   30
Or that some power had chain'd him for a time,
To feel a curse or meditate on crime.
  This known, some curious, some in pity went,
And others question'd—" Wretch, dost thou repent ? "
He heard, he trembled, and in fear resign'd
His boat : new terror fill'd his restless mind ;
Furious he grew, and up the country ran,

And there they seized him—a distemper'd man :—
Him we received, and to a parish-bed,
Follow'd and curs'd, the groaning man was led.

Here when they saw him, whom they used to shun,
A lost, lone man, so harass'd and undone ;
Our gentle females, ever prompt to feel,
Perceived compassion on their anger steal ;
His crimes they could not from their memories blot,
But they were grieved, and trembled at his lot.

A priest too came, to whom his words are told ;   10
And all the signs they shudder'd to behold.

"Look ! look !" they cried ; "his limbs with
    horror shake,
And as he grinds his teeth, what noise they make !
How glare his angry eyes, and yet he's not awake :
See ! what cold drops upon his forehead stand,
And how he clenches that broad bony hand."

The priest attending, found he spoke at times
As one alluding to his fears and crimes :
"It was the fall," he mutter'd, "I can show
The manner how—I never struck a blow : "—   20
And then aloud—"Unhand me, free my chain ;
On oath, he fell—it struck him to the brain :—
Why ask my father ?—that old man will swear
Against my life ; besides, he wasn't there :—
What, all agreed ?—Am I to die to-day ?—
My Lord, in mercy, give me time to pray."

Then, as they watch'd him, calmer he became,
And grew so weak he couldn't move his frame,
But murmuring spake,—while they could see and hear
The start of terror and the groan of fear ;   30
See the large dew-beads on his forehead rise,
And the cold death-drop glaze his sunken eyes ;
Nor yet he died, but with unwonted force
Seem'd with some fancied being to discourse :
He knew not us, or with accustom'd art
He hid the knowledge, yet exposed his heart ;

80

'Twas part confession and the rest defence,
A madman's tale, with gleams of waking sense.
  " I'll tell you all," he said, " the very day
When the old man first placed them in my way :
My father's spirit—he who always tried
To give me trouble, when he lived and died—
When he was gone, he could not be content
To see my days in painful labour spent,
But would appoint his meetings, and he made
Me watch at these, and so neglect my trade.   10
  " 'Twas one hot noon, all silent, still, serene,
No living being had I lately seen ;
I paddled up and down and dipp'd my net,
But (such his pleasure) I could nothing get,—
A father's pleasure, when his toil was done,
To plague and torture thus an only son !
And so I sat and look'd upon the stream,
How it ran on, and felt as in a dream :
But dream it was not ; no !—I fix'd my eyes
On the mid stream and saw the spirits rise ;   20
I saw my father on the water stand,
And hold a thin pale boy in either hand ;
And there they glided ghastly on the top
Of the salt flood, and never touch'd a drop :
I would have struck them, but they knew th' intent,
And smiled upon the oar, and down they went.
  " Now, from that day, whenever I began
To dip my net, there stood the hard old man—
He and those boys : I humbled me and pray'd
They would be gone ;—they heeded not, but stay'd : 30
Nor could I turn, nor would the boat go by,
But gazing on the spirits, there was I :
They bade me leap to death, but I was loth to die ;
And every day, as sure as day arose,
Would these three spirits meet me ere the close ;
To hear and mark them daily was my doom,
And ' Come,' they said, with weak, sad voices, ' come.'

To row away with all my strength I try'd,
But there were they, hard by me in the tide,
The three unbodied forms—and ' Come,' still ' come,'
    they cried.

  " Fathers should pity—but this old man shook
His hoary locks, and froze me by a look :
Thrice, when I struck them, through the water came
A hollow groan, that weaken'd all my frame :
' Father ! ' said I, ' have mercy : '—He replied,
I know not what—the angry spirit lied,—
' Didst thou not draw thy knife ? ' said he :—'Twas
    true,   10
But I had pity and my arm withdrew :
He cried for mercy which I kindly gave,
But he has no compassion in his grave.

  " There were three places, where they ever rose,—
The whole long river has not such as those,—
Places accursed, where, if a man remain,
He'll see the things which strike him to the brain ;
And there they made me on my paddle lean,
And look at them for hours ;—accursed scene !
When they would glide to that smooth eddy-space, 20
Then bid me leap and join them in the place ;
And at my groans each little villain sprite
Enjoy'd my pains and vanish'd in delight.

  " In one fierce summer-day, when my poor brain
Was burning hot, and cruel was my pain,
Then came this father-foe, and there he stood
With his two boys again upon the flood ;
There was more mischief in their eyes, more glee
In their pale faces when they glared at me :
Still did they force me on the oar to rest, 30
And when they saw me fainting and oppress'd,
He, with his hand, the old man, scoop'd the flood,
And there came flame about him mix'd with blood ;
He bade me stoop and look upon the place,
Then flung the hot-red liquor in my face ;

Burning it blazed, and then I roar'd for pain,
I thought the demons would have turn'd my brain.
 " Still there they stood, and forced me to behold
A place of horrors—they cannot be told—
Where the flood open'd, there I heard the shriek
Of tortured guilt—no earthly tongue can speak :
' All days alike ! for ever ! ' did they say,
' And unremitted torments every day '—
Yes, so they said : "—But here he ceased and gazed
On all around, affrighten'd and amazed ;   10
And still he tried to speak, and look'd in dread
Of frighten'd females gathering round his bed ;
Then dropp'd exhausted, and appear'd at rest,
Till the strong foe the vital powers possess'd :
Then with an inward, broken voice he cried,
 " Again they come," and mutter'd as he died.
                                    GEORGE CRABBE

LINES

COMPOSED A FEW MILES ABOVE TINTERN ABBEY, ON REVISITING THE BANKS OF THE WYE DURING A TOUR. JULY 13, 1798

FIVE years have past ; five summers, with the length
Of five long winters ! and again I hear
These waters, rolling from their mountain-springs
With a soft inland murmur.—Once again   20
Do I behold these steep and lofty cliffs,
That on a wild secluded scene impress
Thoughts of more deep seclusion ; and connect
The landscape with the quiet of the sky.
The day is come when I again repose
Here, under this dark sycamore, and view
These plots of cottage-ground, these orchard-tufts,
Which at this season, with their unripe fruits,

Are clad in one green hue, and lose themselves
'Mid groves and copses.   Once again I see
These hedge-rows, hardly hedge-rows, little lines
Of sportive wood run wild : these pastoral farms,
Green to the very door ; and wreaths of smoke
Sent up, in silence, from among the trees !
With some uncertain notice, as might seem
Of vagrant dwellers in the houseless woods,
Or of some Hermit's cave, where by his fire
The Hermit sits alone.   10

                              These beauteous forms,
Through a long absence, have not been to me
As is a landscape to a blind man's eye :
But oft, in lonely rooms, and 'mid the din
Of towns and cities, I have owed to them,
In hours of weariness, sensations sweet,
Felt in the blood, and felt along the heart ;
And passing even into my purer mind,
With tranquil restoration :—feelings too
Of unremembered pleasure : such, perhaps,   20
As have no slight or trivial influence
On that best portion of a good man's life,
His little, nameless, unremembered, acts
Of kindness and of love.   Nor less, I trust,
To them I may have owed another gift,
Of aspect more sublime ; that blessed mood,
In which the burthen of the mystery,
In which the heavy and the weary weight
Of all this unintelligible world,
Is lightened :—that serene and blessed mood,   30
In which the affections gently lead us on,—
Until, the breath of this corporeal frame
And even the motion of our human blood
Almost suspended, we are laid asleep
In body, and become a living soul :
While with an eye made quiet by the power

Of harmony, and the deep power of joy,
We see into the life of things.
                                    If this
Be but a vain belief, yet, oh ! how oft—
In darkness and amid the many shapes
Of joyless daylight ; when the fretful stir
Unprofitable, and the fever of the world,
Have hung upon the beatings of my heart—
How oft, in spirit, have I turned to thee,
O sylvan Wye ! thou wanderer thro' the woods,   10
How often has my spirit turned to thee !

And now, with gleams of half-extinguished thought,
With many recognitions dim and faint,
And somewhat of a sad perplexity,
The picture of the mind revives again :
While here I stand, not only with the sense
Of present pleasure, but with pleasing thoughts
That in this moment there is life and food
For future years.   And so I dare to hope,
Though changed, no doubt, from what I was when first
I came among these hills ; when like a roe   21
I bounded o'er the mountains, by the sides
Of the deep rivers, and the lonely streams,
Wherever nature led : more like a man
Flying from something that he dreads, than one
Who sought the thing he loved.   For nature then
(The coarser pleasures of my boyish days,
And their glad animal movements all gone by)
To me was all in all.—I cannot paint
What then I was.   The sounding cataract   30
Haunted me like a passion : the tall rock,
The mountain, and the deep and gloomy wood,
Their colours and their forms, were then to me
An appetite ; a feeling and a love,
That had no need of a remoter charm,
By thought supplied, nor any interest

Unborrowed from the eye.—That time is past,
And all its aching joys are now no more,
And all its dizzy raptures.   Not for this
Faint I, nor mourn nor murmur ; other gifts
Have followed ; for such loss, I would believe,
Abundant recompense.   For I have learned
To look on nature, not as in the hour
Of thoughtless youth ; but hearing oftentimes
The still, sad music of humanity,
Nor harsh nor grating, though of ample power   10
To chasten and subdue.   And I have felt
A presence that disturbs me with the joy
Of elevated thoughts ; a sense sublime
Of something far more deeply interfused,
Whose dwelling is the light of setting suns,
And the round ocean and the living air,
And the blue sky, and in the mind of man :
A motion and a spirit, that impels
All thinking things, all objects of all thought,
And rolls through all things.   Therefore am I still 20
A lover of the meadows and the woods,
And mountains ; and of all that we behold
From this green earth ; of all the mighty world
Of eye, and ear,—both what they half create,
And what perceive ; well pleased to recognise
In nature and the language of the sense
The anchor of my purest thoughts, the nurse,
The guide, the guardian of my heart, and soul
Of all my moral being.

Nor perchance,   30

If I were not thus taught, should I the more
Suffer my genial spirits to decay :
For thou art with me here upon the banks
Of this fair river ; thou my dearest Friend,
My dear, dear Friend ; and in thy voice I catch
The language of my former heart, and read
My former pleasures in the shooting lights

Of thy wild eyes.   Oh ! yet a little while
May I behold in thee what I was once,
My dear, dear Sister ! and this prayer I make,
Knowing that Nature never did betray
The heart that loved her ; 'tis her privilege,
Through all the years of this our life, to lead
From joy to joy : for she can so inform
The mind that is within us, so impress
With quietness and beauty, and so feed
With lofty thoughts, that neither evil tongues,   10
Rash judgments, nor the sneers of selfish men,
Nor greetings where no kindness is, nor all
The dreary intercourse of daily life,
Shall e'er prevail against us, or disturb
Our cheerful faith, that all which we behold
Is full of blessings.   Therefore let the moon
Shine on thee in thy solitary walk ;
And let the misty mountain-winds be free
To blow against thee : and, in after years,
When these wild ecstasies shall be matured   20
Into a sober pleasure ; when thy mind
Shall be a mansion for all lovely forms,
Thy memory be as a dwelling-place
For all sweet sounds and harmonies ; oh ! then,
If solitude, or fear, or pain, or grief,
Should be thy portion, with what healing thoughts
Of tender joy wilt thou remember me,
And these my exhortations !   Nor, perchance—
If I should be where I no more can hear
Thy voice, nor catch from thy wild eyes these gleams   30
Of past existence—wilt thou then forget
That on the banks of this delightful stream
We stood together ; and that I, so long
A worshipper of Nature, hither came
Unwearied in that service : rather say
With warmer love—oh ! with far deeper zeal
Of holier love.   Nor wilt thou then forget,

That after many wanderings, many years
Of absence, these steep woods and lofty cliffs,
And this green pastoral landscape, were to me
More dear, both for themselves and for thy sake !

WILLIAM WORDSWORTH

RESOLUTION AND INDEPENDENCE

I

THERE was a roaring in the wind all night ;
The rain came heavily and fell in floods ;
But now the sun is rising calm and bright ;
The birds are singing in the distant woods ;
Over his own sweet voice the Stock-dove broods ;
The Jay makes answer as the Magpie chatters ;   10
And all the air is filled with pleasant noise of waters.

II

All things that love the sun are out of doors ;
The sky rejoices in the morning's birth ;
The grass is bright with rain-drops ;—on the moors
The hare is running races in her mirth ;
And with her feet she from the plashy earth
Raises a mist ; that, glittering in the sun,
Runs with her all the way, wherever she doth run.

III

I was a Traveller then upon the moor ;
I saw the hare that raced about with joy ;   20
I heard the woods and distant waters roar ;
Or heard them not, as happy as a boy ;
The pleasant season did my heart employ :
My old remembrances went from me wholly ;
And all the ways of men, so vain and melancholy.

IV

But, as it sometimes chanceth, from the might
Of joy in minds that can no further go,
As high as we have mounted in delight
In our dejection do we sink as low ;
To me that morning did it happen so ;
And fears and fancies thick upon me came ;
Dim sadness—and blind thoughts, I knew not, nor
      could name.

V

I heard the sky-lark warbling in the sky ;
And I bethought me of the playful hare :
Even such a happy Child of earth am I ;   10
Even as these blissful creatures do I fare ;
Far from the world I walk, and from all care ;
But there may come another day to me—
Solitude, pain of heart, distress, and poverty.

VI

My whole life I have lived in pleasant thought,
As if life's business were a summer mood ;
As if all needful things would come unsought
To genial faith, still rich in genial good ;
But how can He expect that others should
Build for him, sow for him, and at his call   20
Love him, who for himself will take no heed at all ?

VII

I thought of Chatterton, the marvellous Boy,
The sleepless Soul that perished in his pride ;
Of Him who walked in glory and in joy
Following his plough, along the mountain-side :
By our own spirits are we deified :

We Poets in our youth begin in gladness ;
But thereof come in the end despondency and madness.

VIII

Now, whether it were by peculiar grace,
A leading from above, a something given,
Yet it befell that, in this lonely place,
When I with these untoward thoughts had striven,
Beside a pool bare to the eye of heaven
I saw a Man before me unawares :
The oldest man he seemed that ever wore grey hairs.

IX

As a huge stone is sometimes seen to lie   10
Couched on the bald top of an eminence ;
Wonder to all who do the same espy,
By what means it could thither come, and whence ;
So that it seems a thing endued with sense :
Like a sea-beast crawled forth, that on a shelf
Of rock or sand reposeth, there to sun itself ;

X

Such seemed this Man, not all alive nor dead,
Nor all asleep—in his extreme old age :
His body was bent double, feet and head
Coming together in life's pilgrimage ;   20
As if some dire constraint of pain, or rage
Of sickness felt by him in times long past,
A more than human weight upon his frame had cast.

XI

Himself he propped, limbs, body, and pale face,
Upon a long grey staff of shaven wood :

And, still as I drew near with gentle pace,
Upon the margin of that moorish flood
Motionless as a cloud the old Man stood,
That heareth not the loud winds when they call ;
And moveth all together, if it move at all.

XII

At length, himself unsettling, he the pond
Stirred with his staff, and fixedly did look
Upon the muddy water, which he conned,
As if he had been reading in a book :
And now a stranger's privilege I took ;   10
And, drawing to his side, to him did say,
" This morning gives us promise of a glorious day."

XIII

A gentle answer did the old Man make,
In courteous speech which forth he slowly drew :
And him with further words I thus bespake,
" What occupation do you there pursue ?
This is a lonesome place for one like you."
Ere he replied, a flash of mild surprise
Broke from the sable orbs of his yet-vivid eyes.

XIV

His words came feebly, from a feeble chest,   20
But each in solemn order followed each,
With something of a lofty utterance drest—
Choice word and measured phrase, above the reach
Of ordinary men ; a stately speech ;
Such as grave Livers do in Scotland use,
Religious men, who give to God and man their
        dues.

XV

He told, that to these waters he had come
To gather leeches, being old and poor :
Employment hazardous and wearisome !
And he had many hardships to endure :
From pond to pond he roamed, from moor to moor ;
Housing, with God's good help, by choice or chance ;
And in this way he gained an honest maintenance.

XVI

The old Man still stood talking by my side ;
But now his voice to me was like a stream
Scarce heard ; nor word from word could I divide ;   10
And the whole body of the Man did seem
Like one whom I had met with in a dream ;
Or like a man from some far region sent,
To give me human strength, by apt admonishment.

XVII

My former thoughts returned : the fear that kills ;
And hope that is unwilling to be fed ;
Cold, pain, and labour, and all fleshly ills ;
And mighty Poets in their misery dead.
—Perplexed, and longing to be comforted,
My question eagerly did I renew,   20
" How is it that you live, and what is it you do ? "

XVIII

,He with a smile did then his words repeat ;
And said that, gathering leeches, far and wide
He travelled ; stirring thus about his feet
The waters of the pools where they abide.
" Once I could meet with them on every side ;

But they have dwindled long by slow decay ;
Yet still I persevere, and find them where I may."

XIX

While he was talking thus, the lonely place,
The old Man's shape, and speech—all troubled me :
In my mind's eye I seemed to see him pace
About the weary moors continually,
Wandering about alone and silently.
While I these thoughts within myself pursued,
He, having made a pause, the same discourse re-
newed.

XX

And soon with this he other matter blended,   10
Cheerfully uttered, with demeanour kind,
But stately in the main ; and, when he ended,
I could have laughed myself to scorn to find
In that decrepit Man so firm a mind.
" God," said I, " be my help and stay secure ;
I'll think of the Leech-gatherer on the lonely Moor ! "

WILLIAM WORDSWORTH

CHRISTABEL

PART THE FIRST

'Tis the middle of night by the castle clock,
And the owls have awakened the crowing cock ;
Tu—whit !——Tu—whoo !
And hark, again ! the crowing cock,   20
How drowsily it crew.

Sir Leoline, the Baron rich,
Hath a toothless mastiff, which
From her kennel beneath the rock
Maketh answer to the clock,

Four for the quarters, and twelve for the hour ;
Ever and aye, by shine and shower,
Sixteen short howls, not over loud ;
Some say, she sees my lady's shroud.

Is the night chilly and dark ?
The night is chilly, but not dark.
The thin grey cloud is spread on high,
It covers but not hides the sky.
The moon is behind, and at the full ;
And yet she looks both small and dull.   10
The night is chill, the cloud is grey :
'Tis a month before the month of May,
And the Spring comes slowly up this way.

The lovely lady, Christabel,
Whom her father loves so well,
What makes her in the wood so late,
A furlong from the castle gate ?
She had dreams all yesternight
Of her own betrothed knight ;
And she in the midnight wood will pray   20
For the weal of her lover that's far away.

She stole along, she nothing spoke,
The sighs she heaved were soft and low,
And naught was green upon the oak,
But moss and rarest mistletoe :
She kneels beneath the huge oak tree,
And in silence prayeth she.
The lady sprang up suddenly,
The lovely lady, Christabel !
It moaned as near, as near can be,   30
But what it is, she cannot tell.—
On the other side it seems to be,
Of the huge, broad-breasted, old oak tree.

The night is chill ; the forest bare ;
Is it the wind that moaneth bleak ?
There is not wind enough in the air
To move away the ringlet curl
From the lovely lady's cheek—
There is not wind enough to twirl
The one red leaf, the last of its clan,
That dances as often as dance it can,
Hanging so light, and hanging so high,
On the topmost twig that looks up at the sky.　　10

Hush, beating heart of Christabel !
Jesu, Maria, shield her well !
She folded her arms beneath her cloak,
And stole to the other side of the oak.
　　What sees she there ?

There she sees a damsel bright,
Drest in a silken robe of white,
That shadowy in the moonlight shone :
The neck that made that white robe wan,
Her stately neck, and arms were bare ;　　20
Her blue-veined feet unsandal'd were
And wildly glittered here and there
The gems entangled in her hair.
I guess, 'twas frightful there to see
A lady so richly clad as she—
Beautiful exceedingly !

" Mary mother, save me now ! "
(Said Christabel) " And who art thou ? "

The lady strange made answer meet,
And her voice was faint and sweet :—　　30
" Have pity on my sore distress,
I scarce can speak for weariness :

Stretch forth thy hand, and have no fear ! "
Said Christabel, " How camest thou here ? "
And the lady, whose voice was faint and sweet,
Did thus pursue her answer meet :—

" My sire is of a noble line,
And my name is Geraldine :
Five warriors seized me yestermorn,
Me, even me, a maid forlorn :
They choked my cries with force and fright,
And tied me on a palfrey white.   10
The palfrey was as fleet as wind,
And they rode furiously behind.
They spurred amain, their steeds were white ;
And once we crossed the shade of night.
As sure as Heaven shall rescue me,
I have no thought what men they be ;
Nor do I know how long it is
(For I have lain entranced I wis)
Since one, the tallest of the five,
Took me from the palfrey's back,   20
A weary woman, scarce alive.
Some muttered words his comrades spoke :
He placed me underneath this oak,
He swore they would return with haste ;
Whither they went I cannot tell—
I thought I heard, some minutes past,
Sounds as of a castle-bell.
Stretch forth thy hand " (thus ended she),
" And help a wretched maid to flee."

Then Christabel stretched forth her hand   30
And comforted fair Geraldine :
" O well, bright dame ! may you command
The service of Sir Leoline ;
And gladly our stout chivalry
Will he send forth and friends withal

To guide and guard you safe and free
Home to your noble father's hall."

She rose : and forth with steps they passed
That strove to be, and were not, fast.
Her gracious stars the lady blest,
And thus spake on sweet Christabel :
" All our household are at rest,
The hall as silent as the cell ;
Sir Leoline is weak in health
And may not well awakened be,   10
But we will move as if in stealth
And I beseech your courtesy,
This night to share your couch with me."

They crossed the moat, and Christabel
Took the key that fitted well ;
A little door she opened straight,
All in the middle of the gate ;
The gate that was ironed within and without,
Where an army in battle array had marched out.
The lady sank, belike through pain,   20
And Christabel with might and main
Lifted her up, a weary weight,
Over the threshold of the gate :
Then the lady rose again,
And moved, as she were not in pain.

So free from danger, free from fear,
They crossed the court : right glad they were.
And Christabel devoutly cried
To the lady by her side,
" Praise we the Virgin all divine   30
Who hath rescued thee from thy distress ! "
" Alas, alas ! " said Geraldine,
" I cannot speak for weariness."

So free from danger, free from fear,
They crossed the court : right glad they were.

Outside her kennel, the mastiff old
Lay fast asleep, in moonshine cold.
The mastiff old did not awake,
Yet she an angry moan did make !
And what can ail the mastiff bitch ?
Never till now she uttered yell
Beneath the eye of Christabel.
Perhaps it is the owlet's scritch :   10
For what can ail the mastiff bitch ?

They passed the hall, that echoes still,
Pass as lightly as you will !
The brands were flat, the brands were dying,
Amid their own white ashes lying ;
But when the lady passed, there came
A tongue of light, a fit of flame ;
And Christabel saw the lady's eye,
And nothing else saw she thereby,
Save the boss of the shield of Sir Leoline tall, 20
Which hung in a murky old niche in the wall.
" O softly tread," said Christabel,
" My father seldom sleepeth well."

Sweet Christabel her feet doth bare,
And jealous of the listening air
They steal their way from stair to stair,
Now in glimmer, and now in gloom,
And now they pass the Baron's room,
As still as death, with stifled breath !
And now have reached her chamber door ;   30
And now doth Geraldine press down
The rushes of the chamber floor.

The moon shines dim in the open air,
And not a moonbeam enters here.
But they without its light can see
The chamber carved so curiously,
Carved with figures strange and sweet,
All made out of the carver's brain,
For a lady's chamber meet :
The lamp with twofold silver chain
Is fastened to an angel's feet.

The silver lamp burns dead and dim ;   10
But Christabel the lamp will trim.
She trimmed the lamp, and made it bright,
And left it swinging to and fro,
While Geraldine, in wretched plight,
Sank down upon the floor below.

" O weary lady, Geraldine,
I pray you, drink this cordial wine !
It is a wine of virtuous powers ;
My mother made it of wild flowers."

" And will your mother pity me,   20
Who am a maiden most forlorn ? "
Christabel answered—" Woe is me !
She died the hour that I was born.
I have heard the grey-haired friar tell,
How on her deathbed she did say,
That she should hear the castle-bell
Strike twelve upon my wedding-day.
O mother dear ! that thou wert here ! "
" I would," said Geraldine, " she were ! "

But soon with altered voice, said she—   30
" Off, wandering mother !   Peak and pine,
I have power to bid thee flee."
Alas ! what ails poor Geraldine ?

Why stares she with unsettled eye ?
Can she the bodiless dead espy ?
And why with hollow voice cries she,
" Off, woman, off ! this hour is mine—
Though thou her guardian spirit be,
Off, woman, off ! 'tis given to me."

Then Christabel knelt by the lady's side,
And raised to heaven her eyes so blue—
" Alas ! " said she, " this ghastly ride—
Dear lady ! it hath wildered you ! "   10
The lady wiped her moist cold brow,
And faintly said, " 'Tis over now ! "

Again the wild-flower wine she drank :
Her fair large eyes 'gan glitter bright,
And from the floor whereon she sank,
The lofty lady stood upright ;
She was most beautiful to see,
Like a lady of a far countrée.

And thus the lofty lady spake—
" All they who live in the upper sky,   20
Do love you, holy Christabel !
And you love them, and for their sake
And for the good which me befell,
Even I in my degree will try,
Fair maiden, to requite you well.
But now unrobe yourself ; for I
Must pray, ere yet in bed I lie."

Quoth Christabel, " So let it be ! "
And as the lady bade, did she.
Her gentle limbs did she undress,   30
And lay down in her loveliness.

But through her brain of weal and woe
So many thoughts moved to and fro,
That vain it were her lids to close ;
So half-way from the bed she rose,
And on her elbow did recline
To look at the lady Geraldine.

Beneath the lamp the lady bowed,
And slowly rolled her eyes around ;
Then drawing in her breath aloud,
Like one that shuddered, she unbound   10
The cincture from beneath her breast :
Her silken robe, and inner vest,
Dropt to her feet, and full in view,
Behold ! her bosom and half her side——
A sight to dream of, not to tell !
O shield her ! shield sweet Christabel !

Yet Geraldine nor speaks nor stirs ;
Ah ! what a stricken look was hers !
Deep from within she seems half-way
To lift some weight with sick assay,   20
And eyes the maid and seeks delay ;
Then suddenly as one defied
Collects herself in scorn and pride,
And lay down by the Maiden's side !—
And in her arms the maid she took,
          Ah wel-a-day !
And with low voice and doleful look
These words did say :
" In the touch of this bosom there worketh a spell,
Which is lord of thy utterance, Christabel !   30
Thou knowest to-night, and wilt know to-morrow,
This mark of my shame, this seal of my sorrow ;
          But vainly thou warrest,
               For this is alone in
               Thy power to declare,

That in the dim forest
Thou heard'st a low moaning,
And found'st a bright lady, surpassingly fair :
And didst bring her home with thee in love and in
    charity,
To shield her and shelter her from the damp air."

THE CONCLUSION TO PART THE FIRST

It was a lovely sight to see
The lady Christabel, when she
Was praying at the old oak tree.
    Amid the jagged shadows
    Of mossy leafless boughs,   10
    Kneeling in the moonlight,
    To make her gentle vows ;
Her slender palms together prest,
Heaving sometimes on her breast ;
Her face resigned to bliss or bale—
Her face, oh, call it fair not pale,
And both blue eyes more bright than clear.
Each about to have a tear.

With open eyes (ah woe is me !)
Asleep, and dreaming fearfully,   20
Fearfully dreaming, yet I wis,
Dreaming that alone, which is—
O sorrow and shame ! Can this be she,
The lady, who knelt at the old oak tree ?
And lo ! the worker of these harms,
That holds the maiden in her arms,
Seems to slumber still and mild,
As a mother with her child.

A star hath set, a star hath risen,
O Geraldine ! since arms of thine   30
Have been the lovely lady's prison.

O Geraldine ! one hour was thine—
Thou'st had thy will !   By tairn and rill,
The night-birds all that hour were still.
But now they are jubilant anew,
From cliff and tower, tu—whoo ! tu—whoo !
Tu—whoo ! tu—whoo ! from wood and fell !

And see ! the lady Christabel
Gathers herself from out her trance ;
Her limbs relax, her countenance
Grows sad and soft ; the smooth thin lids   10
Close o'er her eyes ; and tears she sheds—
Large tears that leave the lashes bright !
And oft the while she seems to smile
As infants at a sudden light !

Yea, she doth smile, and she doth weep,
Like a youthful hermitess,
Beauteous in a wilderness,
Who, praying always, prays in sleep.
And, if she move unquietly,
Perchance, 'tis but the blood so free,   20
Comes back and tingles in her feet.
No doubt, she hath a vision sweet.
What if her guardian spirit 'twere,
What if she knew her mother near ?
But this she knows, in joys and woes,
That saints will aid if men will call :
For the blue sky bends over all !

PART THE SECOND

" Each matin bell," the Baron saith,
" Knells us back to a world of death."
These words Sir Leoline first said,   30
When he rose and found his lady dead :

These words Sir Leoline will say,
Many a morn to his dying day !

And hence the custom and law began,
That still at dawn the sacristan,
Who duly pulls the heavy bell,
Five and forty beads must tell
Between each stroke—a warning knell,
Which not a soul can choose but hear
From Bratha Head to Wyndermere.

Saith Bracy the bard, " So let it knell !   10
And let the drowsy sacristan
Still count as slowly as he can !
There is no lack of such, I ween
As well fill up the space between.
In Langdale Pike and Witch's Lair,
And Dungeon-ghyll so foully rent,
With ropes of rock and bells of air
Three sinful sextons' ghosts are pent,
Who all give back, one after t'other,
The death-note to their living brother ;   20
And oft too, by the knell offended,
Just as their one ! two ! three ! is ended,
The devil mocks the doleful tale
With a merry peal from Borrowdale."

The air is still ! through mist and cloud
That merry peal comes ringing loud ;
And Geraldine shakes off her dread,
And rises lightly from the bed ;
Puts on her silken vestments white,
And tricks her hair in lovely plight,   30
And nothing doubting of her spell
Awakens the lady Christabel.
" Sleep you, sweet lady Christabel ?
I trust that you have rested well."

And Christabel awoke and spied
The same who lay down by her side—
O rather say, the same whom she
Raised up beneath the old oak tree!
Nay, fairer yet ! and yet more fair !
For she belike hath drunken deep
Of all the blessedness of sleep !
And while she spake, her looks, her air
Such gentle thankfulness declare,
That (so it seemed) her girded vests   10
Grew tight beneath her heaving breasts.
" Sure I have sinned ! " said Christabel,
" Now heaven be praised if all be well ! "
And in low faltering tones, yet sweet,
Did she the lofty lady greet
With such perplexity of mind
As dreams too lively leave behind.

So quickly she rose, and quickly arrayed
Her maiden limbs, and having prayed
That He, who on the cross did groan,   20
Might wash away her sins unknown,
She forthwith led fair Geraldine
To meet her sire, Sir Leoline.

The lovely maid and the lady tall
Are pacing both into the hall,
And pacing on through page and groom
Enter the Baron's presence-room.

The Baron rose, and while he prest
His gentle daughter to his breast,
With cheerful wonder in his eyes   30
The lady Geraldine espies,
And gave such welcome to the same,
As might beseem so bright a dame !

But when he heard the lady's tale,
And when she told her father's name,
Why waxed Sir Leoline so pale,
Murmuring o'er the name again,
" Lord Roland de Vaux of Tryermaine ? "

Alas ! they had been friends in youth ;
But whispering tongues can poison truth ;
And constancy lives in realms above ;
And life is thorny ; and youth is vain :
And to be wroth with one we love,   10
Doth work like madness in the brain.
And thus it chanced, as I divine,
With Roland and Sir Leoline.
Each spake words of high disdain
And insult to his heart's best brother :
They parted—ne'er to meet again !
But never either found another
To free the hollow heart from paining—
They stood aloof, the scars remaining,
Like cliffs which had been rent asunder ;   20
A dreary sea now flows between.
But neither heat, nor frost, nor thunder,
Shall wholly do away, I ween,
The marks of that which once hath been.

Sir Leoline, a moment's space,
Stood gazing on the damsel's face :
And the youthful Lord of Tryermaine
Came back upon his heart again.

O then the Baron forgot his age,
His noble heart swelled high with rage ;   30
He swore by the wounds in Jesu's side,
He would proclaim it far and wide
With trump and solemn heraldry,
That they, who thus had wronged the dame,

Were base as spotted infamy !
" And if they dare deny the same,
My herald shall appoint a week
And let the recreant traitors seek
My tourney court—that there and then
I may dislodge their reptile souls
From the bodies and forms of men ! "
He spake : his eye in lightning rolls !
For the lady was ruthlessly seized ; and he kenned
In the beautiful lady the child of his friend !   10
And now the tears were on his face,
And fondly in his arms he took
Fair Geraldine, who met the embrace,
Prolonging it with joyous look.
Which when she viewed, a vision fell
Upon the soul of Christabel,
The vision of fear, the touch and pain !
She shrunk and shuddered, and saw again—
(Ah, woe is me ! Was it for thee,
Thou gentle maid ! such sights to see ?)   20

Again she saw that bosom old,
Again she felt that bosom cold,
And drew in her breath with a hissing sound :
Whereat the Knight turned wildly round,
And nothing saw, but his own sweet maid
With eyes upraised, as one that prayed.

The touch, the sight, had passed away,
And in its stead that vision blest,
Which comforted her after-rest,
While in the lady's arms she lay,   30
Had put a rapture in her breast.
And on her lips and o'er her eyes
Spread smiles like light !
                 With new surprise,
" What ails then my beloved child ? "

The Baron said—His daughter mild
Made answer, " All will yet be well ! "
I ween, she had no power to tell
Aught else : so mighty was the spell.

Yet he, who saw this Geraldine,
Had deemed her such a thing divine.
Such sorrow with such grace she blended,
As if she feared she had offended
Sweet Christabel, that gentle maid !
And with such lowly tones she prayed.   10
She might be sent without delay
Home to her father's mansion.
                                " Nay !
Nay, by my soul ! " said Leoline.
" Ho ! Bracy the bard, the charge be thine !
Go thou, with music sweet and loud,
And take two steeds with trappings proud,
And take the youth whom thou lov'st best
To bear thy harp, and learn thy song,
And clothe you both in solemn vest,   20
And over the mountains haste along,
Lest wandering folk, that are abroad,
Detain you on the valley road.

" And when he has crossed the Irthing flood,
My merry bard ! he hastes, he hastes
Up Knorren Moor, through Halegarth Wood,
And reaches soon that castle good
Which stands and threatens Scotland's wastes.

" Bard Bracy ! bard Bracy ! your horses are fleet,
Ye must ride up the hall, your music so sweet,   30
More loud than your horses' echoing feet !
And loud and loud to Lord Roland call,
' Thy daughter is safe in Langdale hall !
Thy beautiful daughter is safe and free—

Sir Leoline greets thee thus through me.
He bids thee come without delay
With all thy numerous array ;
And take thy lovely daughter home :
And he will meet thee on the way
With all his numerous array
White with their panting palfreys' foam ' :
And by mine honour ! I will say,
That I repent me of the day
When I spake words of fierce disdain   10
To Roland de Vaux of Tryermaine !—
—For since that evil hour hath flown,
Many a summer's sun hath shone ;
Yet ne'er found I a friend again
Like Roland de Vaux of Tryermaine."
The lady fell, and clasped his knees,
Her face upraised, her eyes o'erflowing ;
And Bracy replied, with faltering voice,
His gracious hail on all bestowing ;—
" Thy words, thou sire of Christabel,   20
Are sweeter than my harp can tell ;
Yet might I gain a boon of thee,
This day my journey should not be,
So strange a dream hath come to me ;
That I had vowed with music loud
To clear yon wood from thing unblest,
Warned by a vision in my rest !
For in my sleep I saw that dove,
That gentle bird, whom thou dost love,
And call'st by thy own daughter's name—   30
Sir Leoline ! I saw the same,
Fluttering, and uttering fearful moan,
Among the green herbs in the forest alone.
Which when I saw and when I heard,
I wonder'd what might ail the bird :
For nothing near it could I see,
Save the grass and green herbs underneath the old tree.

" And in my dream, methought, I went
To search out what might there be found ;
And what the sweet bird's trouble meant,
That thus lay fluttering on the ground.
I went and peered, and could descry
No cause for her distressful cry ;
But yet for her dear lady's sake
I stooped, methought, the dove to take,
When lo ! I saw a bright green snake
Coiled around its wings and neck.   10
Green as the herbs on which it couched,
Close by the dove's its head it crouched ;
And with the dove it heaves and stirs,
Swelling its neck as she swelled hers !
I woke ; it was the midnight hour,
The clock was echoing in the tower ;
But though my slumber was gone by,
This dream it would not pass away—
It seems to live upon the eye !
And thence I vowed this selfsame day,   20
With music strong and saintly song
To wander through the forest bare,
Lest aught unholy loiter there."

Thus Bracy said : the Baron, the while,
Half-listening heard him with a smile ;
Then turned to Lady Geraldine,
His eyes made up of wonder and love ;
And said in courtly accents fine,
" Sweet maid, Lord Roland's beauteous dove,
With arms more strong than harp or song,   30
Thy sire and I will crush the snake ! "
He kissed her forehead as he spake,
And Geraldine in maiden wise,
Casting down her large bright eyes,
With blushing cheek and courtesy fine
She turned her from Sir Leoline ;

Softly gathering up her train,
That o'er her right arm fell again;
And folded her arms across her chest,
And couched her head upon her breast,
And looked askance at Christabel——
Jesu, Maria, shield her well !

A snake's small eye blinks dull and shy,
And the lady's eyes they shrunk in her head,
Each shrunk up to a serpent's eye,
And with somewhat of malice, and more of
    dread,   10
At Christabel she looked askance !——
One moment—and the sight was fled !
But Christabel in dizzy trance
Stumbling on the unsteady ground
Shuddered aloud, with a hissing sound ;
And Geraldine again turned round,
And like a thing, that sought relief,
Full of wonder and full of grief,
She rolled her large bright eyes divine
Wildly on Sir Leoline.   20

The maid, alas ! her thoughts are gone,
She nothing sees—no sight but one !
The maid, devoid of guile and sin,
I know not how, in fearful wise,
So deeply had she drunken in
That look, those shrunken serpent eyes,
That all her features were resigned
To this sole image in her mind :
And passively did imitate
That look of dull and treacherous hate !   30
And thus she stood, in dizzy trance,
Still picturing that look askance
With forced unconscious sympathy
Full before her father's view——

As far as such a look could be,
In eyes so innocent and blue !

And when the trance was o'er, the maid
Paused awhile, and inly prayed :
Then falling at the Baron's feet,
" By my mother's soul do I entreat
That thou this woman send away ! "
She said : and more she could not say :
For what she knew she could not tell,
O'er-mastered by the mighty spell.   10

Why is thy cheek so wan and wild,
Sir Leoline ?   Thy only child
Lies at thy feet, thy joy, thy pride,
So fair, so innocent, so mild ;
The same, for whom thy lady died !
O by the pangs of her dear mother
Think thou no evil of thy child !
For her, and thee, and for no other,
She prayed the moment ere she died :
Prayed that the babe, for whom she died,   20
Might prove her dear lord's joy and pride !
    That prayer her deadly pangs beguiled,
            Sir Leoline !
    And wouldst thou wrong thy only child,
            Her child and thine ?

Within the Baron's heart and brain
If thoughts like these had any share,
They only swelled his rage and pain,
And did but work confusion there.
His heart was cleft with pain and rage,   30
His cheeks they quivered, his eyes were wild,
Dishonour'd thus in his old age ;
Dishonour'd by his only child,

And all his hospitality
To the insulted daughter of his friend
By more than woman's jealousy
Brought thus to a disgraceful end—
He rolled his eye with stern regard
Upon the gentle minstrel bard,
And said in tones abrupt, austere—
" Why, Bracy ! dost thou loiter here ?
I bade thee hence ! "   The bard obeyed ;
And turning from his own sweet maid,   10
The aged knight, Sir Leoline,
Led forth the lady Geraldine !

THE CONCLUSION TO PART THE SECOND

A little child, a limber elf,
Singing, dancing to itself,
A fairy thing with red round cheeks
That always finds, and never seeks,
Makes such a vision to the sight
As fills a father's eyes with light ;
And pleasures flow in so thick and fast
Upon his heart, that he at last   20
Must needs express his love's excess
With words of unmeant bitterness.
Perhaps 'tis pretty to force together
Thoughts so all unlike each other ;
To mutter and mock a broken charm,
To dally with wrong that does no harm.
Perhaps 'tis tender too and pretty
At each wild word to feel within
A sweet recoil of love and pity.
And what, if in a world of sin   30
(O sorrow and shame should this be true !)
Such giddiness of heart and brain
Comes seldom save from rage and pain,
So talks as it's most used to do.

SAMUEL TAYLOR COLERIDGE

ADONAIS

I

I WEEP for Adonais—he is dead !
O, weep for Adonais ! though our tears
Thaw not the frost which binds so dear a head !
And thou, sad Hour, selected from all years
To mourn our loss, rouse thy obscure compeers,
And teach them thine own sorrow ; say : " With me
Died Adonais ; till the Future dares
Forget the Past, his fate and fame shall be
An echo and a light unto eternity ! "

II

Where wert thou, mighty Mother, when he lay,   10
When thy Son lay, pierced by the shaft which flies
In darkness ? where was lorn Urania
When Adonais died ?   With veilèd eyes,
'Mid listening Echoes, in her Paradise
She sate, while one, with soft enamoured breath,
Rekindled all the fading melodies,
With which, like flowers that mock the corse beneath,
He had adorned and hid the coming bulk of Death.

III

Oh, weep for Adonais—he is dead !
Wake, melancholy Mother, wake and weep !   20
Yet wherefore ?   Quench within their burning bed
Thy fiery tears, and let thy loud heart keep,
Like his, a mute and uncomplaining sleep ;
For he is gone, where all things wise and fair
Descend ;—oh, dream not that the amorous Deep

Will yet restore him to the vital air ;
Death feeds on his mute voice, and laughs at our
    despair.

IV

Most musical of mourners, weep again !
Lament anew, Urania !—He died,
Who was the Sire of an immortal strain,
Blind, old, and lonely, when his country's pride,
The priest, the slave, and the liberticide,
Trampled and mocked with many a loathèd rite
Of lust and blood ; he went, unterrified,
Into the gulf of death ; but his clear Sprite   10
Yet reigns o'er earth ; the third among the sons of
    light.

V

Most musical of mourners, weep anew !
Not all to that bright station dared to climb ;
And happier they their happiness who knew,
Whose tapers yet burn through that night of time
In which suns perished ; others more sublime,
Struck by the envious wrath of man or god,
Have sunk, extinct in their refulgent prime ;
And some yet live, treading the thorny road,
Which leads, through toil and hate, to Fame's serene
    abode.   20

VI

But now, thy youngest, dearest one, has perished—
The nursling of thy widowhood, who grew,
Like a pale flower by some sad maiden cherished,
And fed with true-love tears, instead of dew ;
Most musical of mourners, weep anew !
Thy extreme hope, the loveliest and the last,
The bloom, whose petals nipped before they blew

Died on the promise of the fruit, is waste ;
The broken lily dies—the storm is overpast.

VII

To that high Capital, where kingly Death
Keeps his pale court in beauty and decay,
He came ; and bought, with price of purest breath,
A grave among the eternal.—Come away !
Haste, while the vault of blue Italian day
Is yet his fitting charnel-roof ! while still
He lies, as if in dewy sleep he lay ;
Awake him not ! surely he takes his fill   10
Of deep and liquid rest, forgetful of all ill.

VIII

He will awake no more, oh, never more !—
Within the twilight chamber spreads apace
The shadow of white Death, and at the door
Invisible Corruption waits to trace
His extreme way to her dim dwelling-place ;
The eternal Hunger sits, but pity and awe
Soothe her pale rage, nor dares she to deface
So fair a prey, till darkness, and the law   19
Of change, shall o'er his sleep the mortal curtain draw.

IX

Oh, weep for Adonais !—The quick Dreams,
The passion-wingèd Ministers of thought,
Who were his flocks, whom near the living streams
Of his young spirit he fed, and whom he taught
The love which was its music, wander not,—
Wander no more, from kindling brain to brain,
But droop there, whence they sprung ; and mourn
          their lot

Round the cold heart, where, after their sweet pain,
They ne'er will gather strength, or find a home
    again.

X

And one with trembling hands clasps his cold head,
And fans him with her moonlight wings, and cries ;
" Our love, our hope, our sorrow, is not dead ;
See, on the silken fringe of his faint eyes,
Like dew upon a sleeping flower, there lies
A tear some Dream has loosened from his brain."
Lost Angel of a ruined Paradise !
She knew not 'twas her own ; as with no stain   10
She faded, like a cloud which had outwept its rain.

XI

One from a lucid urn of starry dew
Washed his light limbs as if embalming them ;
Another clipped her profuse locks, and threw
The wreath upon him, like an anadem,
Which frozen tears instead of pearls begem ;
Another in her wilful grief would break
Her bow and wingèd reeds, as if to stem
A greater loss with one which was more weak ;
And dull the barbèd fire against his frozen cheek. 20

XII

Another Splendour on his mouth alit,
That mouth, whence it was wont to draw the breath
Which gave it strength to pierce the guarded wit,
And pass into the panting heart beneath
With lightning and with music : the damp death
Quenched its caress upon his icy lips ;
And, as a dying meteor stains a wreath

Of moonlight vapour, which the cold night clips,
It flushed through his pale limbs, and passed to its
eclipse.

XIII

And others came . . . Desires and Adorations,
Wingèd Persuasions and veiled Destinies,
Splendours, and Glooms, and glimmering Incarna-
tions
Of hopes and fears, and twilight Phantasies ;
And Sorrow, with her family of Sighs,
And Pleasure, blind with tears, led by the gleam
Of her own dying smile instead of eyes,
Came in slow pomp ;—the moving pomp might
seem   10
Like pageantry of mist on an autumnal stream.

XIV

All he had loved, and moulded into thought,
From shape, and hue, and odour, and sweet sound,
Lamented Adonais.   Morning sought
Her eastern watch-tower, and her hair unbound,
Wet with the tears which should adorn the ground,
Dimmed the aëreal eyes that kindle day ;
Afar the melancholy thunder moaned,
Pale Ocean in unquiet slumber lay,
And the wild Winds flew round, sobbing in their
dismay.   20

XV

Lost Echo sits amid the voiceless mountains,
And feeds her grief with his remembered lay,
And will no more reply to winds or fountains,
Or amorous birds perched on the young green spray,
Or herdsman's horn, or bell at closing day ;

Since she can mimic not his lips, more dear
Than those for whose disdain she pined away
Into a shadow of all sounds :—a drear
Murmur, between their songs, is all the woodmen hear.

XVI

Grief made the young Spring wild, and she threw
    down
Her kindling buds, as if she Autumn were,
Or they dead leaves ; since her delight is flown,
For whom should she have waked the sullen year ?
To Phoebus was not Hyacinth so dear
Nor to himself Narcissus, as to both   10
Thou, Adonais : wan they stand and sere
Amid the faint companions of their youth,
With dew all turned to tears ; odour, to sighing ruth.

XVII

Thy spirit's sister, the lorn nightingale
Mourns not her mate with such melodious pain ;
Not so the eagle, who like thee could scale
Heaven, and could nourish in the sun's domain
Her mighty youth with morning, doth complain,
Soaring and screaming round her empty nest,
As Albion wails for thee : the curse of Cain   20
Light on his head who pierced thy innocent breast,
And scared the angel soul that was its earthly guest !

XVIII

Ah, woe is me ! Winter is come and gone,
But grief returns with the revolving year ;
The airs and streams renew their joyous tone ;
The ants, the bees, the swallows reappear ;
Fresh leaves and flowers deck the dead Seasons' bier;

The amorous birds now pair in every brake,
And build their mossy homes in field and brere ;
And the green lizard, and the golden snake,
Like unimprisoned flames, out of their trance awake.

XIX

Through wood and stream and field and hill and
    Ocean
A quickening life from the Earth's heart has burst
As it has ever done, with change and motion,
From the great morning of the world when first
God dawned on Chaos ; in its stream immersed,
The lamps of Heaven flash with a softer light ;   10
All baser things pant with life's sacred thirst ;
Diffuse themselves ; and spend in love's delight,
The beauty and the joy of their renewèd might.

XX

The leprous corpse, touched by this spirit tender,
Exhales itself in flowers of gentle breath ;
Like incarnations of the stars, when splendour
Is changed to fragrance, they illumine death
And mock the merry worm that wakes beneath ;
Nought we know, dies. Shall that alone which
    knows
Be as a sword consumed before the sheath   20
By sightless lightning ?—the intense atom glows
A moment, then is quenched in a most cold repose.

XXI

Alas ! that all we loved of him should be,
But for our grief, as if it had not been,
And grief itself be mortal ! Woe is me !
Whence are we, and why are we ? of what scene
The actors or spectators ? Great and mean

Meet massed in death, who lends what life must
    borrow.
As long as skies are blue, and fields are green,
Evening must usher night, night urge the morrow,
Month follow month with woe, and year wake year to
    sorrow.

XXII

He will awake no more, oh, never more !
" Wake thou," cried Misery, " childless Mother,
    rise
Out of thy sleep, and slake, in thy heart's core,
A wound more fierce than his, with tears and
    sighs."
And all the Dreams that watched Urania's eyes,
And all the Echoes whom their sister's song   10
Had held in holy silence, cried : " Arise ! "
Swift as a Thought by the snake Memory stung,
From her ambrosial rest the fading Splendour sprung.

XXIII

She rose like an autumnal Night, that springs
Out of the East, and follows wild and drear
The golden Day, which, on eternal wings,
Even as a ghost abandoning a bier,
Had left the Earth a corpse.   Sorrow and fear
So struck, so roused, so rapt Urania ;
So saddened round her like an atmosphere   20
Of stormy mist ; so swept her on her way
Even to the mournful place where Adonais lay.

XXIV

Out of her secret Paradise she sped,
Through camps and cities rough with stone, and
    steel,

And human hearts, which to her aëry tread
Yielding not, wounded the invisible
Palms of her tender feet where'er they fell :
And barbèd tongues, and thoughts more sharp than
   they,
Rent the soft Form they never could repel,
Whose sacred blood, like the young tears of May,
Paved with eternal flowers that undeserving way.

XXV

In the death-chamber for a moment Death,
Shamed by the presence of that living Might,
Blushed to annihilation, and the breath   10
Revisited those lips, and Life's pale light
Flashed through those limbs, so late her dear de-
   light.
" Leave me not wild and drear and comfortless,
As silent lightning leaves the starless night !
Leave me not ! " cried Urania : her distress
Roused Death : Death rose and smiled, and met her
   vain caress.

XXVI

" Stay yet awhile ! speak to me once again ;
Kiss me, so long but as a kiss may live ;
And in my heartless breast and burning brain   19
That word, that kiss, shall all thoughts else survive,
With food of saddest memory kept alive,
Now thou art dead, as if it were a part
Of thee, my Adonais ! I would give
All that I am to be as thou now art !
But I am chained to Time, and cannot thence depart !

XXVII

" O gentle child, beautiful as thou wert,
Why didst thou leave the trodden paths of men
Too soon, and with weak hands though mighty heart
Dare the unpastured dragon in his den ?
Defenceless as thou wert, oh, where was then
Wisdom the mirrored shield, or scorn the spear ?
Or hadst thou waited the full cycle, when
Thy spirit should have filled its crescent sphere,
The monsters of life's waste had fled from thee like
    deer.

XXVIII

The herded wolves, bold only to pursue ;   10
The obscene ravens, clamorous o'er the dead ;
The vultures to the conqueror's banner true,
Who feed where Desolation first has fed,
And whose wings rain contagion ;—how they fled,
When, like Apollo, from his golden bow
The Pythian of the age one arrow sped
And smiled !—The spoilers tempt no second blow,
They fawn on the proud feet that spurn them lying
    low.

XXIX

" The sun comes forth, and many reptiles spawn ;
He sets, and each ephemeral insect then   20
Is gathered into death without a dawn,
And the immortal stars awake again ;
So is it in the world of living men :
A godlike mind soars forth, in its delight
Making earth bare and veiling heaven, and when
It sinks, the swarms that dimmed or shared its light
Leave to its kindred lamps the spirit's awful night."

XXX

Thus ceased she : and the mountain shepherds
    came,
Their garlands sere, their magic mantles rent ;
The Pilgrim of Eternity, whose fame
Over his living head like Heaven is bent,
An early but enduring monument,
Came, veiling all the lightnings of his song
In sorrow ; from her wilds Ierne sent
The sweetest lyrist of her saddest wrong,
And Love taught Grief to fall like music from his
    tongue.

XXXI

Midst others of less note, came one frail Form,   10
A phantom among men ; companionless
As the last cloud of an expiring storm
Whose thunder is its knell ; he, as I guess,
Had gazed on Nature's naked loveliness,
Actaeon-like, and now he fled astray
With feeble steps o'er the world's wilderness,
And his own thoughts, along that rugged way,
Pursued, like raging hounds, their father and their
    prey.

XXXII

A pardlike Spirit beautiful and swift—
A Love in desolation masked ;—a Power   20
Girt round with weakness ;—it can scarce uplift
The weight of the superincumbent hour ;
It is a dying lamp, a falling shower,
A breaking billow ;—even whilst we speak
Is it not broken ? On the withering flower
The killing sun smiles brightly : on a cheek
The life can burn in blood, even while the heart may
    break.

XXXIII

His head was bound with pansies overblown,
And faded violets, white, and pied, and blue ;
And a light spear topped with a cypress cone,
Round whose rude shaft dark ivy-tresses grew
Yet dripping with the forest's noonday dew,
Vibrated, as the ever-beating heart
Shook the weak hand that grasped it ; of that crew
He came the last, neglected and apart ;
A herd-abandoned deer struck by the hunter's dart.

XXXIV

All stood aloof, and at his partial moan   10
Smiled through their tears ; well knew that gentle
        band
Who in another's fate now wept his own,
As in the accents of an unknown land
He sung new sorrow ; sad Urania scanned
The Stranger's mien, and murmured : " Who art
        thou ? "
He answered not, but with a sudden hand
Made bare his branded and ensanguined brow,
Which was like Cain's or Christ's—oh ! that it should
        be so !

XXXV

What softer voice is hushed over the dead ?
Athwart what brow is that dark mantle thrown ? 20
What form leans sadly o'er the white death-bed,
In mockery of monumental stone,
The heavy heart heaving without a moan ?
If it be He, who, gentlest of the wise,
Taught, soothed, loved, honoured the departed one,
Let me not vex, with inharmonious sighs,
The silence of that heart's accepted sacrifice.

XXXVI

Our Adonais has drunk poison—oh !
What deaf and viperous murderer could crown
Life's early cup with such a draught of woe ?
The nameless worm would now itself disown :
It felt, yet could escape, the magic tone
Whose prelude held all envy, hate, and wrong,
But what was howling in one breast alone,
Silent with expectation of the song,
Whose master's hand is cold, whose silver lyre unstrung.

XXXVII

Live thou, whose infamy is not thy fame !   10
Live ! fear no heavier chastisement from me,
Thou noteless blot on a remembered name !
But be thyself, and know thyself to be !
And ever at thy season be thou free
To spill the venom when thy fangs o'erflow :
Remorse and Self-contempt shall cling to thee ;
Hot Shame shall burn upon thy secret brow,
And like a beaten hound tremble thou shalt—as now.

XXXVIII

Nor let us weep that our delight is fled
Far from these carrion kites that scream below ; 20
He wakes or sleeps with the enduring dead ;
Thou canst not soar where he is sitting now—
Dust to the dust ! but the pure spirit shall flow
Back to the burning fountain whence it came,
A portion of the Eternal, which must glow
Through time and change, unquenchably the same,
Whilst thy cold embers choke the sordid hearth of
    shame.

126

XXXIX

Peace, peace ! he is not dead, he doth not sleep—
He hath awakened from the dream of life—
'Tis we, who, lost in stormy visions, keep
With phantoms an unprofitable strife,
And in mad trance strike with our spirit's knife
Invulnerable nothings.—*We* decay
Like corpses in a charnel ; fear and grief
Convulse us and consume us day by day,
And cold hopes swarm like worms within our living
 clay.

XL

He has outsoared the shadow of our night ; 10
Envy and calumny and hate and pain,
And that unrest which men miscall delight,
Can touch him not and torture not again ;
From the contagion of the world's slow stain
He is secure, and now can never mourn
A heart grown cold, a head grown gray in vain ;
Nor, when the spirit's self has ceased to burn,
With sparkless ashes load an unlamented urn.

XLI

He lives, he wakes—'tis Death is dead, not he ;
Mourn not for Adonais.—Thou young Dawn, 20
Turn all thy dew to splendour, for from thee
The spirit thou lamentest is not gone ;
Ye caverns and ye forests, cease to moan !
Cease, ye faint flowers and fountains, and thou Air,
Which like a mourning veil thy scarf hadst thrown
O'er the abandoned Earth, now leave it bare
Even to the joyous stars which smile on its despair !

XLII

He is made one with Nature : there is heard
His voice in all her music, from the moan
Of thunder, to the song of night's sweet bird ;
He is a presence to be felt and known
In darkness and in light, from herb and stone,
Spreading itself where'er that Power may move
Which has withdrawn his being to its own ;
Which wields the world with never-wearied love,
Sustains it from beneath, and kindles it above.

XLIII

He is a portion of the loveliness.   10
Which once he made more lovely : he doth bear
His part, while the one Spirit's plastic stress
Sweeps through the dull dense world, compelling
     there
All new successions to the forms they wear ;
Torturing th' unwilling dross that checks its flight
To its own likeness, as each mass may bear ;
And bursting in its beauty and its might
From trees and beasts and men into the Heavens'
     light.

XLIV

The splendours of the firmament of time
May be eclipsed, but are extinguished not ;   20
Like stars to their appointed height they climb,
And death is a low mist which cannot blot
· The brightness it may veil.   When lofty thought
Lifts a young heart above its mortal lair,
And love and life contend in it, for what
Shall be its earthly doom, the dead live there
And move like winds of light on dark and stormy air.

XLV

The inheritors of unfulfilled renown
Rose from their thrones, built beyond mortal
    thought,
Far in the Unapparent.   Chatterton
Rose pale,—his solemn agony had not
Yet faded from him ; Sidney, as he fought
And as he fell and as he lived and loved
Sublimely mild, a Spirit without spot,
Arose ; and Lucan, by his death approved :
Oblivion as they rose shrank like a thing reproved.

XLVI

And many more, whose names on Earth are dark, 10
But whose transmitted effluence cannot die
So long as fire outlives the parent spark,
Rose, robed in dazzling immortality.
" Thou art become as one of us," they cry,
" It was for thee yon kingless sphere has long
Swung blind in unascended majesty,
Silent alone amid an Heaven of Song.
Assume thy wingèd throne, thou Vesper of our
    throng ! "

XLVII

Who mourns for Adonais ? Oh, come forth,
Fond wretch ! and know thyself and him aright. 20
Clasp with thy panting soul the pendulous Earth ;
As from a centre, dart thy spirit's light
Beyond all worlds, until its spacious might
Satiate the void circumference : then shrink
Even to a point within our day and night ;
And keep thy heart light lest it make thee sink
When hope has kindled hope, and lured thee to the
    brink.

XLVIII

Or go to Rome, which is the sepulchre,
Oh, not of him, but of our joy : 'tis nought
That ages, empires, and religions there
Lie buried in the ravage they have wrought ;
For such as he can lend,—they borrow not
Glory from those who made the world their prey ;
And he is gathered to the kings of thought
Who waged contention with their time's decay,
And of the past are all that cannot pass away.

XLIX

Go thou to Rome,—at once the Paradise,   10
The grave, the city, and the wilderness ;
And where its wrecks like shattered mountains rise,
And flowering weeds, and fragrant copses dress
The bones of Desolation's nakedness
Pass, till the spirit of the spot shall lead
Thy footsteps to a slope of green access
Where, like an infant's smile, over the dead
A light of laughing flowers along the grass is spread ;

L

And gray walls moulder round, on which dull Time
Feeds, like slow fire upon a hoary brand ;   20
And one keen pyramid with wedge sublime,
Pavilioning the dust of him who planned
This refuge for his memory, doth stand
Like flame transformed to marble ; and beneath,
A field is spread, on which a newer band
Have pitched in Heaven's smile their camp of death,
Welcoming him we lose with scarce extinguished
    breath.

LI

Here pause : these graves are all too young as yet
To have outgrown the sorrow which consigned
Its charge to each ; and if the seal is set,
Here, on one fountain of a mourning mind,
Break it not thou ! too surely shalt thou find
Thine own well full, if thou returnest home,
Of tears and gall.   From the world's bitter wind
Seek shelter in the shadow of the tomb.
What Adonais is, why fear we to become ?

LII

The One remains, the many change and pass ;   10
Heaven's light forever shines, Earth's shadows fly ;
Life, like a dome of many-coloured glass,
Stains the white radiance of Eternity,
Until Death tramples it to fragments.—Die,
If thou wouldst be with that which thou dost seek !
Follow where all is fled !—Rome's azure sky,
Flowers, ruins, statues, music, words, are weak
The glory they transfuse with fitting truth to speak.

LIII

Why linger, why turn back, why shrink, my Heart ?
Thy hopes are gone before : from all things here   20
They have departed ; thou shouldst now depart !
A light is passed from the revolving year,
And man, and woman ; and what still is dear
Attracts to crush, repels to make thee wither.
The soft sky smiles,—the low wind whispers near :
'Tis Adonais calls ! oh, hasten thither,
No more let Life divide what Death can join to-
      gether.

LIV

That Light whose smile kindles the Universe,
That Beauty in which all things work and move,
That Benediction which the eclipsing Curse
Of birth can quench not, that sustaining Love
Which through the web of being blindly wove
By man and beast and earth and air and sea,
Burns bright or dim, as each are mirrors of
The fire for which all thirst ; now beams on me,
Consuming the last clouds of cold mortality.

LV

The breath whose might I have invoked in song 10
Descends on me ; my spirit's bark is driven,
Far from the shore, far from the trembling throng
Whose sails were never to the tempest given ;
The massy earth and spherèd skies are riven !
I am borne darkly, fearfully, afar ;
Whilst, burning through the inmost veil of Heaven,
The soul of Adonais, like a star,
Beacons from the abode where the Eternal are.

P. B. SHELLEY

THE EVE OF ST. AGNES

I

ST. AGNES' Eve—Ah, bitter chill it was !
The owl, for all his feathers, was a-cold ;   20
The hare limp'd trembling through the frozen grass,
And silent was the flock in woolly fold :
Numb were the Beadsman's fingers, while he told
His rosary, and while his frosted breath,
Like pious incense from a censer old,
Seem'd taking flight for heaven, without a death,
Past the sweet Virgin's picture, while his prayer he saith.

II

His prayer he saith, this patient, holy man ;
Then takes his lamp, and riseth from his knees,
And back returneth, meagre, barefoot, wan,
Along the chapel aisle by slow degrees :
The sculptur'd dead, on each side, seem to freeze,
Emprison'd in black, purgatorial rails :
Knights, ladies, praying in dumb orat'ries,
He passeth by ; and his weak spirit fails
To think how they may ache in icy hoods and mails.

III

Northward he turneth through a little door,   10
And scarce three steps, ere Music's golden tongue
Flatter'd to tears this aged man and poor ;
But no—already had his deathbell rung :
The joys of all his life were said and sung :
His was harsh penance on St. Agnes' Eve :
Another way he went, and soon among
Rough ashes sat he for his soul's reprieve,
And all night kept awake, for sinners' sake to grieve.

IV

That ancient Beadsman heard the prelude soft ;
And so it chanc'd, for many a door was wide,   20
From hurry to and fro.   Soon, up aloft,
The silver, snarling trumpets 'gan to chide :
The level chambers, ready with their pride,
Were glowing to receive a thousand guests :
The carved angels, ever eager-eyed,
Star'd, where upon their heads the cornice rests,
With hair blown back, and wings put cross-wise on
     their breasts.

V

At length burst in the argent revelry,
With plume, tiara, and all rich array,
Numerous as shadows haunting faerily
The brain, new stuff'd, in youth, with triumphs gay
Of old romance.   These let us wish away,
And turn, sole-thoughted, to one Lady there,
Whose heart had brooded, all that wintry day,
On love, and wing'd St. Agnes' saintly care,
As she had heard old dames full many times declare.

VI

They told her how, upon St. Agnes' Eve,   10
Young virgins might have visions of delight,
And soft adorings from their loves receive
Upon the honey'd middle of the night,
If ceremonies due they did aright ;
As, supperless to bed they must retire,
And couch supine their beauties, lily white ;
Nor look behind, nor sideways, but require
Of Heaven with upward eyes for all that they desire.

VII

Full of this whim was thoughtful Madeline :
The music, yearning like a God in pain,   20
She scarcely heard : her maiden eyes divine,
Fix'd on the floor, saw many a sweeping train
Pass by—she heeded not at all : in vain
Came many a tiptoe, amorous cavalier,
And back retir'd ; not cool'd by high disdain,
But she saw not : her heart was otherwhere :
She sigh'd for Agnes' dreams, the sweetest of the year.

VIII

She danc'd along with vague, regardless eyes,
Anxious her lips, her breathing quick and short :
The hallow'd hour was near at hand : she sighs
Amid the timbrels, and the throng'd resort
Of whisperers in anger, or in sport ;
'Mid looks of love, defiance, hate, and scorn,
Hoodwink'd with faery fancy ; all amort,
Save to St. Agnes and her lambs unshorn,
And all the bliss to be before to-morrow morn.

IX

So, purposing each moment to retire,   10
She linger'd still.   Meantime, across the moors,
Had come young Porphyro, with heart on fire
For Madeline.   Beside the portal doors,
Buttress'd from moonlight, stands he, and implores
All saints to give him sight of Madeline,
But for one moment in the tedious hours,
That he might gaze and worship all unseen ;
Perchance speak, kneel, touch, kiss—in sooth such
        things have been.

X

He ventures in : let no buzz'd whisper tell :
All eyes be muffled, or a hundred swords   20
Will storm his heart, Love's fev'rous citadel :
For him, those chambers held barbarian hordes,
Hyena foemen, and hot-blooded lords,
Whose very dogs would execrations howl
Against his lineage : not one breast affords
Him any mercy, in that mansion foul,
Save one old beldame, weak in body and in soul.

XI

Ah, happy chance ! the aged creature came,
Shuffling along with ivory-headed wand,
To where he stood, hid from the torch's flame,
Behind a broad hall-pillar, far beyond
The sound of merriment and chorus bland :
He startled her ; but soon she knew his face,
And grasp'd his fingers in her palsied hand,
Saying, " Mercy, Porphyro ! hie thee from this
    place :
They are all here to-night, the whole blood-thirsty
    race !

XII

" Get hence ! get hence ! there's dwarfish Hilde- 10
    brand ;
He had a fever late, and in the fit
He cursed thee and thine, both house and land :
Then there's that old Lord Maurice, not a whit
More tame for his gray hairs—Alas me ! flit !
Flit like a ghost away."—" Ah, Gossip dear,
We're safe enough ; here in this arm-chair sit,
And tell me how "—" Good saints ! not here, not
    here ;
Follow me, child, or else these stones will be thy bier."

XIII

He follow'd through a lowly arched way,
Brushing the cobwebs with his lofty plume,   20
And as she mutter'd " Well-a—well-a-day ! "
He found him in a little moonlight room,
Pale, lattic'd, chill, and silent as a tomb.
" Now tell me where is Madeline," said he,
" O tell me, Angela, by the holy loom
Which none but secret sisterhood may see,
When they St. Agnes' wool are weaving piously."

XIV

" St. Agnes !   Ah ! it is St. Agnes' Eve—
Yet men will murder upon holy days :
Thou must hold water in a witch's sieve,
And be liege-lord of all the Elves and Fays,
To venture so : it fills me with amaze
To see thee, Porphyro !—St. Agnes' Eve !
God's help ! my lady fair the conjuror plays
This very night : good angels her deceive !
But let me laugh awhile, I've mickle time to grieve."

XV

Feebly she laugheth in the languid moon,   10
While Porphyro upon her face doth look,
Like puzzled urchin on an aged crone
Who keepeth clos'd a wond'rous riddle-book,
As spectacled she sits in chimney nook.
But soon his eyes grew brilliant, when she told
His lady's purpose : and he scarce could brook
Tears, at the thought of those enchantments cold,
And Madeline asleep in lap of legends old.

XVI

Sudden a thought came like a full-blown rose,
Flushing his brow, and in his pained heart   20
Made purple riot : then doth he propose
A stratagem, that makes the beldame start :
" A cruel man and impious thou art :
Sweet lady, let her pray, and sleep, and dream
Alone with her good angels, far apart
From wicked men like thee.   Go, go !—I deem
Thou canst not surely be the same that thou didst
        seem."

XVII

" I will not harm her, by all saints I swear,"
Quoth Porphyro : " O may I ne'er find grace
When my weak voice shall whisper its last prayer,
If one of her soft ringlets I displace,
Or look with ruffian passion in her face :
Good Angela, believe me by these tears ;
Or I will, even in a moment's space,
Awake, with horrid shout, my foemen's ears,
And beard them, though they be more fang'd than
    wolves and bears."

XVIII

" Ah ! why wilt thou affright a feeble soul ?   10
A poor, weak, palsy-stricken, churchyard thing,
Whose passing-bell may ere the midnight toll ;
Whose prayers for thee, each morn and evening,
Were never miss'd."—Thus plaining, doth she bring
A gentler speech from burning Porphyro ;
So woful, and of such deep sorrowing,
That Angela gives promise she will do
Whatever he shall wish, betide her weal or woe.

XIX

Which was, to lead him, in close secrecy,
Even to Madeline's chamber, and there hide   20
Him in a closet, of such privacy
That he might see her beauty unespied,
And win perhaps that night a peerless bride,
While legion'd faeries pac'd the coverlet,
And pale enchantment held her sleepy-eyed.
Never on such a night have lovers met,
Since Merlin paid his Demon all the monstrous debt.

XX

" It shall be as thou wishest," said the Dame :
" All cates and dainties shall be stored there
Quickly on this feast-night : by the tambour frame
Her own lute thou wilt see : no time to spare,
For I am slow and feeble, and scarce dare
On such a catering trust my dizzy head.
Wait here, my child, with patience ; kneel in
    prayer
The while : Ah ! thou must needs the lady wed,
Or may I never leave my grave among the dead."

XXI

So saying, she hobbled off with busy fear.   10
The lover's endless minutes slowly pass'd ;
The dame return'd, and whispered in his ear
To follow her ; with aged eyes aghast
From fright of dim espial.   Safe at last,
Through many a dusky gallery, they gain
The maiden's chamber, silken, hush'd, and chaste ;
Where Porphyro took covert, pleas'd amain.
His poor guide hurried back with agues in her brain.

XXII

Her falt'ring hand upon the balustrade,
Old Angela was feeling for the stair,   20
When Madeline, St. Agnes' charmed maid,
Rose, like a mission'd spirit, unaware :
With silver taper's light, and pious care,
She turn'd, and down the aged gossip led
To a safe level matting.   Now prepare,
Young Porphyro, for gazing on that bed ;
She comes, she comes again, like ring-dove fray'd and
    fled.

XXIII

Out went the taper as she hurried in ;
Its little smoke, in pallid moonshine, died :
She clos'd the door, she panted, all akin
To spirits of the air, and visions wide :
No uttered syllable, or, woe betide !
But to her heart, her heart was voluble,
Paining with eloquence her balmy side ;
As though a tongueless nightingale should swell
Her throat in vain, and die, heart-stifled, in her dell.

XXIV

A casement high and triple-arch'd there was,   10
All garlanded with carven imag'ries
Of fruits, and flowers, and bunches of knot-grass,
And diamonded with panes of quaint device,
Innumerable of stains and splendid dyes,
As are the tiger-moth's deep-damask'd wings ;
And in the midst, 'mong thousand heraldries,
And twilight saints, and dim emblazonings,
A shielded scutcheon blush'd with blood of queens
        and kings.

XXV

Full on this casement shone the wintry moon,
And threw warm gules on Madeline's fair breast,   20
As down she knelt for heaven's grace and boon ;
Rose-bloom fell on her hands, together prest,
And on her silver cross soft amethyst,
And on her hair a glory, like a saint :
She seem'd a splendid angel, newly drest,
Save wings, for heaven :—Porphyro grew faint :
She knelt, so pure a thing, so free from mortal taint.

XXVI

Anon his heart revives : her vespers done,
Of all its wreathed pearls her hair she frees ;
Unclasps her warmed jewels one by one ;
Loosens her fragrant boddice ; by degrees
Her rich attire creeps rustling to her knees :
Half-hidden, like a mermaid in sea-weed,
Pensive awhile she dreams awake, and sees,
In fancy, fair St. Agnes in her bed,
But dares not look behind, or all the charm is fled.

XXVII

Soon, trembling in her soft and chilly nest,   10
In sort of wakeful swoon, perplex'd she lay,
Until the poppied warmth of sleep oppress'd
Her soothed limbs, and soul fatigued away ;
Flown, like a thought, until the morrow-day ;
Blissfully haven'd both from joy and pain ;
Clasp'd like a missal where swart Paynims pray ;
Blinded alike from sunshine and from rain,
As though a rose should shut, and be a bud again.

XXVIII

Stol'n to this paradise, and so entranced,
Porphyro gazed upon her empty dress,   20
And listen'd to her breathing, if it chanced
To wake into a slumberous tenderness ;
Which when he heard, that minute did he bless,
And breath'd himself : then from the closet crept,
Noiseless as fear in a wide wilderness,
And over the hush'd carpet, silent, stept,
And 'tween the curtains peep'd, where, lo !—how
      fast she slept.

XXIX

Then by the bed-side, where the faded moon
Made a dim, silver twilight, soft he set
A table, and, half anguish'd, threw thereon
A cloth of woven crimson, gold, and jet :—
O for some drowsy Morphean amulet !
The boisterous, midnight, festive clarion,
The kettle-drum, and far-heard clarinet,
Affray his ears, though but in dying tone :—
The hall door shuts again, and all the noise is gone.

XXX

And still she slept an azure-lidded sleep,   10
In blanched linen, smooth, and lavender'd,
While he from forth the closet brought a heap
Of candied apple, quince, and plum, and gourd ;
With jellies soother than the creamy curd,
And lucent syrops, tinct with cinnamon ;
Manna and dates, in argosy transferr'd
From Fez ; and spiced dainties, every one,
From silken Samarcand to cedar'd Lebanon.

XXXI

These delicates he heap'd with glowing hand
On golden dishes and in baskets bright   20
Of wreathed silver : sumptuous they stand
In the retired quiet of the night,
Filling the chilly room with perfume light.—
" And now, my love, my seraph fair, awake !
Thou art my heaven, and I thine eremite :
Open thine eyes, for meek St. Agnes' sake,
Or I shall drowse beside thee, so my soul doth ache."

XXXII

Thus whispering, his warm, unnerved arm
Sank in her pillow. Shaded was her dream
By the dusk curtains :—'twas a midnight charm
Impossible to melt as iced stream :
The lustrous salvers in the moonlight gleam ;
Broad golden fringe upon the carpet lies :
It seem'd he never, never could redeem
From such a stedfast spell his lady's eyes :
So mus'd awhile, entoil'd in woofed phantasies.

XXXIII

Awakening up, he took her hollow lute,—   10
Tumultuous,—and, in chords that tenderest be,
He play'd an ancient ditty, long since mute,
In Provence call'd, " La belle dame sans mercy " :
Close to her ear touching the melody ;—
Wherewith disturb'd, she utter'd a soft moan :
He ceased—she panted quick—and suddenly
Her blue affrayed eyes wide open shone :
Upon his knees he sank, pale as smooth-sculptured
        stone.

XXXIV

Her eyes were open, but she still beheld,
Now wide awake, the vision of her sleep :   20
There was a painful change, that nigh expell'd
The blisses of her dream so pure and deep,
At which fair Madeline began to weep,
And moan forth witless words with many a sigh ;
While still her gaze on Porphyro would keep ;
Who knelt, with joined hands and piteous eye,
Fearing to move or speak, she look'd so dreamingly.

XXXV

" Ah, Porphyro ! " said she, " but even now
Thy voice was at sweet tremble in mine ear,
Made tuneable with every sweetest vow ;
And those sad eyes were spiritual and clear :
How chang'd thou art ! how pallid, chill, and
    drear !
Give me that voice again, my Porphyro,
Those looks immortal, those complainings dear !
Oh leave me not in this eternal woe,
For if thou diest, my Love, I know not where to go."

XXXVI

Beyond a mortal man impassion'd far   20
At these voluptuous accents, he arose,
Ethereal, flush'd, and like a throbbing star
Seen mid the sapphire heaven's deep repose ;
Into her dream he melted, as the rose
Blendeth its odour with the violet,—
Solution sweet : meantime the frost-wind blows
Like Love's alarum pattering the sharp sleet
Against the window-panes ; St. Agnes' moon hath set.

XXXVII

'Tis dark : quick pattereth the flaw-blown sleet :
" This is no dream, my bride, my Madeline ! " 20
'Tis dark : the iced gusts still rave and beat :
" No dream, alas ! alas ! and woe is mine !
Porphyro will leave me here to fade and pine.—
Cruel ! what traitor could thee hither bring ?
I curse not, for my heart is lost in thine,
Though thou forsakest a deceived thing ;—
A dove forlorn and lost with sick unpruned wing."

XXXVIII

" My Madeline ! sweet dreamer ! lovely bride !
Say, may I be for aye thy vassal blest ?
Thy beauty's shield, heart-shap'd and vermeil dyed?
Ah, silver shrine, here will I take my rest
After so many hours of toil and quest,
A famish'd pilgrim,—sav'd by miracle.
Though I have found, I will not rob thy nest
Saving of thy sweet self ; if thou think'st well
To trust, fair Madeline, to no rude infidel.

XXXIX

" Hark ! 'tis an elfin-storm from faery land,   10
Of haggard seeming, but a boon indeed :
Arise—arise ! the morning is at hand ;—
The bloated wassaillers will never heed :—
Let us away, my love, with happy speed ;
There are no ears to hear, or eyes to see,—
Drown'd all in Rhenish and the sleepy mead :
Awake ! arise ! my love, and fearless be,
For o'er the southern moors I have a home for thee."

XL

She hurried at his words, beset with fears,
For there were sleeping dragons all around,   20
At glaring watch, perhaps, with ready spears—
Down the wide stairs a darkling way they found.—
In all the house was heard no human sound.
A chain-droop'd lamp was flickering by each door ;
The arras, rich with horseman, hawk, and hound,
Flutter'd in the besieging wind's uproar ;
And the long carpets rose along the gusty floor.

XLI

They glide, like phantoms, into the wide hall ;
Like phantoms, to the iron porch, they glide ;
Where lay the Porter, in uneasy sprawl,
With a huge empty flaggon by his side :
The wakeful bloodhound rose, and shook his hide,
But his sagacious eye an inmate owns :
By one, and one, the bolts full easy slide :—
The chains lie silent on the footworn stones ;—
The key turns, and the door upon its hinges groans.

XLII

And they are gone : aye, ages long ago   10
These lovers fled away into the storm.
That night the Baron dreamt of many a woe,
And all his warrior-guests, with shade and form
Of witch, and demon, and large coffin-worm,
Were long be-nightmar'd.   Angela the old
Died palsy-twitch'd, with meagre face deform ;
The Beadsman, after thousand aves told,
For aye unsought for slept among his ashes cold.
JOHN KEATS

RUBÁIYÁT OF OMAR KHAYYÁM OF NAISHÁPÚR

I

WAKE !   For the Sun, who scatter'd into flight
The Stars before him from the Field of Night,   20
   Drives Night along with them from Heav'n, and
      strikes
The Sultán's Turret with a Shaft of Light.

II

Before the phantom of False morning died,
Methought a Voice within the Tavern cried,
 " When all the Temple is prepared within,
Why nods the drowsy Worshipper outside ? "

III

And, as the Cock crew, those who stood before
The Tavern shouted—" Open then the Door !
 You know how little while we have to stay,
And, once departed, may return no more."

IV

Now the New Year reviving old Desires,
The thoughtful Soul to Solitude retires,   10
 Where the WHITE HAND OF MOSES on the Bough
Puts out, and Jesus from the Ground suspires.

V

Iram indeed is gone with all his Rose,
And Jamshýd's Sev'n-ring'd Cup where no one
      knows ;
 But still a Ruby kindles in the Vine,
And many a Garden by the Water blows.

VI

And David's lips are lockt ; but in divine
High-piping Pehleví, with " Wine ! Wine ! Wine !
 Red Wine ! "—the Nightingale cries to the Rose
That sallow cheek of hers to' incarnadine.   20

VII

Come, fill the Cup, and in the fire of Spring
Your Winter-garment of Repentance fling :
   The Bird of Time has but a little way
To flutter—and the Bird is on the Wing.

VIII

Whether at Naishápúr or Babylon,
Whether the Cup with sweet or bitter run,
   The Wine of Life keeps oozing drop by drop,
The Leaves of Life keep falling one by one.

IX

Each Morn a thousand Roses brings, you say ;
Yes, but where leaves the Rose of Yesterday ?   10
   And this first Summer month that brings the Rose
Shall take Jamshýd and Kaikobád away.

X

Well, let it take them ! What have we to do
With Kaikobád the Great, or Kaikhosrú ?
   Let Zál and Rustum bluster as they will,
Or Hátim call to Supper—heed not you.

XI

With me along the strip of Herbage strown
That just divides the desert from the sown,
   Where name of Slave and Sultán is forgot—
And Peace to Mahmúd on his golden Throne !   20

XII

A Book of Verses underneath the Bough,
A Jug of Wine, a Loaf of Bread—and Thou
   Beside me singing in the Wilderness—
Oh, Wilderness were Paradise enow !

XIII

Some for the Glories of This World ; and some
Sigh for the Prophet's Paradise to come ;
   Ah, take the Cash, and let the Credit go,
Nor heed the rumble of a distant Drum !

XIV

Look to the blowing Rose about us—" Lo,
Laughing," she says, " into the world I blow, 10
   At once the silken tassel of my Purse
Tear, and its Treasure on the Garden throw."

XV

And those who husbanded the Golden grain,
And those who flung it to the winds like Rain,
   Alike to no such aureate Earth are turn'd
As, buried once, Men want dug up again.

XVI

The Worldly Hope men set their Hearts upon
Turns Ashes—or it prospers ; and anon,
   Like Snow upon the Desert's dusty Face,
Lighting a little hour or two—is gone.   20

XVII

Think, in this batter'd Caravanserai
Whose Portals are alternate Night and Day,
    How Sultán after Sultán with his Pomp
Abode his destined Hour, and went his way.

XVIII

They say the Lion and the Lizard keep
The Courts where Jamshýd gloried and drank deep :
    And Bahrám, that great Hunter—the Wild Ass
Stamps o'er his Head, but cannot break his Sleep.

XIX

I sometimes think that never blows so red
The Rose as where some buried Cæsar bled ;   10
    That every Hyacinth the Garden wears
Dropt in her Lap from some once lovely Head.

XX

And this reviving Herb whose tender Green
Fledges the River-Lip on which we lean—
    Ah, lean upon it lightly ! for who knows
From what once lovely Lip it springs unseen !

XXI

Ah, my Belovéd, fill the Cup that clears
To-day of past Regrets and Future Fears :
    To-morrow !—Why, To-morrow I may be
Myself with Yesterday's Sev'n thousand Years.   20

XXII

For some we loved, the loveliest and the best
That from his Vintage rolling Time hath prest,
  Have drunk their Cup a Round or two before,
And one by one crept silently to rest.

XXIII

And we, that now make merry in the Room
They left, and Summer dresses in new bloom,
  Ourselves must we beneath the Couch of Earth
Descend—ourselves to make a Couch—for whom ?

XXIV

Ah, make the most of what we yet may spend,
Before we too into the Dust descend ;
  Dust into Dust, and under Dust to lie,
Sans Wine, sans Song, sans Singer, and—sans End!

XXV

Alike for those who for TO-DAY prepare,
And those that after some TO-MORROW stare,
  A Muezzín from the Tower of Darkness cries,
" Fools ! your Reward is neither Here nor There."

XXVI

Why, all the Saints and Sages who discuss'd
Of the Two Worlds so wisely—they are thrust
  Like foolish Prophets forth ; their Words to Scorn
Are scatter'd, and their Mouths are stopt with Dust. 20

XXVII

Myself when young did eagerly frequent
Doctor and Saint, and heard great argument
   About it and about : but evermore
Came out by the same door where in I went.

XXVIII

With them the seed of Wisdom did I sow,
And with mine own hand wrought to make it grow ;
   And this was all the Harvest that I reap'd—
" I came like Water, and like Wind I go."

XXIX

Into this Universe, and *Why* not knowing
Nor *Whence*, like Water willy-nilly flowing ;   10
   And out of it, as Wind along the Waste,
I know not *Whither*, willy-nilly blowing.

XXX

What, without asking, hither hurried *Whence* ?
And, without asking, *Whither* hurried hence !
   Oh, many a Cup of this forbidden Wine
Must drown the memory of that insolence !

XXXI

Up from Earth's Centre through the Seventh Gate
I rose, and on the Throne of Saturn sate ;
   And many a Knot unravel'd by the Road ;
But not the Master-knot of Human Fate.   20

XXXII

There was the Door to which I found no Key ;
There was the Veil through which I might not see :
  Some little talk awhile of ME and THEE
There was—and then no more of THEE and ME.

XXXIII

Earth could not answer ; nor the Seas that mourn
In flowing Purple, of their Lord forlorn ;
  Nor rolling Heaven, with all his Signs reveal'd
And hidden by the sleeve of Night and Morn.

XXXIV

Then of the THEE IN ME who works behind
The Veil, I lifted up my hands to find   10
  A lamp amid the Darkness ; and I heard,
As from Without—" THE ME WITHIN THEE BLIND ! "

XXXV

Then to the lip of this poor earthen Urn
I lean'd, the Secret of my Life to learn :
  And Lip to Lip it murmur'd—" While you live,
Drink ! for, once dead, you never shall return."

XXXVI

I think the Vessel, that with fugitive
Articulation answer'd, once did live,
  And drink ; and Ah ! the passive Lip I kiss'd,
How many Kisses might it take—and give !   20

XXXVII

For I remember stopping by the way
To watch a Potter thumping his wet Clay :
   And with its all-obliterated Tongue
It murmur'd—" Gently, Brother, gently, pray ! "

XXXVIII

And has not such a Story from of Old
Down Man's successive generations roll'd
   Of such a clod of saturated Earth
Cast by the Maker into Human mould ?

XXXIX

And not a drop that from our Cups we throw
For Earth to drink of, but may steal below   10
   To quench the fire of Anguish in some Eye
There hidden—far beneath, and long ago.

XL

As then the Tulip for her morning sup
Of Heav'nly Vintage from the soil looks up,
   Do you devoutly do the like, till Heav'n
To Earth invert you—like an empty Cup.

XLI

Perplext no more with Human or Divine,
To-morrow's tangle to the winds resign,
   And lose your fingers in the tresses of
The Cypress-slender Minister of Wine.   20

XLII

And if the Wine you drink, the Lip you press,
End in what All begins and ends in—Yes ;
   Think then you are TO-DAY what YESTERDAY
You were—TO-MORROW you shall not be less.

XLIII

So when that Angel of the darker Drink
At last shall find you by the river-brink,
   And, offering his Cup, invite your Soul
Forth to your Lips to quaff—you shall not shrink.

XLIV

Why, if the Soul can fling the Dust aside,
And naked on the Air of Heaven ride,   10
   Were't not a Shame—were't not a Shame for him
In this clay carcase crippled to abide ?

XLV

'Tis but a Tent where takes his one day's rest
A Sultán to the realm of Death addrest ;
   The Sultán rises, and the dark Ferrásh
Strikes, and prepares it for another Guest.

XLVI

And fear not lest Existence closing your
Account, and mine, should know the like no more ;
   The Eternal Sákí from that Bowl has pour'd
Millions of Bubbles like us, and will pour.   20

XLVII

When You and I behind the Veil are past,
Oh, but the long, long while the World shall last,
   Which of our Coming and Departure heeds
As the Sea's self should heed a pebble-cast.

XLVIII

A Moment's Halt—a momentary taste
Of BEING from the Well amid the Waste—
   And Lo ! the phantom Caravan has reach'd
The NOTHING it set out from—Oh, make haste !

XLIX

Would you that spangle of Existence spend
About THE SECRET—quick about it, Friend !   10
   A Hair perhaps divides the False and True—
And upon what, prithee, may life depend ?

L

A Hair perhaps divides the False and True ;
Yes ; and a single Alif were the clue—
   Could you but find it—to the Treasure-house,
And peradventure to THE MASTER too ;

LI

Whose secret Presence, through Creation's veins
Running Quicksilver-like eludes your pains ;
   Taking all shapes from Máh to Máhi ; and
They change and perish all—but He remains ;   20

LII

A moment guess'd—then back behind the Fold
Immerst of Darkness round the Drama roll'd
  Which, for the Pastime of Eternity,
He doth Himself contrive, enact, behold.

LIII

But if in vain, down on the stubborn floor
Of Earth, and up to Heav'n's unopening Door,
  You gaze TO-DAY, while You are You—how then
TO-MORROW, You when shall be You no more?

LIV

Waste not your Hour, nor in the vain pursuit
Of This and That endeavour and dispute;   10
  Better be jocund with the fruitful Grape
Than sadden after none, or bitter, Fruit.

LV

You know, my Friends, with what a brave Carouse
I made a Second Marriage in my house;
  Divorced old barren Reason from my Bed,
And took the Daughter of the Vine to Spouse.

LVI

For " Is " and " Is-NOT " though with Rule and Line
And " UP-AND-DOWN " by Logic I define,
  Of all that one should care to fathom, I
Was never deep in anything but—Wine.   20

LVII

Ah, but my Computations, People say,
Reduced the Year to better reckoning ?—Nay,
   'Twas only striking from the Calendar
Unborn To-morrow, and dead Yesterday.

LVIII

And lately, by the Tavern Door agape,
Came shining through the Dusk an Angel Shape
   Bearing a Vessel on his Shoulder ; and
He bid me taste of it ; and 'twas—the Grape !

LIX

The Grape that can with Logic absolute
The Two-and-Seventy jarring Sects confute :   10
   The sovereign Alchemist that in a trice
Life's leaden metal into Gold transmute :

LX

The mighty Mahmúd, Allah-breathing Lord,
That all the misbelieving and black Horde
   Of Fears and Sorrows that infest the Soul
Scatters before him with his whirlwind Sword.

LXI

Why, be this Juice the growth of God, who dare
Blaspheme the twisted tendrils as a Snare ?
   A Blessing, we should use it, should we not ?
And if a Curse—why, then, Who set it there ?   20

158

LXII

I must abjure the Balm of Life, I must,
Scared by some After-reckoning ta'en on trust,
    Or lured with Hope of some Diviner Drink,
To fill the Cup—when crumbled into Dust !

LXIII

Oh threats of Hell and Hopes of Paradise !
One thing at least is certain—*This* Life flies ;
    One thing is certain and the rest is Lies ;
The Flower that once has blown for ever dies.

LXIV

Strange, is it not ? that of the myriads who
Before us pass'd the door of Darkness through   10
    Not one returns to tell us of the Road,
Which to discover we must travel too.

LXV

The Revelations of Devout and Learn'd
Who rose before us, and as Prophets burn'd,
    Are all but Stories, which awoke from Sleep
They told their comrades, and to Sleep return'd.

LXVI

I sent my Soul through the Invisible,
Some letter of that After-life to spell :
    And by and by my Soul return'd to me,   19
And answer'd " I Myself am Heav'n and Hell " :

LXVII

Heav'n but the Vision of fulfill'd Desire,
And Hell the Shadow from a Soul on fire,
    Cast on the Darkness into which Ourselves,
So late emerged from, shall so soon expire.

LXVIII

We are no other than a moving row
Of Magic Shadow-shapes that come and go
    Round with the Sun-illumined Lantern held
In Midnight by the Master of the Show ;

LXIX

But helpless Pieces of the Game He plays
Upon this Chequer-board of Nights and Days ; 10
    Hither and thither moves, and checks, and slays,
And one by one back in the Closet lays.

LXX

The Ball no question makes of Ayes and Noes,
But Here or There as strikes the Player goes ;
    And He that toss'd you down into the Field,
He knows about it all—HE knows—HE knows !

LXXI

The Moving Finger writes ; and, having writ,
Moves on : nor all your Piety nor Wit
    Shall lure it back to cancel half a Line,
Nor all your Tears wash out a Word of it. 20

LXXII

And that inverted Bowl they call the Sky,
Whereunder crawling coop'd we live and die,
   Lift not your hands to *It* for help—for It
As impotently moves as you or I.

LXXIII

With Earth's first Clay They did the Last Man knead,
And there of the Last Harvest sow'd the Seed :
   And the first Morning of Creation wrote
What the Last Dawn of Reckoning shall read.

LXXIV

YESTERDAY *This* Day's Madness did prepare ;
TO-MORROW's Silence, Triumph, or Despair :   10
   Drink ! for you know not whence you came, nor
     why :
Drink ! for you know not why you go, nor where.

LXXV

I tell you this—When, started from the Goal,
Over the flaming shoulders of the Foal
   Of Heav'n Parwín and Mushtarí they flung,
In my predestined Plot of Dust and Soul

LXXVI

The Vine had struck a fibre : which about
If clings my being—let the Dervish flout ;
   Of my Base metal may be filed a Key,
That shall unlock the Door he howls without.   20

LXXVII

And this I know : whether the one True Light
Kindle to Love, or Wrath-consume me quite,
   One Flash of It within the Tavern caught
Better than in the Temple lost outright.

LXXVIII

What ! out of senseless Nothing to provoke
A conscious Something to resent the yoke
   Of unpermitted Pleasure, under pain
Of Everlasting Penalties, if broke !

LXXIX

What ! from his helpless Creature be repaid
Pure Gold for what he lent him dross-allay'd— 10
   Sue for a Debt he never did contract,
And cannot answer—Oh the sorry trade !

LXXX

Oh Thou, who didst with pitfall and with gin
Beset the Road I was to wander in,
   Thou wilt not with Predestined Evil round
Enmesh, and then impute my Fall to Sin !

LXXXI

Oh, Thou, who Man of baser Earth didst make,
And ev'n with Paradise devise the Snake :
   For all the Sin wherewith the face of Man
Is blacken'd—Man's forgiveness give—and take ! 20

LXXXII

As under cover of departing Day
Slunk hunger-stricken Ramazán away,
 Once more within the Potter's house alone
I stood, surrounded by the Shapes of Clay.

LXXXIII

Shapes of all Sorts and Sizes, great and small,
That stood along the floor and by the wall ;
 And some loquacious Vessels were ; and some
Listen'd perhaps, but never talk'd at all.

LXXXIV

Said one among them—" Surely not in vain
My substance of the common Earth was ta'en   10
 And to this Figure moulded, to be broke,
Or trampled back to shapeless Earth again."

LXXXV

Then said a Second—" Ne'er a peevish Boy
Would break the Bowl from which he drank in joy ;
 And He that with His hand the Vessel made
Will surely not in after Wrath destroy."

LXXXVI

After a momentary silence spake
Some Vessel of a more ungainly Make :
 " They sneer at me for leaning all awry :
What ! did the Hand then of the Potter shake ? "   20

LXXXVII

Whereat some one of the loquacious Lot—
I think a Súfi pipkin—waxing hot—
    " All this of Pot and Potter—Tell me then,
Who is the Potter, pray, and who the Pot ? "

LXXXVIII

" Why," said another, " Some there are who tell
Of one who threatens he will toss to Hell
    The luckless Pots he marr'd in making—Pish !
He's a Good fellow, and 't will all be well."

LXXXIX

" Well," murmur'd one, " Let whoso make or buy,
My Clay with long Oblivion is gone dry :   10
    But fill me with the old familiar Juice,
Methinks I might recover by and by."

XC

So while the Vessels one by one were speaking,
The little Moon look'd in that all were seeking :
    And then they jogg'd each other, " Brother !
        Brother !
Now for the Porter's shoulder-knot a-creaking ! "

.   .   .   .   .   .

XCI

Ah, with the Grape my fading Life provide,
And wash the Body whence the Life has died,
    And lay me, shrouded in the living Leaf,
By some not unfrequented Garden-side.   20

XCII

That ev'n my buried Ashes such a snare
Of Vintage shall fling up into the Air
   As not a True-believer passing by
But shall be overtaken unaware.

XCIII

Indeed the Idols I have loved so long
Have done my credit in this World much wrong :
   Have drown'd my Glory in a shallow Cup
And sold my Reputation for a Song.

XCIV

Indeed, indeed, Repentance oft before
I swore—but was I sober when I swore ?   10
   And then and then came Spring, and Rose-in-hand
My thread-bare Penitence apieces tore.

XCV

And much as Wine has play'd the Infidel,
And robb'd me of my Robe of Honour—Well,
   I wonder often what the Vintners buy
One half so precious as the stuff they sell.

XCVI

Yet Ah, that Spring should vanish with the Rose !
That Youth's sweet-scented manuscript should close !
   The Nightingale that in the branches sang,
Ah whence, and whither flown again, who knows ! 20

XCVII

Would but the Desert of the Fountain yield
One glimpse—if dimly, yet indeed, reveal'd,
   To which the fainting Traveller might spring,
As springs the trampled herbage of the field !

XCVIII

Would but some wingéd Angel ere too late
Arrest the yet unfolded Roll of Fate,
   And make the stern Recorder otherwise
Enregister, or quite obliterate !

XCIX

Ah Love ! could you and I with Him conspire
To grasp this sorry Scheme of Things entire,   10
   Would not we shatter it to bits—and then
Re-mould it nearer to the Heart's Desire !

     .   .   .

C

Yon rising Moon that looks for us again—
How oft hereafter will she wax and wane ;
   How oft hereafter rising look for us
Through this same Garden—and for *one* in vain !

CI

And when like her, oh Sákí, you shall pass
Among the Guests Star-scatter'd on the Grass,
   And in your joyous errand reach the spot
Where I made One—turn down an empty Glass !   20

TAMÁM

EDWARD FITZGERALD

THE LOTOS-EATERS

" COURAGE ! " he said, and pointed toward the land,
" This mounting wave will roll us shoreward soon."
In the afternoon they came unto a land,
In which it seemed always afternoon.
All round the coast the languid air did swoon,
Breathing like one that hath a weary dream.
Full-faced above the valley stood the moon ;
And like a downward smoke, the slender stream
Along the cliff to fall and pause and fall did seem.

A land of streams ! some, like a downward smoke,　10
Slow-dropping veils of thinnest lawn, did go ;
And some thro' wavering lights and shadows broke,
Rolling a slumbrous sheet of foam below.
They saw the gleaming river seaward flow
From the inner land : far off, three mountain-tops,
Three silent pinnacles of aged snow,
Stood sunset-flush'd : and, dew'd with showery drops,
Up-clomb the shadowy pine above the woven copse.

The charmed sunset linger'd low adown
In the red West : thro' mountain clefts the dale　20
Was seen far inland, and the yellow down
Border'd with palm, and many a winding vale
And meadow, set with slender galingale ;
A land where all things always seem'd the same !
And round about the keel with faces pale,
Dark faces pale against that rosy flame,
The mild-eyed melancholy Lotos-eaters came.

Branches they bore of that enchanted stem,
Laden with flower and fruit, whereof they gave
To each, but whoso did receive of them,　30

And taste, to him the gushing of the wave
Far far away did seem to mourn and rave
On alien shores ; and if his fellow spake,
His voice was thin, as voices from the grave ;
And deep-asleep he seem'd, yet all awake,
And music in his ears his beating heart did make.

They sat them down upon the yellow sand,
Between the sun and moon upon the shore ;
And sweet it was to dream of Father-land,
Of child, and wife, and slave ; but evermore   10
Most weary seem'd the sea, weary the oar,
Weary the wandering fields of barren foam.
Then some one said, " We will return no more " ;
And all at once they sang, " Our island home
Is far beyond the wave ; we will no longer roam."

CHORIC SONG

I

There is sweet music here that softer falls
Than petals from blown roses on the grass,
Or night-dews on still waters between walls
Of shadowy granite, in a gleaming pass ;
Music that gentlier on the spirit lies,   20
Than tir'd eyelids upon tir'd eyes ;
Music that brings sweet sleep down from the blissful
      skies.
Here are cool mosses deep,
And thro' the moss the ivies creep,
And in the stream the long-leaved flowers weep,
And from the craggy ledge the poppy hangs in sleep.

II

Why are we weigh'd upon with heaviness,
And utterly consumed with sharp distress,

168

While all things else have rest from weariness?
All things have rest : why should we toil alone,
We only toil, who are the first of things,
And make perpetual moan,
Still from one sorrow to another thrown :
Nor ever fold our wings,
And cease from wanderings,
Nor steep our brows in slumber's holy balm ;
Nor harken what the inner spirit sings,
" There is no joy but calm ! "   10
Why should we only toil, the roof and crown of things ?

III

Lo ! in the middle of the wood,
The folded leaf is woo'd from out the bud
With winds upon the branch, and there
Grows green and broad, and takes no care,
Sun-steep'd at noon, and in the moon
Nightly dew-fed ; and turning yellow
Falls, and floats adown the air.
Lo ! sweeten'd with the summer light,
The full-juiced apple, waxing over-mellow,   20
Drops in a silent autumn night.
All its allotted length of days,
The flower ripens in its place,
Ripens and fades, and falls, and hath no toil,
Fast-rooted in the fruitful soil.

IV

Hateful is the dark-blue sky
Vaulted o'er the dark-blue sea.
Death is the end of life ; ah, why
Should life all labour be ?
Let us alone.   Time driveth onward fast,   30
And in a little while our lips are dumb.

Let us alone. What is it that will last ?
All things are taken from us, and become
Portions and parcels of the dreadful Past.
Let us alone. What pleasure can we have
To war with evil ? Is there any peace
In ever climbing up the climbing wave ?
All things have rest, and ripen toward the grave
In silence ; ripen, fall and cease :
Give us long rest or death, dark death, or dreamful
      ease.

V

How sweet it were, hearing the downward stream,   10
With half-shut eyes ever to seem
Falling asleep in a half-dream !
To dream and dream, like yonder amber light,
Which will not leave the myrrh-bush on the height ;
To hear each other's whisper'd speech ;
Eating the Lotos day by day,
To watch the crisping ripples on the beach,
And tender curving lines of creamy spray ;
To lend our hearts and spirits wholly
To the influence of mild-minded melancholy ;   20
To muse and brood and live again in memory,
With those old faces of our infancy
Heap'd over with a mound of grass,
Two handfuls of white dust, shut in an urn of brass !

VI

Dear is the memory of our wedded lives,
And dear the last embraces of our wives
And their warm tears : but all hath suffer'd change ;
For surely now our household hearths are cold :
Our sons inherit us : our looks are strange :
And we should come like ghosts to trouble joy.   30
Or else the island princes over-bold

Have eat our substance, and the minstrel sings
Before them of the ten years' war in Troy,
And our great deeds, as half-forgotten things.
Is there confusion in the little isle ?
Let what is broken so remain.
The Gods are hard to reconcile :
'Tis hard to settle order once again.
There *is* confusion worse than death,
Trouble on trouble, pain on pain,
Long labour unto aged breath,   10
Sore task to hearts worn out with many wars
And eyes grown dim with gazing on the pilot-stars.

VII

But, propt on beds of amaranth and moly,
How sweet (while warm airs lull us, blowing lowly)
With half-dropt eyelid still,
Beneath a heaven dark and holy
To watch the long bright river drawing slowly
His waters from the purple hill—
To hear the dewy echoes calling
From cave to cave thro' the thick-twined vine—   20
To watch the emerald-colour'd water falling
Thro' many a wov'n acanthus-wreath divine !
Only to hear and see the far-off sparkling brine,
Only to hear were sweet, stretch'd out beneath the
    pine.

VIII

The Lotos blooms below the barren peak :
The Lotos blows by every winding creek :
All day the wind breathes low with mellower tone :
Thro' every hollow cave and alley lone
Round and round the spicy downs the yellow Lotos-
    dust is blown.
We have had enough of action, and of motion we,   30

Roll'd to starboard, roll'd to larboard, when the surge
    was seething free,
Where the wallowing monster spouted his foam-
    fountains in the sea.
Let us swear an oath, and keep it with an equal mind,
In the hollow Lotos-land to live and lie reclined
On the hills like Gods together, careless of mankind.
For they lie beside their nectar, and the bolts are hurl'd
Far below them in the valleys, and the clouds are
    lightly curl'd
Round their golden houses, girdled with the gleaming
    world :
Where they smile in secret, looking over wasted lands,
Blight and famine, plague and earthquake, roaring
    deeps and fiery sands,   10
Clanging fights, and flaming towns, and sinking ships,
    and praying hands.
But they smile, they find a music centred in a doleful
    song
Steaming up, a lamentation and an ancient tale of
    wrong,
Like a tale of little meaning tho' the words are strong ;
Chanted from an ill-used race of men that cleave the
    soil,
Sow the seed, and reap the harvest with enduring toil,
Storing yearly little dues of wheat, and wine and oil ;
Till they perish and they suffer—some, 'tis whisper'd
    —down in hell
Suffer endless anguish, others in Elysian valleys dwell,
Resting weary limbs at last on beds of asphodel.   20
Surely, surely, slumber is more sweet than toil, the
    shore
Than labour in the deep mid-ocean, wind and wave
    and oar ;
Oh rest ye, brother mariners, we will not wander
    more.

LORD TENNYSON

ULYSSES

IT little profits that an idle king,
By this still hearth, among these barren crags,
Match'd with an aged wife, I mete and dole
Unequal laws unto a savage race,
That hoard, and sleep, and feed, and know not me.
I cannot rest from travel : I will drink
Life to the lees : all times I have enjoy'd
Greatly, have suffer'd greatly, both with those
That loved me, and alone ; on shore, and when
Thro' scudding drifts the rainy Hyades   10
Vext the dim sea : I am become a name ;
For always roaming with a hungry heart
Much have I seen and known ; cities of men
And manners, climates, councils, governments,
Myself not least, but honour'd of them all ;
And drunk delight of battle with my peers,
Far on the ringing plains of windy Troy.
I am a part of all that I have met ;
Yet all experience is an arch wherethro'
Gleams that untravell'd world, whose margin fades 20
For ever and for ever when I move.
How dull it is to pause, to make an end,
To rust unburnish'd, not to shine in use !
As tho' to breathe were life.   Life piled on life
Were all too little, and of one to me
Little remains : but every hour is saved
From that eternal silence, something more,
A bringer of new things ; and vile it were
For some three suns to store and hoard myself,
And this gray spirit yearning in desire   30
To follow knowledge like a sinking star,
Beyond the utmost bound of human thought.
    This is my son, mine own Telemachus,

To whom I leave the sceptre and the isle—
Well-loved of me, discerning to fulfil
This labour, by slow prudence to make mild
A rugged people, and thro' soft degrees
Subdue them to the useful and the good.
Most blameless is he, centred in the sphere
Of common duties, decent not to fail
In offices of tenderness, and pay
Meet adoration to my household gods,
When I am gone.   He works his work, I mine.   10
   There lies the port ; the vessel puffs her sail :
There gloom the dark broad seas.   My mariners,
Souls that have toil'd, and wrought, and thought with
            me—
That ever with a frolic welcome took
The thunder and the sunshine, and opposed
Free hearts, free foreheads—you and I are old ;
Old age hath yet his honour and his toil ;
Death closes all : but something ere the end,
Some work of noble note, may yet be done,
Not unbecoming men that strove with Gods.   20
The lights begin to twinkle from the rocks :
The long day wanes : the slow moon climbs : the
            deep
Moans round with many voices.   Come, my friends,
'Tis not too late to seek a newer world.
Push off, and sitting well in order smite
The sounding furrows ; for my purpose holds
To sail beyond the sunset, and the baths
Of all the western stars, until I die.
It may be that the gulfs will wash us down :
It may be we shall touch the Happy Isles,   30
And see the great Achilles, whom we knew.
Tho' much is taken, much abides ; and tho'
We are not now that strength which in old days
Moved earth and heaven ; that which we are, we
            are ;

TO VIRGIL

One equal temper of heroic hearts,
Made weak by time and fate, but strong in will
To strive, to seek, to find, and not to yield.

LORD TENNYSON

TO VIRGIL

WRITTEN AT THE REQUEST OF THE MANTUANS FOR THE NINETEENTH CENTENARY OF VIRGIL'S DEATH

I

ROMAN VIRGIL, thou that singest
Ilion's lofty temples robed in fire,
Ilion falling, Rome arising,
wars, and filial faith, and Dido's pyre ;

II

Landscape-lover, lord of language
more than he that sang the Works and Days,
All the chosen coin of fancy   10
flashing out from many a golden phrase ;

III

Thou that singest wheat and woodland,
tilth and vineyard, hive and horse and herd ;
All the charm of all the Muses
often flowering in a lonely word ;

IV

Poet of the happy Tityrus
piping underneath his beechen bowers ;
Poet of the poet-satyr
whom the laughing shepherd bound with flowers;

V

Chanter of the Pollio, glorying
    in the blissful years again to be,
Summers of the snakeless meadow,
    unlaborious earth and oarless sea ;

VI

Thou that seëst Universal
    Nature moved by Universal Mind ;
Thou majestic in thy sadness
    at the doubtful doom of human kind ;

VII

Light among the vanish'd ages ;
    star that gildest yet this phantom shore ;   10
Golden branch amid the shadows,
    kings and realms that pass to rise no more ;

VIII

Now thy Forum roars no longer,
    fallen every purple Caesar's dome—
Tho' thine ocean-roll of rhythm
    sound for ever of Imperial Rome—

IX

Now the Rome of slaves hath perish'd,
    and the Rome of freemen holds her place,
I, from out the Northern Island
    sunder'd once from all the human race,   20

X

I salute thee, Mantovano,
  I that loved thee since my day began,
Wielder of the stateliest measure
    ever moulded by the lips of man.
                                    LORD TENNYSON

MY LAST DUCHESS

FERRARA

THAT'S my last Duchess painted on the wall,
Looking as if she were alive ; I call
That piece a wonder, now : Frà Pandolf's hands
Worked busily a day, and there she stands.
Will 't please you sit and look at her ? I said
" Frà Pandolf " by design, for never read   10
Strangers like you that pictured countenance,
The depth and passion of its earnest glance,
But to myself they turned (since none puts by
The curtain I have drawn for you, but I)
And seemed as they would ask me, if they durst,
How such a glance came there ; so, not the first
Are you to turn and ask thus. Sir, 't was not
Her husband's presence only, called that spot
Of joy into the Duchess' cheek : perhaps
Frà Pandolf chanced to say " Her mantle laps   20
Over my Lady's wrist too much," or " Paint
Must never hope to reproduce the faint
Half-flush that dies along her throat ; " such stuff
Was courtesy, she thought, and cause enough
For calling up that spot of joy. She had
A heart . . . how shall I say ? . . . too soon made
    glad,

177

Too easily impressed ; she liked whate'er
She looked on, and her looks went everywhere.
Sir, 't was all one ! My favour at her breast,
The dropping of the daylight in the West,
The bough of cherries some officious fool
Broke in the orchard for her, the white mule
She rode with round the terrace—all and each
Would draw from her alike the approving speech,
Or blush, at least. She thanked men,—good ; but
    thanked
Somehow . . . I know not how . . . as if she ranked 10
My gift of a nine-hundred-years-old name
With anybody's gift. Who'd stoop to blame
This sort of trifling ? Even had you skill
In speech—(which I have not)—to make your will
Quite clear to such an one, and say " Just this
Or that in you disgusts me ; here you miss,
Or there exceed the mark "—and if she let
Herself be lessoned so, nor plainly set
Her wits to yours, forsooth, and made excuse,
—E'en then would be some stooping, and I chuse 20
Never to stoop. Oh, Sir, she smiled, no doubt,
Whene'er I passed her ; but who passed without
Much the same smile ? This grew ; I gave com-
    mands ;
Then all smiles stopped together. There she stands
As if alive. Will 't please you rise ? We'll meet
The company below, then. I repeat,
The Count your Master's known munificence
Is ample warrant that no just pretence
Of mine for dowry will be disallowed ;
Though his fair daughter's self, as I avowed   30
At starting, is my object. Nay, we'll go
Together down, Sir ! Notice Neptune, though,
Taming a sea-horse, thought a rarity,
Which Claus of Innsbruck cast in bronze for me.

ROBERT BROWNING

ANDREA DEL SARTO

(CALLED " THE FAULTLESS PAINTER ")

BUT do not let us quarrel any more,
No, my Lucrezia ; bear with me for once :
Sit down and all shall happen as you wish.
You turn your face, but does it bring your heart ?
I'll work then for your friend's friend, never fear.
Treat his own subject after his own way,
Fix his own time, accept too his own price,
And shut the money into this small hand
When next it takes mine.   Will it ? tenderly ?
Oh, I'll content him,—but to-morrow, Love !   10
I often am much wearier than you think,
This evening more than usual, and it seems
As if—forgive now—should you let me sit
Here by the window with your hand in mine
And look a half-hour forth on Fiesole,
Both of one mind, as married people use,
Quietly, quietly, the evening through,
I might get up to-morrow to my work
Cheerful and fresh as ever.   Let us try.
To-morrow how you shall be glad for this !   20
Your soft hand is a woman of itself,
And mine the man's bared breast she curls inside.
Don't count the time lost, either ; you must serve
For each of the five pictures we require—
It saves a model.   So ! keep looking so—
My serpentining beauty, rounds on rounds !
—How could you ever prick those perfect ears,
Even to put the pearl there ! oh, so sweet—
My face, my moon, my everybody's moon,
Which everybody looks on and calls his,   30
And, I suppose, is looked on by in turn,
While she looks—no one's : very dear, no less !

You smile ? why, there's my picture ready made.
There's what we painters call our harmony !
A common greyness silvers everything,—
All in a twilight, you and I alike
—You, at the point of your first pride in me
(That's gone, you know),—but I, at every point ;
My youth, my hope, my art, being all toned down
To yonder sober pleasant Fiesole.
There 's the bell clinking from the chapel-top ;
That length of convent-wall across the way   10
Holds the trees safer, huddled more inside ;
The last monk leaves the garden ; days decrease
And autumn grows, autumn in everything.
Eh ? the whole seems to fall into a shape
As if I saw alike my work and self
And all that I was born to be and do,
A twilight-piece. Love, we are in God's hand.
How strange now, looks the life He makes us lead !
So free we seem, so fettered fast we are !
I feel He laid the fetter : let it lie !   20
This chamber for example—turn your head—
All that's behind us ! you don't understand
Nor care to understand about my art,
But you can hear at least when people speak ;
And that cartoon, the second from the door
—It is the thing, Love ! so such things should be—
Behold Madonna, I am bold to say.
I can do with my pencil what I know,
What I see, what at bottom of my heart
I wish for, if I ever wish so deep—   30
Do easily, too—when I say perfectly
I do not boast, perhaps : yourself are judge
Who listened to the Legate's talk last week,
And just as much they used to say in France.
At any rate 'tis easy, all of it,
No sketches first, no studies, that's long past—
I do what many dream of all their lives

—Dream ? strive to do, and agonise to do,
And fail in doing. I could count twenty such
On twice your fingers, and not leave this town,
Who strive—you don't know how the others strive
To paint a little thing like that you smeared
Carelessly passing with your robes afloat,—
Yet do much less, so much less, Someone says,
(I know his name, no matter) so much less !
Well, less is more, Lucrezia ! I am judged.
There burns a truer light of God in them,   10
In their vexed, beating, stuffed and stopped-up brain,
Heart, or whate'er else, than goes on to prompt
This low-pulsed forthright craftsman's hand of mine.
Their works drop groundward, but themselves, I know,
Reach many a time a heaven that's shut to me,
Enter and take their place there sure enough,
Though they come back and cannot tell the world.
My works are nearer heaven, but I sit here.
The sudden blood of these men ! at a word—
Praise them, it boils, or blame them, it boils too.   20
I, painting from myself and to myself,
Know what I do, am unmoved by men's blame
Or their praise either.   Somebody remarks
Morello's outline there is wrongly traced,
His hue mistaken—what of that ? or else,
Rightly traced and well ordered—what of that ?
Speak as they please, what does the mountain care ?
Ah, but a man's reach should exceed his grasp,
Or what's a Heaven for ? all is silver-grey
Placid and perfect with my art—the worse !   30
I know both what I want and what might gain—
And yet how profitless to know, to sigh
" Had I been two, another and myself,
Our head would have o'erlooked the world ! " No
        doubt,
Yonder's a work, now, of that famous youth
The Urbinate who died five years ago.

('Tis copied, George Vasari sent it me.)
Well, I can fancy how he did it all,
Pouring his soul, with kings and popes to see,
Reaching, that Heaven might so replenish him,
Above and through his art—for it gives way ;
That arm is wrongly put—and there again—
A fault to pardon in the drawing's lines,
Its body, so to speak : its soul is right,
He means right—that, a child may understand.
Still, what an arm ! and I could alter it. 10
But all the play, the insight and the stretch—
Out of me ! out of me ! And wherefore out ?
Had you enjoined them on me, given me soul,
We might have risen to Rafael, I and you.
Nay, Love, you did give all I asked, I think—
More than I merit, yes, by many times.
But had you—oh, with the same perfect brow,
And perfect eyes, and more than perfect mouth,
And the low voice my soul hears, as a bird
The fowler's pipe, and follows to the snare— 20
Had you, with these the same, but brought a mind !
Some women do so. Had the mouth there urged
" God and the glory ! never care for gain.
The Present by the Future, what is that ?
Live for fame, side by side with Angelo—
Rafael is waiting. Up to God all three ! "
I might have done it for you. So it seems—
Perhaps not. All is as God overrules.
Beside, incentives come from the soul's self ;
The rest avail not. Why do I need you ? 30
What wife had Rafael, or has Angelo ?
In this world, who can do a thing, will not—
And who would do it, cannot, I perceive :
Yet the will's somewhat—somewhat, too, the power—
And thus we half-men struggle. At the end,
God, I conclude, compensates, punishes.
'Tis safer for me, if the award be strict,

That I am something underrated here,
Poor this long while, despised, to speak the truth.
I dared not, do you know, leave home all day,
For fear of chancing on the Paris lords.
The best is when they pass and look aside ;
But they speak sometimes ; I must bear it all.
Well may they speak ! That Francis, that first time,
And that long festal year at Fontainebleau !
I surely then could sometimes leave the ground,
Put on the glory, Rafael's daily wear,   10
In that humane great monarch's golden look,—
One finger in his beard or twisted curl
Over his mouth's good mark that made the smile,
One arm about my shoulder, round my neck,
The jingle of his gold chain in my ear,
I painting proudly with his breath on me,
All his court round him, seeing with his eyes,
Such frank French eyes, and such a fire of souls
Profuse, my hand kept plying by those hearts,—
And, best of all, this, this, this face beyond,   20
This in the background, waiting on my work,
To crown the issue with a last reward !
A good time, was it not, my kingly days ?
And had you not grown restless—but I know—
'Tis done and past ; 'twas right, my instinct said ;
Too live the life grew, golden and not grey,
And I'm the weak-eyed bat no sun should tempt
Out of the grange whose four walls make his world.
How could it end in any other way ?
You called me, and I came home to your heart.   30
The triumph was, to have ended there ; then if
I reached it ere the triumph, what is lost ?
Let my hands frame your face in your hair's gold,
You beautiful Lucrezia that are mine !
  " Rafael did this, Andrea painted that—
The Roman's is the better when you pray,
But still the other's Virgin was his wife—"

Men will excuse me. I am glad to judge
Both pictures in your presence ; clearer grows
My better fortune, I resolve to think.
For, do you know, Lucrezia, as God lives,
Said one day Angelo, his very self,
To Rafael . . . I have known it all these years . . .
(When the young man was flaming out his thoughts
Upon a palace-wall for Rome to see,
Too lifted up in heart because of it)
" Friend, there's a certain sorry little scrub   10
Goes up and down our Florence, none cares how,
Who, were he set to plan and execute
As you are, pricked on by your popes and kings,
Would bring the sweat into that brow of yours ! "
To Rafael's !—And indeed the arm is wrong.
I hardly dare—yet, only you to see,
Give the chalk here—quick, thus the line should go !
Aye, but the soul ! he's Rafael ! rub it out !
Still, all I care for, if he spoke the truth,
(What he ? why, who but Michael Angelo ?   20
Do you forget already words like those ?)
If really there was such a chance, so lost,—
Is, whether you're—not grateful—but more pleased.
Well, let me think so. And you smile indeed !
This hour has been an hour ! Another smile ?
If you would sit thus by me every night
I should work better, do you comprehend ?
I mean that I should earn more, give you more.
See, it is settled dusk now ; there's a star ;
Morello's gone, the watch-lights show the wall,   30
The cue-owls speak the name we call them by.
Come from the window, Love,—come in, at last,
Inside the melancholy little house
We built to be so gay with. God is just.
King Francis may forgive me. Oft at nights
When I look up from painting, eyes tired out,
The walls become illumined, brick from brick

Distinct, instead of mortar, fierce bright gold,
That gold of his I did cement them with !
Let us but love each other.   Must you go ?
That Cousin here again ? he waits outside ?
Must see you—you, and not with me ?   Those loans ?
More gaming debts to pay ? you smiled for that ?
Well, let smiles buy me ! have you more to spend ?
While hand and eye and something of a heart
Are left me, work's my ware, and what's it worth ?
I'll pay my fancy.   Only let me sit   10
The grey remainder of the evening out,
Idle, you call it, and muse perfectly
How I could paint, were I but back in France,
One picture, just one more—the Virgin's face,
Not yours this time !   I want you at my side
To hear them—that is, Michael Angelo—
Judge all I do and tell you of its worth.
Will you ?   To-morrow, satisfy your friend.
I take the subjects for his corridor,
Finish the portrait out of hand—there, there,   20
And throw him in another thing or two
If he demurs ; the whole should prove enough
To pay for this same Cousin's freak.   Beside,
What's better and what's all I care about,
Get you the thirteen scudi for the ruff.
Love, does that please you ? Ah, but what does he,
The Cousin ! what does he to please you more ?

I am grown peaceful as old age to-night.
I regret little, I would change still less.
Since there my past life lies, why alter it ?   30
The very wrong to Francis !—it is true
I took his coin, was tempted and complied,
And built this house and sinned, and all is said.
My father and my mother died of want.
Well, had I riches of my own ? you see
How one gets rich !   Let each one bear his lot.

They were born poor, lived poor, and poor they died :
And I have laboured somewhat in my time
And not been paid profusely.   Some good son
Paint my two hundred pictures—let him try !
No doubt, there's something strikes a balance.   Yes,
You loved me quite enough, it seems to-night.
This must suffice me here.   What would one have ?
In Heaven, perhaps, new chances, one more chance—
Four great walls in the New Jerusalem
Meted on each side by the angel's reed,   10
For Leonard, Rafael, Angelo and me
To cover—the three first without a wife,
While I have mine !   So—still they overcome
Because there's still Lucrezia,—as I choose.

Again the Cousin's whistle !   Go, my Love.
ROBERT BROWNING

THYRSIS

A Monody, *to commemorate the author's friend,*
Arthur Hugh Clough, *who died at Florence,* 1861

How changed is here each spot man makes or fills !
In the two Hinkseys nothing keeps the same ;
    The village street its haunted mansion lacks,
And from the sign is gone Sibylla's name,
    And from the roofs the twisted chimney-stacks— 20
        Are ye too changed, ye hills ?
See, 'tis no foot of unfamiliar men
    To-night from Oxford up your pathway strays !
    Here came I often, often, in old days—
Thyrsis and I ; we still had Thyrsis then.

Runs it not here, the track by Childsworth Farm,
    Past the high wood, to where the elm-tree crowns
        The hill behind whose ridge the sunset flames ?

186

The signal-elm, that looks on Ilsley Downs,
　The Vale, the three lone weirs, the youthful
　　　Thames ?—
　　　This winter-eve is warm,
Humid the air ! leafless, yet soft as spring,
　The tender purple spray on copse and briers !
　And that sweet city with her dreaming spires,
She needs not June for beauty's heightening,

Lovely all times she lies, lovely to-night !—
　Only, methinks, some loss of habit's power
　　Befalls me wandering through this upland dim. 10
Once pass'd I blindfold here, at any hour ;
　Now seldom come I, since I came with him.
　　That single elm-tree bright
Against the west—I miss it ! is it gone ?
　We prized it dearly ; while it stood, we said,
　Our friend, the Gipsy-Scholar, was not dead ;
While the tree lived, he in these fields lived on.

Too rare, too rare, grow now my visits here,
　But once I knew each field, each flower, each stick ;
　　And with the country-folk acquaintance made 20
By barn in threshing-time, by new-built rick.
　Here, too, our shepherd pipes we first assay'd.
　　Ah me ! this many a year
My pipe is lost, my shepherd's holiday !
　Needs must I lose them, needs with heavy heart
　Into the world and wave of men depart ;
But Thyrsis of his own will went away.

It irk'd him to be here, he could not rest.
　He loved each simple joy the country yields,
　　He loved his mates ; but yet he could not keep, 30
For that a shadow lour'd on the fields,
　Here with the shepherds and the silly sheep.
　　Some life of men unblest

187

He knew, which made him droop, and fill'd his head.
He went ; his piping took a troubled sound
  Of storms that rage outside our happy ground ;
He could not wait their passing, he is dead.

So, some tempestuous morn in early June,
  When the year's primal burst of bloom is o'er,
  Before the roses and the longest day—
When garden-walks and all the grassy floor
  With blossoms red and white of fallen May
    And chestnut-flowers are strewn—   10
So have I heard the cuckoo's parting cry,
  From the wet field, through the vext garden-trees,
  Come with the volleying rain and tossing breeze :
The bloom is gone, and with the bloom go I !

Too quick despairer, wherefore wilt thou go ?
  Soon will the high Midsummer pomps come on,
  Soon will the musk carnations break and swell,
Soon shall we have gold-dusted snapdragon,
  Sweet-William with his homely cottage-smell,
    And stocks in fragrant blow ;   20
Roses that down the alleys shine afar,
  And open, jasmine-muffled lattices,
  And groups under the dreaming garden-trees,
And the full moon, and the white evening-star.

He hearkens not ! light comer, he is flown !
  What matters it ? next year he will return,
  And we shall have him in the sweet spring-days,
With whitening hedges, and uncrumpling fern,
  And blue-bells trembling by the forest-ways,
    And scent of hay new-mown.   30
But Thyrsis never more we swains shall see ;
  See him come back, and cut a smoother reed,
  And blow a strain the world at last shall heed—
For Time, not Corydon, hath conquer'd thee !

Alack, for Corydon no rival now !—
　　But when Sicilian shepherds lost a mate,
　　　Some good survivor with his flute would go,
Piping a ditty sad for Bion's fate ;
　　　And cross the unpermitted ferry's flow,
　　　　And relax Pluto's brow,
　　And make leap up with joy the beauteous head
　　　Of Proserpine, among whose crowned hair
　　　Are flowers first open'd on Sicilian air,
　　And flute his friend, like Orpheus, from the dead.　10

O easy access to the hearer's grace
　　When Dorian shepherds sang to Proserpine !
　　　For she herself had trod Sicilian fields,
　　She knew the Dorian water's gush divine,
　　　She knew each lily white which Enna yields,
　　　　Each rose with blushing face ;
　　She loved the Dorian pipe, the Dorian strain.
　　　But ah, of our poor Thames she never heard !
　　　Her foot the Cumner cowslips never stirr'd ;
　　And we should tease her with our plaint in vain !　20

Well ! wind-dispersed and vain the words will be,
　　Yet, Thyrsis, let me give my grief its hour
　　　In the old haunt, and find our tree-topp'd hill !
Who, if not I, for questing here hath power ?
　　　I know the wood which hides the daffodil,
　　　　I know the Fyfield tree,
　　I know what white, what purple fritillaries
　　　The grassy harvest of the river-fields,
　　　Above by Ensham, down by Sandford, yields,
　　And what sedged brooks are Thames's tributaries ;　30

I know these slopes ; who knows them if not I ?—
　　But many a dingle on the loved hill-side,
　　　With thorns once studded, old, white-blossom'd
　　　　trees,

Where thick the cowslips grew, and far descried
   High tower'd the spikes of purple orchises,
     Hath since our day put by
The coronals of that forgotten time ;
   Down each green bank hath gone the ploughboy's
     team,
   And only in the hidden brookside gleam
Primroses, orphans of the flowery prime.

Where is the girl, who by the boatman's door,
   Above the locks, above the boating throng,
     Unmoor'd our skiff when through the Wytham
      flats,   10
   Red loosestrife and blond meadow-sweet among
   And darting swallows and light water-gnats,
     We track'd the shy Thames shore ?
Where are the mowers, who, as the tiny swell
   Of our boat passing heaved the river-grass,
   Stood with suspended scythe to see us pass ?—
They all are gone, and thou art gone as well !

Yes, thou are gone ! and round me too the night
   In ever-nearing circle weaves her shade.
     I see her veil draw soft across the day,   20
   I feel her slowly chilling breath invade
   The cheek grown thin, the brown hair sprent with
     grey ;
     I feel her finger light
Laid pausefully upon life's headlong train ;—
   The foot less prompt to meet the morning dew,
   The heart less bounding at emotion new,
And hope, once crush'd, less quick to spring again.

And long the way appears, which seem'd so short
   To the less practised eye of sanguine youth ;
     And high the mountain-tops, in cloudy air,   30
   The mountain-tops where is the throne of Truth,

Tops in life's morning-sun so bright and bare !
  Unbreachable the fort
Of the long-batter'd world uplifts its wall ;
  And strange and vain the earthly turmoil grows,
  And near and real the charm of thy repose,
And night as welcome as a friend would fall.

But hush ! the upland hath a sudden loss
  Of quiet !—Look, adown the dusk hill-side,
  A troop of Oxford hunters going home,
As in old days, jovial and talking, ride !   10
    From hunting with the Berkshire hounds they
      come.
      Quick ! let me fly, and cross
Into yon farther field !—'Tis done ; and see,
  Back'd by the sunset, which doth glorify
  The orange and pale violet evening-sky,
Bare on its lonely ridge, the Tree ! the Tree !

I take the omen ! Eve lets down her veil,
  The white fog creeps from bush to bush about,
  The west unflushes, the high stars grow bright,
And in the scatter'd farms the lights come out.   20
    I cannot reach the signal-tree to-night,
      Yet, happy omen, hail !
Hear it from thy broad lucent Arno-vale
  (For there thine earth-forgetting eyelids keep
  The morningless and unawakening sleep
Under the flowery oleanders pale),

Hear it, O Thyrsis, still our tree is there !—
  Ah, vain ! These English fields, this upland dim,
  These brambles pale with mist engarlanded,
That lone, sky-pointing tree, are not for him ;   30
    To a boon southern country he is fled,
      And now in happier air,

Wandering with the great Mother's train divine
　　(And purer or more subtle soul than thee,
　　　I trow, the mighty Mother doth not see)
Within a folding of the Apennine,

Thou hearest the immortal chants of old !—
　　Putting his sickle to the perilous grain
　　　In the hot cornfield of the Phrygian king,
For thee the Lityerses-song again
　　　Young Daphnis with his silver voice doth sing ;
　　　　Sings his Sicilian fold,　　　　　　　　　10
His sheep, his hapless love, his blinded eyes—
　　And how a call celestial round him rang,
　　And heavenward from the fountain-brink he
　　　　sprang,
And all the marvel of the golden skies.

There thou art gone, and me thou leavest here
　　Sole in these fields ! yet will I not despair.
　　　Despair I will not, while I yet descry
Neath the mild canopy of English air
　　　That lonely tree against the western sky.
　　　　Still, still these slopes, 'tis clear,　　　20
Our Gipsy-Scholar haunts, outliving thee !
　　Fields where soft sheep from cages pull the hay,
　　Woods with anemonies in flower till May,
Know him a wanderer still ; then why not me ?

A fugitive and gracious light he seeks,
　　Shy to illumine ; and I seek it too.
　　　This does not come with houses or with gold,
With place, with honour, and a flattering crew ;
　　　'Tis not in the world's market bought and sold—
　　　　But the smooth-slipping weeks　　　　30
Drop by, and leave its seeker still untired ;
　　Out of the heed of mortals he is gone,
　　He wends unfollow'd, he must house alone ;
Yet on he fares, by his own heart inspired.

Thou too, O Thyrsis, on like quest wast bound ;
  Thou wanderedst with me for a little hour !
    Men gave thee nothing ; but this happy quest,
  If men esteem'd thee feeble, gave thee power,
    If men procured thee trouble, gave thee rest.
      And this rude Cumner ground,
  Its fir-topped Hurst, its farms, its quiet fields,
    Here cam'st thou in thy jocund youthful time,
    Here was thine height of strength, thy golden
      prime !
And still the haunt beloved a virtue yields.   10

What though the music of thy rustic flute
  Kept not for long its happy, country tone ;
    Lost it too soon, and learnt a stormy note
  Of men contention-tost, of men who groan,
    Which task'd thy pipe too sore, and tired thy
      throat—
      It fail'd, and thou wast mute !
Yet hadst thou alway visions of our light,
  And long with men of care thou couldst not stay,
  And soon thy foot resumed its wandering way,
Left human haunt, and on alone till night.   20

Too rare, too rare, grow now my visits here !
  'Mid city-noise, not, as with thee of yore,
    Thyrsis ! in reach of sheep-bells, is my home.
  —Then through the great town's harsh, heart-
      wearying roar,
    Let in thy voice a whisper often come,
      To chase fatigue and fear :
  Why faintest thou ? I wander'd till I died.
  Roam on ! The light we sought is shining still.
  Dost thou ask proof ? Our tree yet crowns the hill,
Our Scholar travels yet the loved hill-side.   30
            MATTHEW ARNOLD

THE BLESSED DAMOZEL

THE blesséd damozel leaned out
　　From the gold bar of Heaven ;
Her eyes were deeper than the depth
　　Of waters stilled at even ;
She had three lilies in her hand,
　　And the stars in her hair were seven.

Her robe, ungirt from clasp to hem,
　　No wrought flowers did adorn,
But a white rose of Mary's gift,
　　For service meetly worn ;　　　　　10
Her hair that lay along her back
　　Was yellow like ripe corn.

Herseemed she scarce had been a day
　　One of God's choristers ;
The wonder was not yet quite gone
　　From that still look of hers ;
Albeit, to them she left, her day
　　Had counted as ten years.

(To one, it is ten years of years.
　　. . . Yet now, and in this place　　　20
Surely she leaned o'er me—her hair
　　Fell all about my face . . .
Nothing : the autumn fall of leaves.
　　The whole year sets apace.)

It was the rampart of God's house
　　That she was standing on ;
By God built over the sheer depth
　　The which is Space begun ;

So high, that looking downward thence
    She scarce could see the sun.

It lies in Heaven, across the flood
    Of ether, as a bridge.
Beneath, the tides of day and night
    With flame and darkness ridge
The void, as low as where this earth
    Spins like a fretful midge.

Heard hardly, some of her new friends
    Amid their loving games   10
Spake evermore among themselves
    Their virginal chaste names ;
And the souls mounting up to God
    Went by her like thin flames.

And still she bowed herself and stooped
    Out of the circling charm ;
Until her bosom must have made
    The bar she leaned on warm,
And the lilies lay as if asleep
    Along her bended arm.   20

From the fixed place of Heaven she saw
    Time like a pulse shake fierce
Through all the worlds. Her gaze still strove
    Within the gulf to pierce
Its path ; and now she spoke as when
    The stars sang in their spheres.

The sun was gone now ; the curled moon
    Was like a little feather
Fluttering far down the gulf ; and now
    She spoke through the still weather.   30
Her voice was like the voice the stars
    Had when they sang together.

(Ah sweet !   Even now, in that bird's song,
    Strove not her accents there,
Fain to be hearkened ?   When those bells
    Possessed the mid-day air,
Strove not her steps to reach my side
    Down all the echoing stair ?)

" I wish that he were come to me,
    For he will come," she said.
" Have I not prayed in Heaven ?—on earth,
    Lord, Lord, has he not prayed ?   10
Are not two prayers a perfect strength ?
    And shall I feel afraid ?

" When round his head the aureole clings,
    And he is clothed in white,
I'll take his hand and go with him
    To the deep wells of light ;
We will step down as to a stream,
    And bathe there in God's sight.

" We two will stand beside that shrine,
    Occult, withheld, untrod,   20
Whose lamps are stirred continually
    With prayer sent up to God ;
And see our old prayers, granted, melt
    Each like a little cloud.

" We two will lie i' the shadow of
    That living mystic tree,
Within whose secret growth the Dove
    Is sometimes felt to be,
While every leaf that His plumes touch
    Saith His Name audibly.   30

" And I myself will teach to him,
    I myself, lying so,

196

The song I sing here ; which his voice
    Shall pause in, hushed and slow,
And find some knowledge at each pause,
    Or some new thing to know."

(Alas ! We two, we two, thou say'st !
    Yea, one wast thou with me
That once of old. But shall God lift
    To endless unity
The soul whose likeness with thy soul
    Was but its love for thee ?)   10

" We two," she said, " will seek the groves
    Where the lady Mary is,
With her five handmaidens, whose names
    Are five sweet symphonies,
Cecily, Gertrude, Magdalen,
    Margaret and Rosalys.

" Circlewise sit they, with bound locks
    And foreheads garlanded ;
Into the fine cloth white like flame
    Weaving the golden thread,   20
To fashion the birth-robes for them
    Who are just born, being dead.

" He shall fear, haply, and be dumb :
    Then will I lay my cheek
To his, and tell about our love,
    Not once abashed or weak :
And the dear Mother will approve
    My pride, and let me speak.

" Herself shall bring us, hand in hand,
    To Him round whom all souls   30
Kneel, the clear-ranged unnumbered heads
    Bowed with their aureoles :

And angels meeting us shall sing
　　To their citherns and citoles.

"There will I ask of Christ the Lord
　　Thus much for him and me :—
Only to live as once on earth
　　With Love,—only to be,
As then awhile, for ever now
　　Together, I and he."

She gazed and listened and then said,
　　Less sad of speech than mild,—　　　　10
"All this is when he comes." She ceased.
　　The light thrilled towards her, filled
With angels in strong level flight.
　　Her eyes prayed, and she smiled.

(I saw her smile.) But soon their path
　　Was vague in distant spheres:
And then she cast her arms along
　　The golden barriers,
And laid her face between her hands,
　　And wept. (I heard her tears.)　　　　20

D. G. ROSSETTI

CHORUSES FROM "ATALANTA IN CALYDON"

I

WHEN the hounds of spring are on winter's traces,
　　The mother of months in meadow or plain
Fills the shadows and windy places
　　With lisp of leaves and ripple of rain ;
And the brown bright nightingale amorous
Is half assuaged for Itylus,

For the Thracian ships and the foreign faces,
   The tongueless vigil, and all the pain.

Come with bows bent and with emptying of quivers
   Maiden most perfect, lady of light,
With a noise of winds and many rivers,
   With a clamour of waters, and with might ;
Bind on thy sandals, O thou most fleet,
Over the splendour and speed of thy feet ;
For the faint east quickens, the wan west shivers,   9
   Round the feet of the day and the feet of the night.

Where shall we find her, how shall we sing to her,
   Fold our hands round her knees, and cling ?
O that man's heart were as fire and could spring to her,
   Fire, or the strength of the streams that spring !
For the stars and the winds are unto her
As raiment, as songs of the harp-player ;
For the risen stars and the fallen cling to her,
   And the southwest-wind and the west-wind sing.

For winter's rains and ruins are over,
   And all the season of snows and sins ;   20
The days dividing lover and lover,
   The light that loses, the night that wins ;
And time remembered is grief forgotten,
And frosts are slain and flowers begotten,
And in green underwood and cover
   Blossom by blossom the spring begins.

The full streams feed on flower of rushes,
   Ripe grasses trammel a travelling foot,
The faint fresh flame of the young year flushes
   From leaf to flower and flower to fruit ;   30
And fruit and leaf are as gold and fire,
And the oat is heard above the lyre,
And the hoofèd heel of a satyr crushes
   The chestnut-husk at the chestnut-root.

And Pan by noon and Bacchus by night,
    Fleeter of foot than the fleet-foot kid,
Follows with dancing and fills with delight
    The Mænad and the Bassarid ;
And soft as lips that laugh and hide
The laughing leaves of the trees divide,
And screen from seeing and leave in sight
    The god pursuing, the maiden hid.

The ivy falls with the Bacchanal's hair
    Over her eyebrows hiding her eyes ;   10
The wild vine slipping down leaves bare
    Her bright breast shortening into sighs ;
The wild vine slips with the weight of its leaves,
But the berried ivy catches and cleaves
To the limbs that glitter, the feet that scare
    The wolf that follows, the fawn that flies.

A. C. SWINBURNE

II

Before the beginning of years
    There came to the making of man
Time, with a gift of tears ;
    Grief, with a glass that ran ;   20
Pleasure, with pain for leaven ;
    Summer, with flowers that fell ;
Remembrance fallen from heaven,
    And madness risen from hell ;
Strength without hands to smite ;
    Love that endures for a breath :
Night, the shadow of light,
    And life, the shadow of death.
And the high gods took in hand
    Fire, and the falling of tears,   30
And a measure of sliding sand
    From under the feet of the years ;

And froth and drift of the sea ;
  And dust of the labouring earth ;
And bodies of things to be
  In the houses of death and of birth ;
And wrought with weeping and laughter,
  And fashioned with loathing and love
With life before and after
  And death beneath and above,
For a day and a night and a morrow,
  That his strength might endure for a span   10
With travail and heavy sorrow,
  The holy spirit of man.

From the winds of the north and the south
  They gathered as unto strife ;
They breathed upon his mouth,
  They filled his body with life ;
Eyesight and speech they wrought
  For the veils of the soul therein,
A time for labour and thought,
  A time to serve and to sin ;   20
They gave him light in his ways,
  And love, and a space for delight,
And beauty and length of days,
  And night, and sleep in the night.
His speech is a burning fire ;
  With his lips he travaileth ;
In his heart is a blind desire,
  In his eyes foreknowledge of death ;
He weaves, and is clothed with derision ;
  Sows, and he shall not reap ;   30
His life is a watch or a vision
  Between a sleep and a sleep.

                              A. C. SWINBURNE

THE SACRILEGE

A Ballad-Tragedy

(*Circa* 182–)

Part I

" I have a Love I love too well
Where Dunkery frowns on Exon Moor ;
I have a Love I love too well,
    To whom, ere she was mine,
' Such is my love for you,' I said,
' That you shall have to hood your head
A silken kerchief crimson-red,
    Wove finest of the fine.'

" And since this Love, for one mad moon,
On Exon Wild by Dunkery Tor,   10
Since this my Love for one mad moon
    Did clasp me as her king,
I snatched a silk-piece red and rare
From off a stall at Priddy Fair,
For handkerchief to hood her hair
    When we went gallanting.

" Full soon the four weeks neared their end
Where Dunkery frowns on Exon Moor ;
And when the four weeks neared their end,
    And their swift sweets outwore,   20
I said, ' What shall I do to own
Those beauties bright as tulips blown,
And keep you here with me alone
    As mine for evermore ? '

" And as she drowsed within my van
On Exon Wild by Dunkery Tor—

And as she drowsed within my van,
  And dawning turned to day
She heavily raised her sloe-black eyes
And murmured back in softest wise,
' One more thing, and the charms you prize
  Are yours henceforth for aye.

" ' And swear I will I'll never go
While Dunkery frowns on Exon Moor
To meet the Cornish Wrestler Joe
  For dance and dallyings,   10
If you'll to yon cathedral shrine,
And finger from the chest divine
Treasure to buy me ear-drops fine,
  And richly jewelled rings.'

" I said : ' I am one who has gathered gear
From Marlbury Downs to Dunkery Tor,
Who has gathered gear for many a year
  From mansion, mart and fair ;
But at God's house I've stayed my hand,
Hearing within me some command— 20
Curbed by a law not of the land
  From doing damage there ! '

" Whereat she pouts, this Love of mine,
As Dunkery pouts to Exon Moor,
And still she pouts, this Love of mine,
  So cityward I go.
But ere I start to do the thing,
And speed my soul's imperilling
For one who is my ravishing
  And all the joy I know,   30

" I come to lay this charge on thee—
On Exon Wild by Dunkery Tor—
I come to lay this charge on thee
  With solemn speech and sign :

Should things go ill, and my life pay
For botchery in this rash assay,
You are to take hers likewise—yea,
    The month the law takes mine.

" For should my rival, Wrestler Joe,
Where Dunkery frowns on Exon Moor—
My reckless rival, Wrestler Joe,
    My Love's bedwinner be,
My rafted spirit would not rest,
But wander weary and distrest   10
Throughout the world in wild protest :
    The thought nigh maddens me ! "

PART II

Thus did he speak—this brother of mine—
On Exon Wild by Dunkery Tor,
Born at my birth of mother of mine,
    And forthwith went his way
To dare the deed some coming night . . .
I kept the watch with shaking sight,
The moon at moments breaking bright,
    At others glooming gray.   20

For three full days I heard no sound
Where Dunkery frowns on Exon Moor,
I heard no sound at all around
    Whether his fay prevailed,
Or one more foul the master were,
Till some afoot did tidings bear
How that, for all his practised care,
    He had been caught and jailed.

They had heard a crash when twelve had chimed
By Mendip east of Dunkery Tor,   30
When twelve had chimed and moonlight climbed ;
    They watched, and he was tracked

THE SACRILEGE

By arch and aisle and saint and knight
Of sculptured stonework sheeted white
In the cathedral's ghostly light,
    And captured in the act.

Yes ; for this Love he loved too well
Where Dunkery sights the Severn shore,
All for this Love he loved too well
    He burst the holy bars,
Seized golden vessels from the chest
To buy her ornaments of the best,   10
At her ill-witchery's request
    And lure of eyes like stars. . . .

When blustering March confused the sky
In Toneborough Town by Exon Moor,
When blustering March confused the sky
    They stretched him ; and he died.
Down in the crowd where I, to see
The end of him, stood silently,
With a set face he lipped to me—
    " Remember." " Ay ! " I cried.   20

By night and day I shadowed her
From Toneborough Deane to Dunkery Tor,
I shadowed her asleep, astir,
    And yet I could not bear—
Till Wrestler Joe anon began
To figure as her chosen man,
And took her to his shining van—
    To doom a form so fair !

He made it handsome for her sake—
And Dunkery smiled to Exon Moor—   30
He made it handsome for her sake,
    Painting it out and in ;

205

And on the door of apple-green
A bright brass knocker soon was seen,
And window-curtains white and clean
    For her to sit within.

And all could see she clave to him
As cleaves a cloud to Dunkery Tor,
Yea, all could see she clave to him,
    And every day I said,
" A pity it seems to part those two
That hourly grow to love more true :   10
Yet she's the wanton woman who
    Sent one to swing till dead ! "

That blew to blazing all my hate,
While Dunkery frowned on Exon Moor,
And when the river swelled, her fate
    Came to her pitilessly. . . .
I dogged her, crying : " Across that plank
They use as bridge to reach yon bank
A coat and hat lie limp and dank ;
    Your goodman's, can they be ? "   20

She paled, and went, I close behind—
And Exon frowned to Dunkery Tor,
She went, and I came up behind
    And tipped the plank that bore
Her, fleetly flitting across to eye
What such might bode. She slid awry ;
And from the current came a cry,
    A gurgle ; and no more.

How that befell no mortal knew
From Marlbury Downs to Exon Moor ;   30
No mortal knew that deed undue
    But he who schemed the crime,

Which night still covers. . . . But in dream
Those ropes of hair upon the stream
He sees, and he will hear that scream
　　　　Until his judgment-time.

THOMAS HARDY

ELEGY

ON A LADY WHOM GRIEF FOR THE DEATH OF HER BETROTHED KILLED

ASSEMBLE, all ye maidens, at the door,
And all ye loves, assemble ; far and wide
Proclaim the bridal, that proclaimed before
Has been deferred to this late eventide :
　　　　For on this night the bride,
　　　The days of her betrothal over,　　　　　10
　　Leaves the parental hearth for evermore ;
To-night the bride goes forth to meet her lover.

Reach down the wedding-vesture, that has lain
　　Yet all unvisited, the silken gown :
Bring out the bracelets, and the golden chain
　　Her dearer friends provided : sere and brown
　　　　Bring out the festal crown,
　　　And set it on her forehead lightly :
　　Though it be withered, twine no wreath again ;
This only is the crown she can wear rightly.　　20

Cloke her in ermine, for the night is cold,
And wrap her warmly, for the night is long,
In pious hands the flaming torches hold,
While her attendants, chosen from among
　　　　Her faithful virgin throng,
　　　May lay her in her cedar litter,
　　Decking her coverlet with sprigs of gold,
Roses, and lilies white that best befit her.

Sound flute and tabor, that the bridal be
Not without music, nor with these alone ;
But let the viol lead the melody,
With lesser intervals, and plaintive moan
  Of sinking semitone ;
    And, all in choir, the virgin voices
  Rest not from singing in skilled harmony
The song that aye the bridegroom's ear rejoices.

Let the priests go before, arrayed in white,
And let the dark-stoled minstrels follow slow,   10
Next they that bear her, honoured on this night,
And then the maidens, in a double row,
    Each singing soft and low,
  And each on high a torch upstaying :
Unto her lover lead her forth with light,
With music, and with singing, and with praying.

'Twas at this sheltering hour he nightly came,
And found her trusty window open wide,
And knew the signal of the timorous flame,
That long the restless curtain would not hide   20
    Her form that stood beside ;
  As scarce she dared to be delighted,
  Listening to that sweet tale, that is no shame
To faithful lovers, that their hearts have plighted.

But now for many days the dewy grass
Has shown no markings of his feet at morn :
And watching she has seen no shadow pass
The moonlit walk, and heard no music borne
    Upon her ear forlorn.
    In vain has she looked out to greet him ;   30
  He has not come, he will not come, alas !
So let us bear her out where she must meet him.

Now to the river bank the priests are come :
The bark is ready to receive its freight :
Let some prepare her place therein, and some
Embark the litter with its slender weight :
    The rest stand by in state,
    And sing her a safe passage over ;
  While she is oared across to her new home,
Into the arms of her expectant lover.

And thou, O lover, that art on the watch,
Where, on the banks of the forgetful streams, 10
The pale indifferent ghosts wander, and snatch
The sweeter moments of their broken dreams,—
    Thou, when the torchlight gleams,
    When thou shalt see the slow procession,
And when thine ears the fitful music catch,
Rejoice, for thou art near to thy possession.
                      ROBERT BRIDGES

THE HOUND OF HEAVEN

I FLED Him, down the nights and down the days ;
  I fled Him, down the arches of the years ;
I fled Him, down the labyrinthine ways
  Of my own mind ; and in the mist of tears 20
I hid from Him, and under running laughter.
      Up vistaed hopes, I sped ;
      And shot, precipitated,
Adown Titanic glooms of chasmèd fears,
  From those strong Feet that followed, followed after.
      But with unhurrying chase,
      And unperturbèd pace,
Deliberate speed, majestic instancy,
      They beat—and a Voice beat
      More instant than the Feet— 30
" All things betray thee, who betrayest Me."

I pleaded, outlaw-wise,
By many a hearted casement, curtained red,
    Trellised with intertwining charities ;
(For, though I knew His love Who followèd,
        Yet was I sore adread
Lest, having Him, I must have naught beside.)
But, if one little casement parted wide,
    The gust of His approach would clash it to.
    Fear wist not to evade, as Love wist to pursue.
Across the margent of the world I fled,   10
    And troubled the gold gateways of the stars,
    Smiting for shelter on their clangèd bars ;
        Fretted to dulcet jars
And silvern chatter the pale ports o' the moon.
I said to Dawn : Be sudden—to Eve : Be soon ;
    With thy young skiey blossoms heap me over
        From this tremendous Lover—
Float thy vague veil about me, lest He see !
    I tempted all His servitors, but to find
My own betrayal in their constancy,   20
In faith to Him their fickleness to me,
    Their traitorous trueness, and their loyal deceit.
To all swift things for swiftness did I sue ;
    Clung to the whistling mane of every wind.
    But whether they swept, smoothly fleet,
    The long savannahs of the blue ;
        Or whether, Thunder-driven,
    They clanged his chariot 'thwart a heaven
Plashy with flying lightnings round the spurn o' their
        feet :—
    Fear wist not to evade as Love wist to pursue.   30
        Still with unhurrying chase,
        And unperturbèd pace,
    Deliberate speed, majestic instancy,
        Came on the following Feet,
        And a Voice above their beat—
    " Naught shelters thee, who wilt not shelter Me."

I sought no more that after which I strayed
      In face of man or maid ;
But still within the little children's eyes
      Seems something, something that replies,
They at least are for me, surely for me !
I turned me to them very wistfully ;
But, just as their young eyes grew sudden fair
      With dawning answers there,
Their angel plucked them from me by the hair.
" Come then, ye other children, Nature's—share   10
With me " (said I) " your delicate fellowship ;
          Let me greet you lip to lip,
          Let me twine with you caresses,
              Wantoning
          With our Lady-Mother's vagrant tresses,
              Banqueting
          With her in her wind-walled palace,
          Underneath her azured daïs,
          Quaffing as your taintless way is,
              From a chalice   20
Lucent-weeping out of the day-spring."
      So it was done :
I in their delicate fellowship was one—
Drew the bolt of Nature's secrecies.
      I knew all the swift importings
      On the wilful face of skies ;
      I knew how the clouds arise
      Spumèd of the wild sea-snortings ;
          All that's born or dies
      Rose and drooped with ; made them shapers
Of mine own moods, or wailful or divine ;   31
      With them joyed and was bereaven.
      I was heavy with the even,
      When she lit her glimmering tapers
      Round the day's dead sanctities.
      I laughed in the morning's eyes.
I triumphed and I saddened with all weather,

Heaven and I wept together,
And its sweet tears were salt with mortal mine ;
Against the red throb of its sunset heart
   I laid my own to beat,
   And share commingling heat ;
But not by that, by that, was eased my human smart.
In vain my tears were wet on Heaven's grey cheek.
For ah ! we know not what each other says
   These things and I ; in sound *I* speak—
Their sound is but their stir, they speak by silences. 10
Nature, poor stepdame, cannot slake my drouth ;
   Let her, if she would owe me,
Drop yon blue bosom-veil of sky, and show me
   The breasts o' her tenderness :
Never did any milk of hers once bless
   My thirsting mouth.
   Nigh and nigh draws the chase
   With unperturbèd pace,
 Deliberate speed, majestic instancy ;
   And past those noisèd Feet   20
   A voice comes yet more fleet—
 " Lo ! naught contents thee, who content'st not
  Me."

Naked I wait Thy love's uplifted stroke !
My harness piece by piece Thou hast hewn from
  me,
   And smitten me to my knee ;
   I am defenceless utterly.
   I slept, methinks, and woke,
And, slowly gazing, find me stripped in sleep.
In the rash lustihead of my young powers,
   I shook the pillaring hours   30
And pulled my life upon me ; grimed with smears,
I stand amid the dust o' the mounded years—
My mangled youth lies dead beneath the heap.
My days have crackled and gone up in smoke,

Have puffed and burst as sun-starts on a stream.
      Yea, faileth now even dream
The dreamer, and the lute the lutanist ;
Even the linked fantasies, in whose blossomy twist
I swung the earth a trinket at my wrist,
Are yielding ; cords of all too weak account
For earth with heavy griefs so overplussed.
      Ah ! is Thy love indeed
A weed, albeit an amaranthine weed,
Suffering no flowers except its own to mount ?   10
      Ah ! must—
      Designer infinite !—
Ah ! must Thou char the wood ere Thou canst limn
    with it ?
My freshness spent its wavering shower i' the dust ;
And now my heart is as a broken fount,
Wherein tear-drippings stagnate, spilt down ever
      From the dank thoughts that shiver
    Upon the sighful branches of my mind.
      Such is ; what is to be ?
The pulp so bitter, how shall taste the rind ?   20
I dimly guess what Time in mists confounds ;
Yet ever and anon a trumpet sounds
From the hid battlements of Eternity ;
Those shaken mists a space unsettle, then
Round the half glimpsèd turrets slowly wash again.
      But not ere him who summoneth
      I first have seen, enwound
With glooming robes purpureal, cypress-crowned ;
His name I know, and what his trumpet saith.
Whether man's heart or life it be which yields   30
      Thee harvest, must Thy harvest-fields
      Be dunged with rotten death ?

      Now of that long pursuit
      Comes on at hand the bruit ;
   That Voice is round me like a bursting sea :

"And is thy earth so marred,
    Shattered in shard on shard?
Lo, all things fly thee, for thou fliest Me!
    Strange, piteous, futile thing,
Wherefore should any set thee love apart?
Seeing none but I makes much of naught" (He said),
"And human love needs human meriting:
        How hast thou merited—
Of all man's clotted clay the dingiest clot?
        Alack, thou knowest not   10
How little worthy of any love thou art!
Whom wilt thou find to love ignoble thee,
        Save Me, save only Me?
All which I took from thee I did but take,
        Not for thy harms,
But just that thou might'st seek it in My arms.
        All which thy child's mistake
Fancies as lost, I have stored for thee at home:
        Rise, clasp my hand, and come!"

        Halts by me that footfall: 20
        Is my gloom, after all,
Shade of His hand, outstretched caressingly?
        "Ah, fondest, blindest, weakest,
        I am He Whom thou seekest!
Thou dravest love from thee, who dravest Me."
                        FRANCIS THOMPSON

LEPANTO

WHITE founts falling in the courts of the sun,
And the Soldan of Byzantium is smiling as they run;
There is laughter like the fountains in that face of all
        men feared,   28
It stirs the forest darkness, the darkness of his beard,
It curls the blood-red crescent, the crescent of his lips,

For the inmost sea of all the earth is shaken with his
    ships.
They have dared the white republics up the capes of
    Italy,
They have dashed the Adriatic round the Lion of the
    Sea,
And the Pope has cast his arms abroad for agony and
    loss,
And called the kings of Christendom for swords about
    the Cross.
The cold queen of England is looking in the glass ;
The shadow of the Valois is yawning at the Mass ;
From evening isles fantastical rings faint the Spanish
    gun,
And the Lord upon the Golden Horn is laughing in
    the sun.

Dim drums throbbing, in the hills half heard,   10
Where only on a nameless throne a crownless prince
    has stirred,
Where, risen from a doubtful seat and half-attainted
    stall,
The last knight of Europe takes weapons from the wall,
The last and lingering troubadour to whom the bird
    has sung,
That once went singing southward when all the world
    was young.
In that enormous silence, tiny and unafraid,
Comes up along a winding road the noise of the
    Crusade.
Strong gongs groaning as the guns boom far,
Don John of Austria is going to the war,
Stiff flags straining in the night-blasts cold,   20
In the gloom black-purple, in the glint old-gold,
Torchlight crimson on the copper kettle-drums,
Then the tuckets, then the trumpets, then the cannon,
    and he comes.

Don John laughing in the brave beard curled.
Spurning of his stirrups like the thrones of all the world,
Holding his head up for a flag of all the free.
Love-light of Spain—hurrah !
Death-light of Africa !
Don John of Austria
Is riding to the sea.

Mahound is in his paradise above the evening star,
(*Don John of Austria is going to the war.*)
He moves a mighty turban on the timeless houri's knees, 10
His turban that is woven of the sunsets and the seas.
He shakes the peacock gardens as he rises from his ease,
And he strides among the tree-tops and is taller than the trees,
And his voice through all the garden is a thunder sent to bring
Black Azrael and Ariel and Ammon on the wing.
Giants and the Genii,
Multiplex of wing and eye,
Whose strong obedience broke the sky
When Solomon was king.

They rush in red and purple from the red clouds of the morn, 20
From temples where the yellow gods shut up their eyes in scorn ;
They rise in green robes roaring from the green hells of the sea
Where fallen skies and evil hues and eyeless creatures be ;
On them the sea-valves cluster and the grey sea-forests curl,
Splashed with a splendid sickness, the sickness of the pearl ;

They swell in sapphire smoke out of the blue cracks of
 the ground,—
They gather and they wonder and give worship to
 Mahound.
And he saith, " Break up the mountains where the
 hermit-folk may hide,
And sift the red and silver sands lest bone of saint
 abide,
And chase the Giaours flying night and day, not giving
 rest,
For that which was our trouble comes again out of the
 west.
We have set the seal of Solomon on all things under
 sun,
Of knowledge and of sorrow and endurance of things
 done,
But a noise is in the mountains, in the mountains, and
 I know
The voice that shook our palaces—four hundred years
 ago :   10
It is he that saith not ' Kismet ' ; it is he that knows
 not Fate ;
It is Richard, it is Raymond, it is Godfrey in the gate !
It is he whose loss is laughter when he counts the
 wager worth :
Put down your feet upon him, that our peace be on
 the earth."
For he heard drums groaning and he heard guns jar,
(*Don John of Austria is going to the war.*)
Sudden and still—hurrah !
Bolt from Iberia !
Don John of Austria
Is gone by Alcalar.   20

St. Michael's on his Mountain in the sea-roads of the
 north
(*Don John of Austria is girt and going forth.*)

Where the gray seas glitter and the sharp tides shift
And the sea folk labour and the red sails lift.
He shakes his lance of iron and he claps his wings of
    stone ;
The noise is gone through Normandy ; the noise is
    gone alone ;
The North is full of tangled things and texts and
    aching eyes,
And dead is all the innocence of anger and surprise,
And Christian killeth Christian in a narrow dusty
    room,
And Christian dreadeth Christ that hath a newer face
    of doom,
And Christian hateth Mary that God kissed in Galilee,
But Don John of Austria is riding to the sea.   10
Don John calling through the blast and the eclipse,
Crying with the trumpet, with the trumpet of his
    lips,
Trumpet that sayeth ha !
Domino gloria !
Don John of Austria
Is shouting to the ships.

King Philip's in his closet with the Fleece about his
    neck,
(*Don John of Austria is armed upon the deck.*)
The walls are hung with velvet that is black and soft
    as sin,
And little dwarfs creep out of it and little dwarfs
    creep in.   20
He holds a crystal phial that has colours like the moon,
He touches, and it tingles, and he trembles very soon,
And his face is as a fungus of a leprous white and grey,
Like plants in the high houses that are shuttered from
    the day,
And death is in the phial, and the end of noble work,
But Don John of Austria has fired upon the Turk.

Don John's hunting, and his hounds have bayed—
Booms away past Italy the rumour of his raid.
Gun upon gun, ha ! ha !
Gun upon gun, hurrah !
Don John of Austria
Has loosed the cannonade.

The Pope was in his chapel before day or battle broke,
(*Don John of Austria is hidden in the smoke.*)
The hidden room in a man's house where God sits all
    the year,
The secret window whence the world looks small and
    very dear.   10
He sees as in a mirror on the monstrous twilight sea
The crescent of his cruel ships whose name is mystery ;
They fling great shadows foe-wards, making Cross and
    Castle dark,
They veil the plumèd lions on the galleys of St. Mark ;
And above the ships are palaces of brown, black-
    bearded chiefs,
And below the ships are prisons, where with multi-
    tudinous griefs,
Christian captives sick and sunless, all a labouring race
    repines
Like a race in sunken cities, like a nation in the mines.
They are lost like slaves that swat, and in the skies of
    morning hung
The stairways of the tallest gods when tyranny was
    young.   20
They are countless, voiceless, hopeless as those fallen
    or fleeing on
Before the high Kings' horses in the granite of
    Babylon.
And many a one grows witless in his quiet room in
    hell
Where a yellow face looks inward through the lattice
    of his cell,

And he finds his God forgotten, and he seeks no more
    a sign—
(But Don John of Austria has burst the battle line !)
Don John pounding from the slaughter-painted poop,
Purpling all the ocean like a bloody pirate's sloop,
Scarlet running over on the silvers and the golds,
Breaking of the hatches up and bursting of the holds,
Thronging of the thousands up that labour under sea
White for bliss and blind for sun and stunned for
    liberty.
Vivat Hispania !
Domino Gloria !   10
Don John of Austria
Has set his people free !

Cervantes on his galley sets the sword back in the
    sheath
(Don John of Austria rides homeward with a wreath.)
And he sees across a weary land a straggling road in
    Spain,
Up which a lean and foolish knight forever rides in
    vain,
And he smiles, but not as Sultans smile, and settles
    back the blade . . .
(But Don John of Austria rides home from the Crusade.)
                               G. K. CHESTERTON

INDIGNATION

AN ODE

I

THERE was an anger among men
    In the old days ; and it was as a sword   20
    In the hands of the Spirit then
    To hew the ambusht villainy out of his path

And in its thievish lurking kill the fraud.
And all the greeds of hell kept to their den
When the Spirit in his hands took wrath.
But lately, when there smiting should have been,
    Who has a weapon seen ?
The Spirit stands and looks on infamy,
And unashamed the faces of the pit
    Snarl at their enemy,
Finding him wield no insupportable light
And no whirled edge of blaze to hit   10
Backward their impudence, and hammer them to
    flight ;
    Although ready is he,
Wearing the same righteous steel
Upon his limbs, helmed as he was then
    When he made olden war ;
Yet cannot now with foulness fiercely deal.
There is no indignation among men,
    The Spirit has no scimetar.

II

Wilt thou not come again, thou godly sword,
    Into the Spirit's hands ?   20
That he may be a captain of the Lord
    Again, and mow out of our lands
        The crop of wicked men.
    O thou forged anger, sword
    Made of the holy rage
That went out against the old sick fen
Of being and on disorder warr'd
And fought it into fire and white stars,
When God made Heavens out of the unwholesome age
And maladies of existence, into good   30
Hunting all that liked not to be glad,—
In what armoury art thou now uplaid,
    And is the rust upon thy blade ?

These many years unhelpt has stood
The Spirit, weaponless against bad,
  Having no sharpness and no heat
Of indignation wherewith to meet
And battle with the vile banners, his great
Beleaguerment of fiends.   But to his hands
  Come thou and clear our lands.
Let him exult to feel the weight
Of wrath swinging with his arm abroad,
And the air about him burn'd with a sword.   10
Let there be fire, and the anger of the Lord.

III

The Mind of Man has been a sacred place,
  And into it the evil race
Would trespass warily, much afraid
Of sorely-felt assaults upon them made
  By statures of great wind that came
  Terribly using a huge flame
    Intolerably white.
But now that wrath comes never out to fight,
The fiendish bands go lording in the day   20
And openly possess the mind of man.
With meaningless scurries of their insane feet
  They have rutted the helpless ground
  Like baggage-travell'd clay.
And when the climate of man's thought they found
Blue air, a road for immortal lights—
Days like the house of God, and hosted nights
Held by the champions of eternity—
  With evil fires the swarms began
To make a weather they could understand   30
Of yellow dusk and smoky enormous bale
  To grieve over the land
  And make the sunlight fail.

Till a low roof of dirty storm they brought
  To hang upon the mind of man :
Who cannot see that man's huge thought
  Is now a dark calamity ?

IV

  But how long shall the Spirit see
The Life of Man, wherein with such delight
He walkt his glebe, and in his ways would sing
  To do his pleasant gardening,
How long see his own especial ground
Vext in a season of disastrous blight,   10
Trampled and staled and trodden filthily
By troops of insolence, the beasts of hell ?
But the Spirit now is built up narrowly,
  And kept within a shameful pound
  Walled in with folly and stupid greed
    Lest he should come to plead
  Against our ugly wickedness,
Against our wanton dealing of distress,
The forced defilement of humanity,
  The foundries and the furnaces   20
  That straddle over the human place.
  Nothing comes to rebuke us for
The hearts we wound with laws grievously,
  The souls our commerce clutches
Cunningly into inescapable lime,
Embruted in wicked streets, made debase
  In villainous alleys and foul hutches,
    There trapt in vice and crime,
And for the wrong we did, who made them poor,
Set to pay infamous penalties in jails ;   30
Not even for this the Spirit breaks his pales.
And shall there be no end to life's expense
  In mills and yards and factories,
    With no more recompense

Than sleep in warrens and low styes,
　　And undelighted food ?
Shall still our ravenous and unhandsome mood
Make men poor and keep them poor ?
Either to starve or work in deadly shops
　　Where the damn'd wisdom of the wheels
Fearfully fascinates men's wit and steals,
With privy embezzlement that never stops,
The worker's conscience into their spinning roar,—
　　Until men are the dead stuff there, 10
　　And the engines are aware ?
Shall we not think of Beauty any more
　　In our activities ?
Or do no better than to God complain ?—
I would that to the world would come again
That indignation, that anger of the Lord,
　　Which once was known among us men.
　　For terrible and upright then
The Spirit would stand suddenly out of his ways
　　Of crouching grief and tears, 20
As by a hilt handling the wrathful blaze,
　　Having again a sword.
And he would ruin all the mischievous walls
That had been raised up of materials
　　Darkly quarried in hell, to hedge
And fence him out of the life of man ;
　　But he with anger's shining edge
Would mightily cut the built iniquities,
Commerce, and all the policies
Of ownership and avarice ; 30
And they would buckle at his stroke,
Perishing into flights of smoke.
Then he with a dreadful song, a sound
To put a howling fear in the bad horde,
Would step again on his own ground,
　　He and his indignant sword,
And the golden havoc would begin.

Those foul ghosts encampt in man
Would run from the stabbing light of his blade.
Caught in the anger's burning wheel,
The huge scything of the tempered zeal,
This clumsy unlit shed we have made,
Money, to house our being in,
Would travel like a wind-blown thing.
In that fanning as motes would be,
The sword-thresht fabric of our trade,
Our happy greed, our healthy wrong,   10
Our villainous prosperity.
And ript out of its cursèd rind
Of laidly duties, that did wring
And clamp in ignominy man's whole mind,
This iron scurf of labour torn away,
Thought would walk again like a sacred king
The shining space of immortality.
    O for that anger in the hands
    Of Spirit ! To us, O righteous sword,
      Come thou and clear our lands,   20
O fire, O indignation of the Lord !
                          LASCELLES ABERCROMBIE

THE SONG OF HONOUR

I CLIMBED a hill as light fell short,
And rooks came home in scramble sort,
And filled the trees and flapped and fought
And sang themselves to sleep ;
An owl from nowhere with no sound
Swung by and soon was nowhere found,
I heard him calling half-way round,
Holloing loud and deep ;
A pair of stars, faint pins of light,   30
Then many a star, sailed into sight,
And all the stars, the flower of night,

225

Were round me at a leap ;
To tell how still the valleys lay
I heard a watchdog miles away,
And bells of distant sheep.

I heard no more of bird or bell,
The mastiff in a slumber fell,
I stared into the sky,
As wondering men have always done
Since beauty and the stars were one,
Though none so hard as I.   10

It seemed, so still the valleys were,
As if the whole world knelt at prayer,
Save me and me alone ;
So pure and wide that silence was
I feared to bend a blade of grass,
And there I stood like stone.

There, sharp and sudden, there I heard—
Ah ! some wild lovesick singing bird
Woke singing in the trees ?
The nightingale and babble-wren   20
Were in the English greenwood then,
And you heard one of these ?

The babble-wren and nightingale
Sang in the Abyssinian vale
That season of the year !
Yet, true enough, I heard them plain,
I heard them both again, again,
As sharp and sweet and clear
As if the Abyssinian tree
Had thrust a bough across the sea,   30
Had thrust a bough across to me
With music for my ear !

THE SONG OF HONOUR

I heard them both, and oh ! I heard
The song of every singing bird
That sings beneath the sky,
And with the song of lark and wren
The song of mountains, moths and men
And seas and rainbows vie !

I heard the universal choir,
The Sons of Light exalt their Sire
With universal song,
Earth's lowliest and loudest notes,   10
Her million times ten million throats
Exalt Him loud and long,
And lips and lungs and tongues of Grace
From every part and every place
Within the shining of His face,
The universal throng.

I heard the hymn of being sound
From every well of honour found
In human sense and soul :
The song of poets when they write   20
The testament of Beautysprite
Upon a flying scroll,
The song of painters when they take
A burning brush for Beauty's sake
And limn her features whole—

The song of men divinely wise
Who look and see in starry skies
Not stars so much as robins' eyes,
And when these pale away
Hear flocks of shiny pleiades   30
Among the plums and apple trees
Sing in the summer day—

The song of all both high and low
To some blest vision true,
The song of beggars when they throw
The crust of pity all men owe
To hungry sparrows in the snow,
Old beggars hungry too—
The song of kings of kingdoms when
They rise above their fortune Men,
And crown themselves anew—

The song of courage, heart and will   10
And gladness in a fight,
Of men who face a hopeless hill
With sparking and delight,
The bells and bells of song that ring
Round banners of a cause or king
From armies bleeding white—

The song of sailors every one
When monstrous tide and tempest run
At ships like bulls at red,
When stately ships are twirled and spun   20
Like whipping tops and help there's none
And mighty ships ten thousand ton
Go down like lumps of lead—

And song of fighters stern as they
At odds with fortune night and day,
Crammed up in cities grim and grey
As thick as bees in hives,
Hosannas of a lowly throng
Who sing unconscious of their song,
Whose lips are in their lives—   30

And song of some at holy war
With spells and ghouls more dread by far
Than deadly seas and cities are

Or hordes of quarrelling kings—
The song of fighters great and small,
The song of pretty fighters all
And high heroic things—

The song of lovers—who knows how
Twitched up from place and time
Upon a sigh, a blush, a vow,
A curve or hue of cheek or brow,
Borne up and off from here and now
Into the void sublime !   10

And crying loves and passions still
In every key from soft to shrill
And numbers never done,
Dog-loyalties to faith and friend,
And loves like Ruth's of old no end,
And intermission none—

And burst on burst for beauty and
For numbers not behind,
From men whose love of motherland
Is like a dog's for one dear hand,   20
Sole, selfless, boundless, blind—
And song of some with hearts beside
For men and sorrows far and wide,
Who watch the world with pity and pride
And warm to all mankind—

And endless joyous music rise
From children at their play,
And endless soaring lullabies
From happy, happy mothers' eyes,
And answering crows and baby-cries,   30
How many who shall say !
And many a song as wondrous well
With pangs and sweets intolerable

From lonely hearths too grey to tell,
God knows how utter grey !
And song from many a house of care
When pain has forced a footing there
And there's a Darkness on the stair
Will not be turned away—

And song—that song whose singers come
With old kind tales of pity from
The Great Compassion's lips,
That make the bells of Heaven to peal   10
Round pillows frosty with the feel
Of Death's cold finger tips—

The song of men all sorts and kinds,
As many tempers, moods and minds
As leaves are on a tree,
As many faiths and castes and creeds,
As many human bloods and breeds
As in the world may be ;

The song of each and all who gaze
On Beauty in her naked blaze,   20
Or see her dimly in a haze,
Or get her light in fitful rays
And tiniest needles even,
The song of all not wholly dark,
Not wholly sunk in stupor stark
Too deep for groping Heaven—

And alleluias sweet and clear
And wild with beauty men mishear,
From choirs of song as near and dear
To Paradise as they,   30
The everlasting pipe and flute
Of wind and sea and bird and brute,

And lips deaf men imagine mute
In wood and stone and clay :

The music of a lion strong
That shakes a hill a whole night long,
A hill as loud as he,
The twitter of a mouse among
Melodious greenery,
The ruby's and the rainbow's song,
The nightingale's—all three,
The song of life that wells and flows   10
From every leopard, lark, and rose
And everything that gleams or goes
Lack-lustre in the sea.

I heard it all, each, every note
Of every lung and tongue and throat,
Ay, every rhythm and rhyme
Of everything that lives and loves
And upward, ever upward moves
From lowly to sublime !
Earth's multitudinous Sons of Light,   20
I heard them lift their lyric might
With each and every chanting sprite
That lit the sky that wondrous night
As far as eye could climb !

I heard it all, I heard the whole
Harmonious hymn of being roll
Up through the chapel of my soul
And at the altar die,
And in the awful quiet then
Myself I heard, Amen, Amen,   30
Amen I heard me cry !
I heard it all and then although
I caught my flying senses, Oh,
A dizzy man was I !

I stood and stared ; the sky was lit,
The sky was stars all over it,
I stood, I knew not why,
Without a wish, without a will,
I stood upon that silent hill
And stared into the sky until
My eyes were blind with stars and still
I stared into the sky.

RALPH HODGSON

THEATRE OF VARIETIES

CIRCLE on circle the hanging gardens descend,
Sloping from upper darkness, each flower face   10
Open, turned to the light and laughter and life
Of the sun-like stage.   And all the space between,
Like the hot fringes of a summer sky,
Is quick with trumpets, beats with the pulse of drums,
Athwart whose sultry thunders rise and fall
Flute fountains and the swallow flight of strings.
Music, the revelation and marvellous lie !
On the bright trestles tumblers, tamers of beasts,
Dancers and clowns affirm their fury of life.

" The World-Renowned Van Hogen Mogen in   20
   The Master Mystery of Modern times."

He talks, he talks ; more powerfully than even
Music his quick words hammer on men's minds.
" Observe this hat, ladies and gentlemen ;
Empty, observe, empty as the universe
Before the Head for which this Hat is made
Was or could think.   Empty, observe, observe."
The rabbit kicks ; a bunch of paper flowers
Blooms in the limelight ; paper tape unrolls,
Endless, a clue.   " Ladies and gentlemen . . ."   30

Sharp, sharp on malleable minds his words
Hammer.   The little Indian boy
Enters the basket.   Bright, an Ethiop's sword
Transfixes it and bleeding is withdrawn.
Death draws and petrifies the watching faces.
" Ladies and gentlemen " : the great Van Hogen
    Mogen
Smiles and is kind.   A puddle of dark blood
Slowly expands.   " The irremediable
Has been and is no more."
Empty of all but blood, the basket gapes.   10
" Arise ! " he calls, and blows his horn.   " Arise ! "
And bird-like from the highest gallery
The little Indian answers.
Shout upon shout, the hanging gardens reverberate.
Happy because the irremediable is healed,
Happy because they have seen the impossible,
Because they are freed from the dull daily law,
They shout, they shout.   And great Van Hogen
    Mogen
Modestly bows, graciously smiles.   The band
Confirms the lie with cymbals and bassoons,   20
The curtain falls.   How quickly the walls recede,
How soon the petrified gargoyles re-become
Women and men ! who fill the warm thick air
With rumour of their loves and discontents,
Not suffering even great Hogen Mogen—
Only begetter out of empty hats
Of rose and rabbit, raiser from the dead—
To invade the sanctity of private life.

The Six Aerial Sisters Polpetini
Dive dangerously from trapeze to far   30
Trapeze, like stars, and know not how to fall.
For if they did and if, of his silver balls,
Sclopis, the juggler, dropped but one—but one
Of all the flying atoms which he builds

233

With his quick throwing into a solid arch—
What panic then would shake the pale flower faces
Blooming so tranquilly in their hanging beds !
What a cold blast of fear !   But patrons must not,
And since they must not, cannot be alarmed.
Hence Sclopis, hence (the proof is manifest)
The Six Aerial Ones infallibly
Function, and have done, and for ever will.

Professor Chubb's Automaton performs
Upon the viols and virginals, plays chess,   10
Ombre and loo, mistigri, tric-trac, pushpin,
Sings Lilliburlero in falsetto, answers
All questions put to it, and with its rubber feet
Noiselessly dances the antique heydiguy.
" Is it a man ? " the terrible infant wonders.
And " no," they say, whose business it is
To say such infants nay.   And " no " again
They shout when, after watching Dobbs and Debs
Step simultaneously through intricate dances,
Hammer the same tune with their rattling clogs   20
In faultless unison, the infant asks,
" And they, are they machines ? "

Music, the revelation and marvellous lie,
Rebuilds in the minds of all a suave and curving
Kingdom of Heaven, where the saxophone
Affirms everlasting loves, the drums deny
Death, and where great Tenorio, when he sings,
Makes Picardy bloom only with perfumed roses,
And never a rotting corpse in all its earth.
Play, music, play !   In God's bright limelight eyes 30
An angel walks and with one rolling glance
Blesses each hungry flower in the hanging gardens.
" Divine," they cry, having no words by which
To call the nameless spade a spade, " Divine
Zenocrate ! "   There are dark mysteries

Whose name is beauty, strange revelations called
Love, and a gulph of pleasure and of awe
Where words fall vain and wingless in the dark ;
The seen Ineffable, the felt but all-Unknown
And Undescribed, is God.   " Divine, divine ! "
The god-intoxicated shout goes up.
" Divine Zenocrate ! "
" Father," the terrible infant's voice is shrill,
" Say, father, why does the lady wear no skirts ? "
She wears no skirts ; God's eyes have never been
    brighter.   10
The face flowers open in her emanation.
She is the suave and curving Kingdom of Heaven
Made visible, and in her sugared song
The ear finds paradise.   Divine, divine !
    Her foot is feat with diamond toes
    And she—divine Zenocrate—
    And she on legs of ruby goes.
The face flowers tremble in the rushing wind
Of her loud singing.   A poet in the pit
Jots down in tears the words of her Siren song.   20
    So every spirit as it is most pure,
    And hath in it the more of heavenly light,
    So it the rarer body doth procure
    To habit in, and is more fairly dight
    With cheerful grace and amiable sight :
    For of the soul the body form doth take ;
    And soul is form and doth the body make.
" Now, boys, together.   All with me," she cries
Through the long sweet suspense of dominant chords ;
" For of the soul," her voice is paradise,   30
" For of the soul the body form doth take ;
And soul is form and doth the body make."
Zenocrate, alone, alone divine !

God save the King.   Music's last practical joke
Still bugling in their ears of war and glory,

The folk emerge into the night.
Already next week's bills are being posted :—
Urim and Thummim, cross-talk comedians ;
Ringpok, the Magian of Tibet ;
The Two Bedelias ; Ruby and Truby Dix ;
Sam Foy and Troupe of Serio-Comic Cyclists . . .
Theatre of immemorial varieties,
Old mummery, but mummers never the same !
Twice nightly every night from now till doomsday
The hanging gardens, bedded with pale flower faces, 10
Young flowers in the old old gardens, will echo
With ever new, with ever new delight.

ALDOUS HUXLEY

TRISTAN DA CUNHA

SNORE in the foam : the night is vast and blind,
The blanket of the mist around your shoulders,
Sleep your old sleep of rock, snore in the wind,
Snore in the spray ! The storm your slumber lulls,
His wings are folded on your nest of boulders
As on their eggs the grey wings of your gulls.

No more as when, ten thousand years ago,
You hissed a giant cinder from the ocean— 20
Around your rocks you furl the shawling snow,
Half sunk in your own darkness, vast and grim,
And round you on the deep with surly motion
Pivot your league-long shadow as you swim.

Why should you haunt me thus but that I know
My surly heart is in your own displayed,
Round whom such wastes in endless circuit flow,
Whose hours in such a gloomy compass run—
A dial with its league-long arm of shade
Slowly revolving to the moon and sun. 30

TRISTAN DA CUNHA

My heart has sunk, like your grey fissured crags,
By its own strength o'ertoppled and betrayed :
I too have burned the wind with fiery flags,
Who now am but a roost for empty words—
An island of the sea whose only trade
Is in the voyages of its wandering birds.

Did you not, when your strength became your pyre,
Deposed and tumbled from your flaming tower,
Awake in gloom from whence you sank in fire
To find Antaeus-like, more vastly grown,   10
A throne in your own darkness, and a power
Sheathed in the very coldness of your stone ?

Your strength is that you have no hope or fear,
You march before the world without a crown :
The nations call you back, you do not hear :
The cities of the earth grow grey behind you,
You will be there when their great flames go down
And still the morning in the van will find you.

You march before the continents : you scout
In front of all the earth : alone you scale   20
The masthead of the world, a lorn look-out,
Waving the snowy flutter of your spray
And gazing back in infinite farewell
To suns that sink, and shores that fade away.

From your grey tower what long regrets you fling
To where, along the low horizon burning,
The great swan-breasted seraphs soar and sing,
And suns go down, and trailing splendours dwindle,
And sails on lonely errands unreturning,
Glow with a gold no sunrise can rekindle.   30

Turn to the Night, these flames are not for you
Whose steeple for the thunder swings its bells :

Grey Memnon, to the tempest only true,
Turn to the night, turn to the shadowing foam,
And let your voice, the saddest of farewells,
With sullen curfew toll the grey wings home.

The wind your mournful syren haunts the gloom :
The rocks, spray-clouded, are your signal-guns
Whose stony nitre, puffed with flying spume,
Rolls forth in grim salute your broadside hollow,
Over the gorgeous burials of suns,
To sound the tocsin of the storms that follow.   10

Plunge forward ; like a ship to battle hurled,
Slip the long cables of the failing light,
The level rays that moor you to the world :
Sheathed in your armour of eternal frost,
Plunge forward, in the thunder of the fight
To lose yourself as I would fain be lost.

Exiled, like you, and severed from my race
By the cold ocean of my own disdain,
Do I not freeze in such a wintry space,
Do I not travel through a storm as vast   20
And rise at times, victorious from the main,
To fly the sunrise at my shattered mast ?

Your path is but a desert where you reap
Only the bitter knowledge of your soul,
You fish with nets of seaweed in the deep
As fruitlessly as I with nets of rhyme,
Yet forth you stride : yourself the way, the goal,
The surges are your strides, your path is time.

Hurled by what aim to what tremendous range !
A missile from the great sling of the past   30
Your passage leaves its track of death and change
And ruin on the world : you fly beyond,

TRISTAN DA CUNHA

Leaping the current of the ages vast
As lightly as a pebble skims a pond.

The years are undulations in your flight
Whose awful motion we can only guess :
Too swift for sense, too terrible for sight,
We only know how fast behind you darken
Our days like lonely beacons of distress :
We know that you stride on and will not harken.

Now in the eastern sky the fairest planet
Pierces the dying wave with dangled spear,   10
And in the whirring hollows of your granite
That vaster Sea, to which you are a shell,
Sighs with a ghostly rumour like the drear
Moan of the nightwind in a hollow cell.

We shall not meet again : over the wave
Our ways divide, and yours is straight and endless—
But mine is short and crooked to the grave :
Yet what of these dark crowds, amid whose flow
I battle like a rock, aloof and friendless—
Are not their generations, vague and endless,   20
The waves, the strides, the feet on which I go ?
                                        ROY CAMPBELL

NOTES

The Pardoner's Tale.

Geoffrey Chaucer (1340 ?–1400) was born in London, took service as a page in the household of the Duke of Clarence, served in the Hundred Years' War, and probably entered the Royal Household. His early poems follow the fashion of the prevailing French romances, and " The Book of the Duchess," dedicated to the wife of his patron, John of Gaunt, is typical of the artificial allegories of the time. In 1378 he undertook one of several diplomatic missions to Italy, where he may have met Petrarch. The more human influence of Italy now in turn dominated his work, and led him in the direction of free artistry. " Troilus and Cressida " is an adaptation from Boccaccio, in which Chaucer's native humour begins to shine through, and his growing command of flowing narrative verse to mature. His circumstances seem to have become more prosperous about the same time : he was appointed Comptroller of Petty Customs in the Port of London in 1382, and four years later was appointed a knight of the shire (M.P.) for Kent. Chaucer was now in every way ready to discard his models and launch into his own vein. Political events seem to have provided a period of enforced leisure, which produced the greater part of " The Canterbury Tales." " The Prologue," which describes the pilgrims in detail, is the apex of Chaucer's work, and the best example of his mature powers of humour, irony, and the quiet but accurate observation of contemporary life and manners. The sudden blooming, in Chaucer, of facility of verse and a modern outlook, entitle him justly " The Father of English Poetry."

P. 1, l. 1. *Whilom :* formerly.
  l. 2. *Haunteden :* practised.
  l. 6. *Erst er primè :* before six A.M.
  l. 7. *Hem :* them, themselves.
  l. 8. *A bellè :* formerly rung before the corpse, to give notice to pray for the soul of the dead.

241

l. 10. *Knave :* boy, servant.

l. 11. *Bet :* better, more quickly.

 Axè : ask.

l. 14. *Deel :* whit.

l. 16. *Pardee : par Dieu :* a common oath.

l. 18. *For-dronke :* very drunk.

l. 19. *Clepeth :* call.

l. 21. *Atwo :* in two.

l. 25. *Me thynketh :* it seems to me.

P. 2, l. 1. *War :* wary.

l. 6. *Henne :* hence.

l. 7. *Hyne :* hind, servant.

l. 9. *Avysèd :* advised.

l. 14. *Dignè :* worthy.

l. 21. *Han :* have.

 Hir : their.

l. 24. *Stirte :* started.

l. 28. *To-rente :* rent to pieces, in swearing by its parts.

l. 29. *Hente :* seize.

l. 33. *Grette :* greeted.

l. 36. *Carl :* fellow.

 With sory grace : " you cursed fellow " (Pollard).

l. 37. *Artow :* art thou.

 For-wrappèd : wrapped up, covered up.

P. 3, l. 7. *Moot :* must.

l. 11. *Moodrès :* mother's.

l. 13. *Leevè :* dear.

l. 16. *Cheste :* box containing his wealth. He would exchange it for a coffin.

l. 18. *Heyrè-clowt :* hair-cloth, hair-shirt.

l. 20. *Welkèd :* withered.

l. 22. *Vileynye :* vulgar language.

l. 23. *But :* unless.

ll. 25-26. *Agayns . . . arise :* Leviticus xix. 32 : " Thou shalt rise up before the hoary head and honour the face of the old man."

 Yeve : give.

 Reed : advice.

l. 28. *Namoorè :* no more.

l. 33. *Hasardour :* gambler.

l. 35. *Thilkè :* the same, that same.

P. 4, l. 1. *Abye :* pay for.

l. 3. *Assent :* plot, agreement.

l. 5. *Leef :* desirous, willing.

l. 7. *Fey :* faith.

l. 13. *Evèrich :* each.

l. 22. *Kepê :* heed.

l. 23. *Wit :* wisdom, intelligence.

    Bourde : jest.

l. 25. *Joliftee :* enjoyment.

l. 27. *Wende :* thought.

l. 34. *Seyn :* say.

l. 35. *Doon us honge :* get us hanged.

P. 5, l. 1. *Rede :* advise.

    Cut : lot.

l. 4. *Swithe :* quickly.

l. 16. *Swornè brother :* one who has interchanged oaths of friendship and loyalty with another.

l. 18. *Woost :* knowest.

l. 20. *Departed :* divided.

l. 21. *Nathêlees :* nevertheless.

l. 27. *Conseil :* a matter on which you will keep counsel, *i.e.* be secret.

    Shrewe : scoundrel.

l. 31. *Biwreye :* betray.

P. 6, l. 16. *Attè :* at the.

l. 19. *For-why :* because.

l. 20. *Levè :* leave.

l. 26. *Quelle :* kill.

l. 27. *Hawe :* yard enclosed by a hedge.

l. 28. *Y-slawe :* slain.

l. 34. *Confiture :* mixture.

l. 35. *Montance :* amount.

    Corn : grain.

l. 36. *Forlete :* give up.

l. 37. *Sterve :* die.

P. 7, l. 1. *A-paas :* at a walking pace.

l. 3. *Y-hent :* taken.

l. 4. *Sith :* afterwards.

l. 9. *Shoope hym :* planned.

    Swynke : toil.

l. 11. *With sory grace :* with evil intention, with an ill favour.

l. 20. *Par cas :* by chance.

l. 23. *Storven :* died.

Lycidas.

John Milton (1608–72), after an education at St. Paul's School, London, and at Cambridge, where his appearance and manners earned him the title of " the Lady of Christ's," retired to Horton, in Buckinghamshire. There he continued his studies and wrote his early poems, " Hymn on the Morning of Christ's Nativity," " Il Penseroso," " L'Allegro," and the masque, " Comus." In 1638 he made a tour on the Continent, especially in Italy. During the Civil War his literary work was confined to pamphlets in support of the Parliamentary cause, and on general political and social questions. Under Cromwell he acted as Latin Secretary. On the Restoration of Charles II, he again retired from active life, and devoted himself to the ambition of his life—a great heroic poem. " Paradise Lost " appeared in 1667, and was followed by the unfinished " Paradise Regained." In both, Milton seems to have felt that the subject had not proved altogether satisfactory, since the issue was predetermined against the actual protagonist, Satan. This feeling probably decided the subject of his final effort, " Samson Agonistes," a drama in which the balance is weighted more evenly.

Milton's preoccupation with the classics produced the involved Latin structure which makes his prose so unwieldy, but which adds dignity by its rolling periods to his later poetry ; while the influence of the Italian Renascence prevented his strong inherent Puritanism from developing its characteristic narrowness. Under these influences he became our chief English poet of " the grand style."

Lycidas : the name of a shepherd in Theocritus and Virgil.

P. 7, l. 24. *Once more :* a reference to Milton's return to poetry, which he had laid aside since the writing of " Comus " in 1634.

ll. 24-25. *Laurels, Myrtles, Ivy :* emblems of distinction in poetry.

Sear : withered.

l. 27. *Forc'd :* unwilling (to write poetry so soon).

Rude : rough.

l. 28. *Mellowing year :* autumn—a reference to his immaturity as a poet.

P. 8, l. 1. *Dear :* costing Milton dear, painful.

l. 2. *Season :* time.

l. 6. *To sing :* i.e. how to sing, to write poetry—a Latin idiom.

l. 9. *Meed :* tribute.

Melodious tear : tearful melody, elegy.

l. 10.   *Sisters of the sacred well :* the Muses, daughters of Jove, who were supposed to haunt the Pierian spring at the foot of Mt. Olympus, where they were born.

l. 11.   *Seat of Jove :* Mt. Olympus.

l. 15.   *Lucky :* bringing good luck.

   Destin'd Urn : " the urn I destine for his ashes, the elegy I am writing " ; or, alternatively, " the urn destined for me."

l. 18.   *The self-same hill :* Christ's College, Cambridge, where Milton and King studied together.

l. 20.   *Lawns :* pastures.

l. 23.   *What time :* when.

   The Gray-fly : the trumpet-fly, which makes a sharp humming sound, about midday.

l. 24.   *Batt'ning :* feeding plentifully.

l. 25.   *The Star . . . :* Venus, or Hesperus, the evening-star.

ll. 25-26.   *Till . . . sloped his . . . wheel :* i.e. till morning.

l. 27.   *Rural ditties :* the early poems of Milton and King.

l. 28.   *Temper'd :* attuned.

   Oaten : of straw. The oaten flute is the shepherd's pipe.

l. 29.   *Satyrs, Fauns :* the students and Fellows of Cambridge. In Greek mythology, the Satyrs represented the luxuriance of nature ; the Fauns, in Roman mythology, were conceived as half man, half goat, like their chief, Faunus or Pan.

l. 31.   *Damoetas :* in Theocritus and Virgil, a general name for a shepherd ; here—a Cambridge tutor of Milton and King.

l. 35.   *Gadding :* straggling.

P. 9. l. 3.   *Fanning :* waving.

l. 4.   *Canker :* the canker-worm, a caterpillar that destroys buds and leaves.

l. 5.   *Taint-worm :* a small red spider.

   Weanling : just weaned.

l. 7.   *White thorn :* hawthorn.

l. 11.   *The steep :* perhaps Penmaenmawr, a mountain in Carnarvon, where the Druids were buried.

l. 12.   *Druids :* the poets and priests of the ancient Britons.

l. 13.   *Mona :* the island of Anglesey, once thickly wooded. It rises towards the interior.

l. 14.   *Deva . . . wisard stream :* the Dee, the boundary

between Wales and England. It was supposed to forebode ill-fortune to the country towards which it changed its course. King sailed from Chester, near its mouth.

l. 15. *Ay me :* alas !

    Fondly : foolishly.

l. 17. *The Muse . . . that Orpheus bore :* Calliope, mother of Orpheus, and the Muse of epic poetry.

l. 18. *Inchanting :* Orpheus enchanted beasts and trees with his music.

l. 20. *Rout :* disorderly crowd, mob.

ll. 20-22. *The rout . . . shore :* on the final loss of his wife Eurydice, Orpheus treated the Thracian women with contempt. In revenge they tore him to pieces, and threw his head into the Hebrus, down which it rolled to the sea, and was carried across to Lesbos.

l. 23. *What boots it ? :* Of what use is it ?

l. 25. *Meditate the . . . Muse :* cultivate poetry.

l. 26. *As others use :* as others are accustomed to do.

ll. 27-28. *Amaryllis, Neaera :* general names for the heroines of love poetry ; taken from Virgil's " Eclogues."

l. 28. *With :* probably = *withe*—to twist.

    Tangles : curls, locks.

l. 29. *Clear :* noble, pure.

l. 30. *Last infirmity :* the last temptation on the path to nobility of mind.

l. 32. *Guerdon :* reward.

l. 34. *The blind Fury :* correctly—Fate. In Greek mythology, there were three Fates, who determined human destiny under the figure of spinning. Clotho span the thread, Lachesis wound it for each individual, Atropos cut it off blindly, without regard to merit or justice.

l. 35. *Thin spun :* and therefore fragile.

    But not the praise : " but slits [cuts short] not the praise."

l. 36. *Phoebus :* Apollo, the god of poetry.

    My trembling ears : the ears of me trembling.

P. 10, l. 2. *Foil :* a thin metal leaf placed under a jewel to set it off by increasing its lustre.

l. 3. *Set off :* is set off.

l. 4. *By :* according as it is judged by.

l. 5. *Witnes :* judgment and bearing witness.

l. 6. *Lastly :* finally.

l. 8. *Arethuse :* a Sicilian fountain, in the island of Ortygia, near Syracuse. It is used here as a symbol of the poetry of Theocritus, a native of Syracuse. He was the greatest Greek pastoral poet.

l. 9. *Mincius :* on an island in this river stands Mantua, the home of the greatest Latin pastoral poet, Virgil.

l. 10. *That strain :* the reply of Phoebus, just concluded.

l. 11. *My Oate :* pipe, pastoral song.

l. 12. *Herald of the Sea :* Triton, son of the sea-god Neptune. He carried a trumpet made from a shell, which he blew at Neptune's command to still the sea.

l. 14. *Fellon :* treacherous.

l. 19. *Hippotades :* son of Hippotes, or Aeolus, god of the winds.

l. 22. *Panope :* a Nereid or sea-nymph.

l. 23. *Fatall :* appointed by fate, fated : or deadly, doom-fraught.

l. 24. *Built in th'eclipse :* and therefore unlucky.

l. 25. *Sacred :* devoted to death.

l. 26. *Camus :* the river Cam, hence Cambridge and its ancient University.

l. 27. *Mantle hairy :* the river-weed floating on the Cam.

l. 28. *Figures dim :* the markings on the sedge leaves.

l. 29. *Sanguine :* blood-red.

Flower : the Hyacinth or iris, which sprang, according to Greek legend, from the blood of Hyacinthus, a beautiful youth beloved by Apollo, who accidentally killed him with a quoit. Natural markings on the hyacinth petals were supposed by the Greeks to resemble the words AI AI (alas ! alas !).

l. 30. *Reft :* snatched away.

Pledge : child.

l. 32. *The Pilot of the Galilean lake :* Saint Peter, who was at first a fisherman on the Sea of Galilee. He is introduced to represent the Church, which Edward King intended to enter.

l. 33. *Two . . . Keyes :* St. Peter is regarded as Head of the Church. Christ gave him " the keys of the kingdom of heaven " (Matt. xvi. 19).

l. 34. *Amain :* forcibly.

l. 35. *Miter'd locks :* wearing the mitre, or bishop's head-dress, since he was the first bishop.

l. 37. *Anow :* enough.

P. 11, l. 1. *The fold :* the English Church.

l. 3. *Feast :* the " plums " or richly endowed positions in the Church.

l. 4. *The worthy bidden guest :* cf. St. Matthew xxii. 8.

I

l. 5. *Blind mouthes:* they ought, as bishops, to see (*episkopein*—to oversee) and, as pastors, to feed (*pascere*—to feed) ; instead they are blind and eat.

l. 8. *What recks it them?:* What do they care ?
They are sped: they have attained their object.

l. 9. *Songs:* sermons, delivered when it suits them.

l. 10. *Scrannel:* thin.

l. 14. *The grim Woolf:* Roman Catholicism, making secret converts.

l. 16. *That two-handed engine:* the shepherd's staff, furnished with a crook at one end, and a mattock at the other.
The door: sc. of the sheepfold.

l. 18. *Alpheus:* a stream in Southern Greece, supposed to flow underseas to join the fountain Arethuse in Sicily. Here it symbolizes, like Arethuse, the pastoral strain, renewed now that "the dread voice" of St. Peter "is past."

l. 22. *Use:* frequent, dwell.

l. 24. *The swart Star:* the Dogstar, Sirius, which appeared in the heat of summer, when the complexion became "swart" or dark.
Sparely looks: hardly affects (with heat).

l. 25. *Eyes:* flowers.

l. 28. *Rathe:* early (comparative—"rather").
Forsaken: sc. by the sun, since it grows in shady places.

l. 29. *Crow-toe:* crow-foot.

l. 30. *Freakt:* streaked.

l. 32. *Well attir'd Woodbine:* the honeysuckle with its "tire" or head-dress of flowers.

l. 35. *Amaranthus:* a plant with richly coloured foliage, and long in withering.

P. 12, l. 2. *Laureat Herse:* tomb covered with laurel, since Lycidas was a poet.

l. 4. *False surmise:* that we are able so to "strew the Laureat Herse," having recovered his body.

l. 9. *Monstrous:* full of monsters.

l. 10. *Moist vows:* tearful prayers.

l. 11. *Fable:* the fabled abode.
Bellérus: a giant. The name was apparently coined by Milton from Bellerium, the Roman name for Land's End, in Cornwall.

l. 12. *The great vision . . . Mount:* St. Michael is supposed to have appeared on the hill, hence called St.

248

Michael's Mount, in Mount's Bay in Cornwall. He is conceived by Milton as still " guarding " the Mount, and thence looking to the south from the rock called St. Michael's Chair.

l. 13. *Namancos and Bayona's hold :* places in the north of Spain, near Cape Finisterre, and thus south from St. Michael's Mount. In old atlases Namancos is marked with a tower and Bayona with a castle, or " hold."

l. 15. *Dolphins :* an allusion to the story of Arion, a Greek musician, who, when thrown overboard, was carried to shore by dolphins he had charmed with his music. Lycidas, a poet, might well expect their assistance.

l. 19. *The day-star :* the sun.

l. 21. *Tricks :* displays, sets off.

Ore : golden rays.

l. 24. *Walk'd the waves :* St. Matthew xiv. 25.

l. 26. *Nectar :* the drink of the gods.

l. 27. *Unexpressive :* inexpressible.

Nuptiall Song : Revelation xix. 9. ". . . the marriage supper of the Lamb."

l. 32. *Wipe the tears :* Revelation vii. 17, and Isaiah xxv. 8.

l. 34. *Genius :* guardian spirit.

l. 35. *In . . . recompense :* " as a recompense to thee."

P. 13, l. 1. *Uncouth :* unskilled.

The . . . Swain : Milton.

l. 3. *Various Quills :* reeds : a reference to the various moods or themes of the poem.

l. 4. *Dorick :* pastoral. The Doric dialect of Greek was that in which the pastoral poetry of Theocritus and his successors was written.

l. 5. *The hills :* the shadows of the hills.

l. 7. *Twitch'd :* drew or hitched round him.

l. 8. *Fresh woods :* a reference to Milton's proposed journey to Italy.

Cymon and Iphigenia.

John Dryden (1631–1700). In an age when authors of no independent means depended largely on the patronage of the Court, Dryden was put to many political shifts to maintain his position. He began by writing verses in praise of Cromwell. With the Restoration (1660) he turned to drama, a taste for which Charles II had acquired during his exile in France. He wrote

" heroic plays," and blank verse tragedies, of which his best is " All for Love." He was appointed Poet Laureate in 1670. He excelled in satiric poetry and found scope for his talent in the political controversies that arose round the Earl of Shaftesbury and the Duke of Monmouth's succession to the throne. He satirised Shaftesbury (in favour of Charles's brother, the Duke of York) in " Absalom and Achitophel " (1681). Perhaps with an eye to the future of politics (James was a Catholic), Dryden became a Catholic in the same year and wrote " The Hind and the Panther " defending the Church of Rome against the Church of England. Dryden's prose imported clearness and precision from France, and " An Essay of Dramatic Poesie " (1668), with the Prefaces to his poems, earned him the title of " The Father of English Prose."

P. 13, l. 9. *That sweet isle . . . :* Cyprus, one of the seats of the worship of Venus.

l. 29. *Wit :* intelligence.

P. 14, l. 11. *Swains :* peasants.

l. 17. *Quarter-staff :* a long staff used as a weapon, and grasped at the middle and at a quarter-length from the end.

l. 28. *Dian :* the goddess of hunting.

Nymphs : maidens.

l. 29. *Eurotas :* a river in southern Greece. Sparta lies in its valley.

l. 30. *Expressed :* represented.

l. 34. *Decent :* becoming, suitable.

l. 35. *Cymarr :* a loose, light dress.

P. 15, l. 23. *Brutal :* brutish.

P. 17, l. 6. *Double day :* from both eyes.

l. 8. *Cudden :* a born fool.

P. 18, l. 29. *The better hand :* in the right direction.

l. 35. *Bishoped :* ordained.

P. 19, l. 5. *Rhodian :* of Rhodes, an island west of Cyprus.

l. 8. *Speed :* be successful.

l. 10. *Prevent :* anticipate.

l. 32. *Prove :* try.

l. 36. *Grapples :* grappling-irons.

P. 21, l. 1. *The Spartan spouse :* Helen, wife of Menelaus, King of Sparta. She was carried off by Paris, Prince of Troy : hence arose the Trojan war.

l. 8. *Candy :* Candia, a town in Crete.

l. 24. *Counterbuffed :* checked by a blow.

l. 25. *The proud archangel fell :* Lucifer's fall from Heaven, in Milton's " Paradise Lost."

P. 23, l. 3. . *Cheer :* countenance.

l. 35. *Rested :* remained.

P. 25, l. 11. *Praetor :* magistrate.

l. 12. *Event :* result.

l. 19. *Menage :* to husband, be careful of.

P. 26, l. 35. *Neuter :* neutral.

P. 27, l. 1. *Provoke :* call forth.

l. 14. *Suborn :* prepare secretly.

P. 28, l. 8. *Harpies :* fabulous birds with maidens' heads and long claws. They tormented blind Phineus by carrying off meals placed before him or rendering them unfit for eating.

l. 19. *Purchased :* obtained by labour.

P. 29, l. 4. *Buxom :* yielding, elastic.

l. 14. *Darts :* javelins.

l. 19. *Jove's Isle :* Crete, where Jove, or Jupiter, was said to have been born and brought up.

The Rape of the Lock.

Alexander Pope (1688–1744) attained early to great perfection of rhythm and expression—he " lisp'd in numbers "—but his mind received an odd twist from the facts that he was practically a cripple and that he suffered certain disabilities through being a Catholic. He found fittest expression in satire. He excelled in the use of the heroic couplet, which he perfected as a satirical weapon in the mock-heroic " Rape of the Lock " (1712) and " The Dunciad " (1728). His " Essay on Criticism " (1711) and " Essay on Man " (1734) are clever re-statements of other men's ideas. Pope completed verse translations of Homer's " Iliad " (1720) and " Odyssey " (1726), which made his fortune. His poetry has a matchless glitter and, after Shakespeare, his poetic aphorisms are probably more often quoted than those of any other English poet.

P. 30, l. 3. *Caryll :* John Caryll (1666–1736), a friend of Pope and a cousin of Lord Petre, " the Baron." It was he who suggested to Pope the subject of the poem.

l. 13. *Sol :* the sun.

l. 20. *Sylph :* a spirit that inhabits the air.

l. 23. *A birth-night beau :* a handsome young man such as she would have met at a ball held on a royal birthday.

l. 32. *The silver token :* a coin left by fairies in the slippers of industrious maids.

The circled green : the circle of turf on which the fairies danced.

P. 31, l. 12. *The box : i.e.* in the theatre.

The ring : in Hyde Park ; a favourite resort for driving or horsemanship.

l. 14. *A chair :* a sedan-chair, carried by two Pages. It consisted of a sort of covered box, with poles for the carriers projecting behind and before.

l. 24. *Ombre :* a card-game for three (Spanish *el hombre*, the man). The " ombre " played against the other two.

l. 26. *Their first elements :* the four elements, in Greek philosophy, were earth, air, fire, and water. From these, mixed in varying proportions, all things were believed to be made. In human beings one element generally predominated over the others, and determined the main quality of their character.

l. 28. *Salamander :* a Spirit of fire.

l. 30. *Nymph :* a Spirit of water.

Elemental tea : made with water — the element appropriate to the Nymphs.

P. 32, l. 16. *Garters, Stars :* emblems of knighthood.

Coronets : small crowns worn by dukes, marquises, earls, viscounts or barons.

l. 17. *Your Grace :* a title of ceremony used in addressing a duke or duchess.

l. 32. *Sword-knot :* a ribbon tied to the hilt of a sword.

l. 36. *Thy protection claim :* claim to protect thee.

P. 33, l. 3. *Ruling star :* the star which was in the ascendant at a person's birth and was supposed to " rule " his life and destiny by its influence.

l. 13. *Billet-doux :* love-letter.

l. 33. *Patches :* small pieces of black silk stuck on the face to bring out the complexion by contrast. They were commonly worn in Pope's day.

P. 34, l. 7. *Betty :* Belinda's maid.

l. 10. *The rival :* Belinda.

l. 32. *Springes :* snares in the form of a spring-noose.

P. 35, l. 9. *Phoebus :* the sun.

l. 15. *Pyre :* a pile of wood on which a dead body was burned.

l. 19. *Half his pray'r : i.e.* " soon to obtain " the prize.

P. 36, l. 10. *Sylphids :* female sylphs.

l. 37. *Furbelow :* the plaited border of a gown or petticoat.

P. 37, l. 13.   *Drops :* ear-drops, ear-rings.

l. 31.   *Styptics :* substances, like alum, that cause contraction.

l. 32.   *Rivelled :* wrinkled, shrivelled.

l. 33.   *Ixion :* for treachery to his father-in-law and ingratitude to Zeus (Jupiter), Ixion was chained by Hermes to a wheel, that revolved perpetually.

l. 35.   *Chocolate :* cocoa.

P. 38, l. 8.   *Structure :* Hampton Court.

P. 39, l. 1.   *The sacred nine :* the nine Muses. Each of the three hands at ombre held nine cards.

l. 4.   *Matadores :* the three best trumps : the Ace of Spades (*Spadillio*), the 2 of trumps (*Manillio*), and the Ace of Clubs (*Basto*).

l. 12.   *Succinct :* girt up.

l. 17.   *Trumps :* Belinda, as " ombre," declared trumps.

ll. 20–24.   *Spadillio, Manillio, Basto :* See note on " Matadores " above.

ll. 32–33.   *Mighty Pam . . . Loo :* the Knave of Clubs, the highest card in the game of Loo.

P. 40, l. 2.   *Amazon :* the Queen of Spades, the only remaining trump. The Amazons were a fabulous race of female warriors, believed to have come from the Caucasus and to have settled in Asia Minor.

l. 4.   *Club's . . . tyrant :* the King of Clubs.

l. 9.   *The globe :* he alone carries an orb.

l. 11.   *Th' embroider'd King . . . :* the King of Diamonds.

l. 19.   *Habit :* dress.

l. 27.   *Codille :* whichever of the adversaries wins the game, gives *Codille* to the Ombre.

l. 29.   *One nice trick :* the game is so *nicely* or finely balanced that this trick decides the game.

ll. 30–33.   *The King . . . Ace :* in a red suit, unless it was declared trumps, the ace ranked below the knave.

P. 41, l. 4.   *The berries . . . the mill :* coffee-beans and coffee-mill.

l. 5.   *Altars of Japan :* japanned or lacquered trays.

l. 8.   *China's earth :* china cups.

ll. 20–22.   *Scylla's fate . . . Nisus' . . . hair :* Scylla, daughter of Nisus, fell in love with Minos, who was besieging her father's capital, Megára, and promised to deliver the city into his hands. She pulled out from her father's head the golden hair on which his life depended. Nisus died, and Minos took the city. He was so disgusted, however, with Scylla's treachery that he abandoned her, and she threw herself into the sea. She was changed into a lark, Nisus into a hawk.

P. 42, l. 8. *Forfex :* a pair of scissors.

l. 13. *But airy substance . . . :* " See Milton, lib. vi. of Satan cut asunder by the Angel Michael." (P.).

l. 26. *Atalantis :* a book of " Secret Memoirs and Manners of Several Persons of Quality of Both sexes. From the New Atalantis." It was published in 1709, and written by Mrs. Manley, a friend of Swift.

l. 28. *Solemn days :* the days on which festivals fell annually.

P. 43, l. 18. *Spleen :* the organ supposed to be the seat of melancholy and bad temper ; here personified as a goddess living in a cave.

l. 26. *Megrim :* low spirits, migraine.

l. 27. *Wait :* attend on.

l. 32. *Lampoons :* personal satires.

P. 44, l. 11. *On rolling spires :* in spirals.

l. 13. *Elysian :* heavenly.

l. 14. *Machines :* stage contrivances for effecting the entry or descent on the stage of a supernatural person.

l. 19. *Pipkin :* a small earthen pot.

Homer's tripod : " Iliad," xviii. 373-6. " The tripods are perhaps meant to carry trays and serve as tables at the feasts of the gods. They were made by Hephaestus for his own home " (W. Leaf).

l. 24. *Spleenwort :* a fern supposed to cure attacks of spleen.

P. 45, l. 1. *Citron-waters :* brandy flavoured with lemon peel.

l. 9. *The goddess :* Spleen.

ll. 11–12. *Bag . . . Ulysses . . . the winds :* the bag, containing the winds, given to Ulysses by Aeolus.

l. 24. *Thalestris :* a Queen of the Amazons.

l. 31. *Fillet :* a small band tied round the head.

l. 32. *Loads of lead :* used in curling the hair.

P. 46, ll. 7–9. *Through crystal . . . blaze :* in a diamond ring.

l. 10. *Hyde Park Circus :* a well-known thoroughfare in London.

l. 11. *In the sound of Bow :* Bow-bells were those of St. Mary-le-Bow, and had one of the most celebrated peals in London. They were nearly in the centre of the city : a wit would lodge in the West End.

l. 17. *Clouded :* variegated with spots.

P. 47, l. 13. *Chariot :* coach.

NOTES

l. 14. *Bohea :* tea.

P. 48, l. 5. *The Trojan . . . :* Aeneas, who, according to Virgil, persevered in his intention to leave Carthage, in spite of the entreaties of Queen Dido and her sister Anna.

l. 14. *The side-box :* the gentlemen who sat there.

l. 17. *The front-box :* the ladies.

P. 49, l. 11. *So when bold Homer . . . :* "Homer, *Il.* xx." (P.)

l. 13. *Pallas :* the Greek goddess of wisdom.

Mars : the Roman god of war.

Latona : daughter of the Titan Coeus and Phoebe, and mother of Apollo.

Hermes : Mercury, the herald and messenger of the gods.

l. 14. *Olympus :* a mountain in Greece, supposed to be the home of the gods.

l. 16. *Neptune :* the god of the sea.

l. 31. *Maeander :* a river in Asia Minor.

P. 50, l. 35. *Othello :* the Shakespearean protagonist whose jealousy of Desdemona, his wife, was aggravated by seeing her handkerchief in the possession of another.

P. 51, l. 6. *The Lunar sphere . . . :* the moon ; a reference to the derivation of "lunatic."

l. 15. *Tomes of casuistry :* volumes dealing with cases of conscience, and enabling a decision to be made between conflicting claims.

l. 16. *The Muse :* the goddess of poetry.

l. 19. *Proculus :* a Roman senator, to whom Romulus, after his death, is said to have appeared, and whom he informed that the Roman people were thereafter to honour him as a god.

l. 22. *Berenice :* the wife of Ptolemy III, who dedicated her hair for her husband's safe and victorious return from an expedition into Syria. The hair was hung in the temple of the war-god, but was stolen, and was believed to have become a constellation.

l. 26. *The beau monde :* the fashionable world.

The Mall : Pall Mall, a fashionable street in London : (*pron.* pel-mel) "on the north side of St. James's Park."

l. 28. *Venus :* the goddess of love.

l. 29. *Rosamonda's lake :* in St. James's Park : a favourite trysting-place. The lake is now filled up.

l. 30. *Partridge :* "John Partridge was a ridiculous Star-gazer, who in his Almanacks every year never

255

fail'd to predict the downfall of the Pope, and the King of France, then at war with the English " (P.).

l. 31. *Galileo :* a great Italian astronomer and physicist (*d.* 1642), imprisoned by the Inquisition.

The Bard.

Thomas Gray (1716–71) was educated at Cambridge, where he remained as Professor of History. During a life of scholarly retirement he published only a few meticulously chiselled poems, almost all of which have become classics. By training and contemporary tradition a classicist, he has, by his melancholy, his accurate observation of nature, and his praise of the simple country life, distinct affinities with the coming Romantic Revival.

This Ode, says Gray, " is founded on a tradition current in Wales, that Edward the First, when he completed the conquest of that country, ordered all the Bards, that fell into his hands, to be put to death." The tradition has been shown to have no foundation.

In 1277, Edward I summoned Llewellyn, Prince of Wales, to do homage to him. He refused. Edward invaded North Wales, and forced Llewellyn to do homage and cede a part of his territory. In 1282 Llewellyn rose in revolt. Wales was again invaded, Llewellyn killed in 1283, and by the Statute of Wales, the country was annexed to England. Edward's eldest son, who was born at Carnarvon in 1284, was given the title Prince of Wales.

Pindaric : Pindar (522–442 B.C.) was the greatest lyric poet of Greece. His odes, the structure of which is imitated by Gray, consist of groups of three irregular stanzas, known as strophe, antistrophe, and epode. In " The Bard," the groups will be found to resemble each other in length of corresponding stanzas, in metre, and in rhyme-scheme. Each group, also, forms a kind of paragraph or section of the ode, and deals with one aspect of the main theme. Thus " The Bard " deals with

(*a*) The curse of the poet on Edward I.

(*b*) The fulfilment of the curse in the misfortunes of Edward's descendants, the Plantagenets.

(*c*) The contrasted glory of the Tudors, who were of Welsh descent.

P. 52, l. 8. *Ruthless King :* Edward I, King of England (reigned 1272–1307).

l. 9.   *Confusion :* destruction.

l. 12. *Hauberk's twisted mail :* " The Hauberk was a tex-
ture of steel ringlets, or rings interwoven, forming a coat
of mail, that sat close to the body, and adapted itself to
every motion " (G.).

l. 14. *Secret :* inmost.
    Nightly : nocturnal, at night.

l. 15. *Cambria :* Wales.

l. 18. *Snowdon :* " a name given by the Saxons to that
mountainous tract, which . . . included all the highlands
of Caernarvonshire and Merionethshire, as far east as
the river Conway " (G.).

l. 20. *Glo'ster :* " Gilbert de Clare, surnamed the Red,
Earl of Gloucester and Hertford, son-in-law to King
Edward " (G.).

l. 21. *Mortimer :* Lord of Wigmore. Both Mortimer
and Gloucester " were *Lords-Marchers*, whose lands lay
on the borders of Wales, and probably accompanied
the King in this expedition " (G.).

l. 23. *Conway :* a swift river in N.W. Wales, near
Snowdon.

P. 53, l. 8.   *Vocal :* resounding.

l. 9.   *Hoel :* son of Owain Gwynedd, Prince of North
Wales.
    Llewellyn : the last native Prince of Wales. He was
murdered in 1282, while Edward I was leading the
expedition against him.

ll. 10–12. *Cadwallo, Urien :* Welsh kings and bards of the
sixth or seventh century. None of their poetry has
survived.

l. 14. *Modred :* a Welsh bard. The exact reference is
uncertain.

l. 15. *Plinlimmon :* a mountain in Montgomeryshire.

l. 16. *Arvon's shore :* " the shores of Caernarvonshire
opposite to the isle of Anglesey " (G.).

l. 25. *Griesly :* grisly, horrible.

l. 28. *Join :* pron. " jine."

l. 29. *Weave . . . the tissue :* in Norse mythology the
three Norns or Fates, representing Past, Present and
Future, weave the web of fate.

l. 30. *Warp . . . woof :* the threads running lengthwise
and crosswise respectively.

P. 53, l. 30–P. 55, l. 20.   These lines are " the dreadful
harmony."

P. 54, l. 2.   *Characters :* symbols, writing.

ll. 5–6. *Berkley's roofs . . . King:* Edward II was dethroned by his wife, Isabella, the "she-wolf of France," and her favourite, Roger, Lord Mortimer; and his young son made King in his place. Edward was imprisoned in Berkeley Castle, in Gloucestershire, and there murdered by Mortimer's orders in 1327.

ll. 9–10. *Who . . . Heav'n:* Edward III, who scourged France, his mother's native country, in the first phase of the Hundred Years' War.

ll. 10–11. *Terrors . . . Flight:* Edward III routed the French at Cressy in 1346, captured Calais in 1347, and won the battle of Poitiers in 1356.

l. 11. *Amazement:* extreme terror.

ll. 12–16. *Sorrow . . . solitude . . . obsequies:* "Death of that King [Edward III], abandon'd by his Children, and even robbed in his last moments by his Courtiers and his Mistress" (G.).

l. 17. *The sable Warriour:* Edward III's eldest son, "Edward, the Black Prince, dead some time [a year] before his Father" (G.).

l. 19. *The Swarm:* the younger courtiers.

l. 20. *The rising Morn:* Richard II, who succeeded his grandfather, Edward III, in 1377.

l. 23. *The gilded Vessel:* the ship of state, and the "magnificence of Richard the Second's reign" (G.).

l. 24. *Youth on the prow:* Richard II was only eleven at his accession.

Pleasure at the helm: Richard II was governed by his favourites, who considered their own pleasure before the good of the country.

l. 25. *The . . . Whirlwind:* Richard II was deposed in 1399 by Henry Bolingbroke, his cousin. He had "sown the wind"; he was now "reaping the whirlwind."

P. 55, l. 1. *Thirst and Famine:* after his deposition Richard was imprisoned in Pomfret (or Pontefract) Castle, where he died of starvation six months after.

l. 5. *Years of havock:* the Wars of the Roses (1455–1485).

l. 6. *Kindred squadrons:* the houses of York and Lancaster were descended from sons of Edward III—John of Gaunt, Duke of Lancaster, and Edmund, Duke of York.

l. 7. *Towers of Julius:* the Tower of London. "The oldest part of that structure is vulgarly attributed to Julius Caesar" (G.).

l. 8. *Midnight murther :* " Henry the Sixth, George Duke of Clarence, Edward the Fifth, and Richard Duke of York, &c. believed to be murthered secretly in the Tower of London " (G.).

l. 9. *Consort :* " Margaret of Anjou, a woman of heroic spirit, who struggled hard to save her Husband and her Crown " (G.).

Father : Henry V, famous for his French wars, and especially for his victory at Agincourt.

l. 10. *The . . . Usurper's holy head :* " Henry the Sixth very near being canonized. The line of Lancaster had no right inheritance to the Crown " (G.). Henry VI was not himself exactly a usurper, but was the grandson of the usurping Henry IV, who deposed Richard II.

ll. 11–12. *The rose of snow, . . . foe :* " The white and red roses, devices of York and Lancaster " (G.).

Twined : perhaps a reference to the marriage of Edward IV, a Yorkist, to Elizabeth Woodville, a Lancastrian.

l. 13. *The bristled Boar in infant-gore wallows :* " The silver Boar was the badge of Richard the Third ; whence he was usually known in his own time by the name of *The Boar* " (G.). He is suspected of murdering his two nephews in the Tower, and so ensuring his own succession to the crown.

l. 19. *Half of thy heart :* Queen Eleanor, wife of Edward I, died at Grantham in 1290. This is the first fulfilment of the Bard's call for vengeance.

Consecrate : to bless for a sacred purpose ; here, for sacrifice.

l. 21. *Stay :* the ghosts vanish.

l. 29. *Arthur :* " It was the common belief of the Welch nation, that King Arthur was still alive in Fairy-Land, and should return again to reign over Britain " (G.). Henry VII named his eldest son Arthur, in deference to Welsh sentiment.

l. 30. *Ye genuine Kings :* the Tudors, who were descended from the ancient Welsh or " British " princes. " Both Merlin and Taliessin had prophesied, that the Welch should regain their sovereignty over this island ; which seemed to be accomplished in the House of Tudor " (G.).

l. 32. *Sublime :* aloft.

Fronts : foreheads.

P. 56, l. 3. *A Form divine :* Queen Elizabeth.

l. 5. *Lyon-port :* proud carriage or deportment.

l. 6. *Attemper'd . . . to :* attuned, mixed in due proportion.

ll. 7-8. *Strings symphonious . . . vocal transport :* the music and lyric poetry of the Elizabethan age.

l. 9. *Taliessin :* " Taliessin, Chief of the Bards, flourished in the VIth Century " (G.).

ll. 14-15. *Fierce War . . . Fiction :* " Fierce wars and faithful loves shall moralize my song. *Spenser's Proëme to the Fairy Queen* " (G.).

l. 16. *Buskin'd measures :* tragic verse. The buskin was a high boot worn in Greek and Roman tragedies. The reference here is to Shakespeare's tragedies.

ll. 19-20. *A Voice . . . Eden :* Milton, in " Paradise Lost."

l. 21. *Distant warblings :* " The succession of Poets after Milton's time " (G.).

l. 23. *Sanguine :* red with blood.

Yon . . . cloud : the massacre of the bards.

l. 25. *Repairs :* renews, restores.

The Deserted Village.

Oliver Goldsmith (1728–1774) was the son of an Irish clergyman—the kindly Mr. Primrose of " The Vicar of Wakefield." After desultory studies at Dublin, Edinburgh, and Leyden, he travelled on foot over France, Switzerland, and Italy, earning his living by his flute. On his return to London, he produced various types of work : essays, collected in " The Citizen of the World " ; a novel, " The Vicar of Wakefield " ; two plays, " The Good-natured Man " and " She Stoops to Conquer " ; and a few poems, including " The Traveller " and " The Deserted Village." His kindly humour and universal good-nature shines through all he wrote, and a natural and limpid style of exquisite charm has placed his work among the classics.

P. 57, l. 1. *Auburn :* the description of this village owes some of its details to Goldsmith's native hamlet of Lissoy, in Westmeath, Ireland.

P. 58, l. 11. *Bittern :* a wading bird of the heron family.

l. 24. *England's griefs :* depopulation, enclosures, the rise of industry.

P. 59, l. 12. *Tangling :* with overgrowth.

P. 61, l. 6. *Passing :* very (surpassingly).

l. 13. *The vagrant train :* beggars.

l. 15. *Long-remember'd :* here meaning "with a long memory or store of memories."

P. 63, l. 3. *Cypher :* to count, do arithmetic.

l. 5. *Gauge :* to measure (volume).

l. 27. *The twelve good rules :* maxims supposed to have been found in the study of Charles I after his death, and commonly printed in pamphlet form or framed on a single sheet.

Royal game of goose : a game of chance in which counters were moved from one compartment on a board to another, the right to a double move being secured when the card bearing the picture of a goose was reached.

l. 29. *Fennel :* a fragrant plant with yellow flowers.

P. 64, l. 9. *The mantling bliss :* the drink, mantled with froth.

P. 65, l. 31. *Common :* a stretch of open land, used in common by the inhabitants of a town.

P. 66 l. 7. *Brocade :* a silk material embroidered with figures.

P. 67, l. 1. *Altama :* Altamaha, in Georgia, U.S.A.

l. 14. *Tornado :* a violent hurricane, moving in circles or eddies.

P. 69, l. 5. *Torno :* Tornea, a river that flows into the Gulf of Bothnia, and divides Sweden from Finland.

Pambamarca : a mountain near Quito, in Ecuador, South America.

l. 6. *Equinoctial fervours :* equatorial heat. The sun crosses the equator at the equinox, *i.e.* when day and night are equal.

l. 15. *Labour'd :* made with great labour.

Mole : breakwater.

On the Receipt of my Mother's Picture.

William Cowper (1731–1800), the son of a clergyman of Great Berkhampstead, was educated at Westminster School, and articled to the law. His serious, melancholy temper which turned at times into madness, appears in "The Castaway" and "On the Receipt of my Mother's Picture." Occasionally he turned for relief to lighter humorous themes, as in "John Gilpin." His quiet years of retirement are mirrored in poems on his various pets, "Epitaph on a Hare," "The Retired Cat," and in his chief poem, "The Task." In order to divert his mind from melancholy he undertook a blank verse translation of Homer. His " Letters " are notable.

My mother : Ann, daughter of Roger Donne, of Ludham Hall, in Norfolk. She died in 1737, when William was six years old.

Ann Bodham : or Anne Donne, Cowper's early playmate.

P. 70, l. 4. *As :* as if.

l. 7. *Elysian :* delightful. According to the Greeks, Elysium was the abode of the blessed after death.

l. 12. *Wretch even then :* Cowper's health was delicate even in childhood, and he was always sensitively shy and despondent. At school he was ridiculed and often cruelly ill-treated.

l. 24. *Maidens :* maid-servants.

l. 27. *Still :* always, constantly.

P. 71, l. 4. *The past'ral house :* the rectory at Great Berkhampstead, Hertfordshire. His father held the living of the parish.

l. 18. *Humour :* caprice, temper.

l. 22. *Numbers :* verses, poetry.

P. 72, l. 1. *Unbound spirit :* the spirit freed from the bonds of the body.

l. 11. *" Where tempests never . . . roar " :* a quotation from Garth (*c.* 1660–1719), a physician and poet of the age of Anne. His best work is the mock-heroic poem, " The Dispensary."

l. 12. *Consort :* Cowper's father died in 1756.

l. 16. *Devious :* " from my course."

Peter Grimes.

George Crabbe (1754–1832) was born at Aldeburgh, in Suffolk, and apprenticed to a surgeon, but left home to venture on literature in London. Later he took holy orders, and found more comfort and security in the living of Trowbridge. His poetry is of a piece—realistic and accurate descriptions of nature and tales of the lives of country people, somewhat similar to those of his great contemporary, Wordsworth. His artificial style, however, and his lack of humour, imagination, or idealism, group him rather with the earlier eighteenth century.

" Peter Grimes " is one of the tales included in " The Borough," published in 1810.

P. 73, l. 23. *Assert the man :* assert his manhood, that he had reached manhood.

l. 26. *The sacrilegious blow :* profaning sacred things : here, the fifth Commandment.

l. 32. *Settle :* a long, high-backed bench with arms.

P. 74, l. 29. *Parish-boys :* boys from the workhouse.

Bind : to engage, to apprentice.

P. 76, l. 33. *Draught :* a haul of fish.

P. 78, l. 3. *Tides . . . neap :* at the lowest.

l. 17. *Golden-eye :* a kind of duck that makes a loud clanging or whistling sound with the rapid beating of its wings.

l. 18. *What time :* at the time when (a Latin construction).

l. 19. *Bittern :* a wading bird of the heron family.

l. 30. *Reach :* a stretch of the river between two bends.

P. 80, l. 1. *Distemper'd :* with mind deranged or diseased.

l. 25. *All agreed ? :* i.e. all the jury.

l. 26. *My Lord :* i.e. the judge.

Tintern Abbey.

William Wordsworth (1770–1850) was born and educated in the Lake District, where he spent a free and happy childhood. After a short period at Cambridge University, he travelled abroad, chiefly in France, just after the outbreak of the Revolution. His enthusiasm for France and the ideas of the Revolution suffered a severe shock with the September Massacres in 1792, and for the next few years he was in a state of deep depression and uncertainty. These years were spent at Nether Stowey, in Somerset, in the society of his sister Dorothy and his friend Coleridge. Through their influence and by his renewed contact with Nature, he gradually returned to his healthy youthful outlook, and in 1798 began the great period of his poetic production. In that year he issued " Lyrical Ballads," in collaboration with Coleridge. The book is a turning-point in literary history. Wordsworth discarded the artificial style of Pope and Johnson, and wrote of ordinary men and their primary emotions in the natural language of everyday life. Both emotions and language he found in their purest state in the country : hence his poems deal almost entirely with incidents and characters taken from country life.

" Tintern Abbey " was published in 1798, in " Lyrical Ballads."

Tintern Abbey : an old Cistercian abbey, founded in

1131, and now in ruins. It stands in a situation of great natural beauty, about five miles from the mouth of the Wye, in South Wales.

P. 83, l. 17. *Five years :* in 1793, Wordsworth had previously visited Tintern Abbey, in the course of a walking tour in Somerset and South Wales.

P. 87, l. 3. *My . . . Sister :* Dorothy Wordsworth. Her " Journal " shows an observation of nature as faithful as her brother's, and more delicate. Her influence was sane and healthy, and was particularly beneficial during Wordsworth's years of melancholy depression between 1793 and 1797.

Resolution and Independence.

P. 88, l. 16. *Plashy :* watery, soaked.

P. 89, l. 22. *Chatterton :* Thomas Chatterton (1752–1770) was born in Bristol. At the age of sixteen he issued a collection of forged poems, archaic in style, which he claimed to have found in the church of St. Mary Redcliffe, in Bristol, and to be the work of a monk named Thomas Rowley. Chatterton then went to London to try his fortune as a poet, but lapsed into penury and poisoned himself.

ll. 24–25. *Him . . . following his plough :* Robert Burns (1759–1796) who was brought up as a ploughman on his father's farm in Ayrshire. On the success of his poems, he obtained a post in the Excise, and took a farm near Dumfries. Drink and fame were his ruin, and he died, soon after, prematurely aged, at Dumfries.

P. 90, l. 10. *A huge stone :* an erratic, or boulder carried and deposited by ice.

P. 92, l. 2. *Leeches :* bloodsucking aquatic worms used by doctors to draw blood from a patient.

Christabel.

Samuel Taylor Coleridge (1772–1834), son of the Vicar at Ottery St. Mary, Devonshire, was educated at Christ Hospital and Jesus College, Cambridge. At the outbreak of the French Revolution, he engaged, with his friend Southey, in an idealistic plan for a new settlement in America, but he was too unpractical ever to carry out the project. He made friends with Wordsworth, with whom he issued " Lyrical Ballads " in 1798, Coleridge treating supernatural subjects and Wordsworth themes from everyday life. He lived for some time near Wordsworth, at Keswick ; and later he moved to London, where he lectured on Shakespeare. Towards the end of his life he became a victim to opium, which deadened his intellectual powers. He successfully overcame this habit, however, and spent the last years of his life contentedly at Highgate.

In the Preface, Coleridge says, " The metre of Christabel is not, properly speaking, irregular, though it may seem so from its being founded on a new principle : namely, that of counting in each line the accents, not the syllables. Though the latter may vary from seven to twelve, yet in each line the accents will be found to be only four. Nevertheless, this occasional variation in number of syllables is not introduced wantonly, or for the mere ends of convenience, but in correspondence with some transition, in the nature of the imagery or passion."

Gillman, in his " Life of Coleridge," gives the following report of how the poem was to have been finished :

" Over the mountains, the Bard, as directed by Sir Leoline, hastes with his disciple ; but in consequence of one of those inundations supposed to be common to this country, the spot only where the castle once stood is discovered—the edifice itself being washed away. He determines to return. Geraldine being acquainted with all that is passing, like the weird sisters in Macbeth, vanishes. Reappearing, however, she awaits the return of the Bard, exciting in the meantime, by her wily arts, all the anger she could rouse in the Baron's breast, as well as that jealousy of which he is described to have been susceptible. The old Bard and the youth at length arrive, and therefore she can no longer personate the character of Geraldine, the daughter of Lord Roland de Vaux, but changes her appearance to that of the accepted though absent lover of Christabel. Now ensues a courtship most distressing to Christabel, who feels, she knows not why, great disgust for her once favoured knight. This coldness is very painful to the Baron, who has no more conception than herself of the supernatural transformation. She at last yields to her father's entreaties, and consents to approach the altar with this hated suitor. The real lover returning, enters at this moment, and produces the ring which she had once given him in sign of her betrothment. Thus defeated, the supernatural being Geraldine disappears. As predicted, the castle bell tolls, the mother's voice is heard, and to the exceeding great joy of the parties, the rightful marriage takes place, after which follows a reconciliation and explanation between the father and daughter."

P. 96. l. 18. *I wis :* = *ywis*, certainly.

P. 99, l. 17. *Cordial :* that revives or stimulates the heart.

l. 18. *Virtuous :* strong, efficacious.

l. 31. *Wandering mother :* the spirit of Christabel's mother, seeking to guard her against the spells of Geraldine.

Peak : become sickly, pine away.

P. 103, l. 2. *Tairn:* tarn, a small lake among the mountains.

P. 104, l. 9. *Bratha Head :* the source of the river Brathay, that flows into Lake Windermere.

l. 15. *Langdale Pike :* or Pikes : a group of hills west of Ambleside.

l. 16. *Dungeon-ghyll :* a small stream rising near Langdale Pikes ; or the valley containing it.

l. 24. *Borrowdale :* the valley of the river Derwent from near its source to its entering Derwent Water.

P. 106, l. 5. *Tryermaine :* near the head of Thirlmere.

P. 108, l. 24. *Irthing :* a tributary of the Eden.

P. 113, l. 13. *Limber :* lithe.

Adonais.

Percy Bysshe Shelley (1792–1822) was educated at Eton and Oxford. He early adopted the rationalist ideas of William Godwin, whose daughter he afterwards married. With her he settled in Italy near to his friend Byron. On the death of Keats he wrote the elegy "Adonais." Like Keats, he died prematurely, being drowned while sailing in the Gulf of Spezzia. Shelley and Keats are both buried in the Protestant Cemetery in Rome.

Matthew Arnold said of Shelley that his proper sphere was not poetry but music. Certainly the superb rhythm and cadence of his verse are in essence musical, but when, as in " The Cenci," he set himself to treat a concrete theme his work is as thoughtful as such lyrics as " The Skylark " and the " Ode to the West Wind " are musical. Shelley's early death deprived England of one of the finest, if not the finest, of her lyric poets.

Adonais : a variant of *Adonis*. The elegy is an imitation of the elegy on Adonis by the Greek poet Bion, and of that on Bion by Moschus.

P. 114, l. 5. *Obscure compeers :* the other Hours.

l. 10. *Mighty Mother :* Aphrodite Urania, the Greek goddess representing ideal or spiritual love.

P. 115, l. 4. *He died : i.e.* Milton.

l. 11. *The third . . . :* the third great epic poet. Shelley elsewhere mentions Homer as the first, and Dante as the second.

l. 22. *Thy widowhood :* the period since the death of Milton.

P. 116, l. 3. *That high Capital :* Rome.

l. 6. *Come away ! :* addressed to the imaginary mourners.

P. 117, l. 15. *Anadem :* a band or fillet bound round the head.

P. 118, l. 1. *Clips :* embraces.

ll. 15–16. *Her hair . . . ground :* wisps of cloud, in due course to drop as rain.

P. 119, l. 2. *Those for whose disdain she pined :* the lips of Narcissus, whom she (Echo) loved, but who loved only the reflection of his own face.

l. 9. *Phoebus . . . Hyacinth :* Phoebus, or Apollo, loved Hyacinthus. See note to P. 10, l. 29.

l. 11. *Sere :* withered.

l. 14. *The lorn nightingale :* a reference to Keats's " Ode to a Nightingale."

ll. 16–18. *The eagle . . . morning :* an echo of one of Shelley's favourite passages in Milton :

" Methinks I see in my mind a noble and puissant nation rousing herself like a strong man after sleep, and shaking her invincible locks ; methinks I see her as an eagle, mewing her mighty youth, and kindling her undazzled eyes at the full mid-day beam ; purging and unscaling her long-abused sight at the fountain itself of heavenly radiance ; while the whole noise of timorous and flocking birds, with those also that love the twilight, flutter about, amazed at what she means."

l. 20. *Albion :* England.

P. 121, l. 10. *Their sister's song :* the " Echo " mentioned above (P. 118, l. 21).

P. 123, l. 4. *The unpastured dragon :* the uncultured and tyrannical.

l. 6. *The mirrored shield . . . the spear :* the shield that blinded by its brightness and the spear that conquered at a touch, described by Ariosto ("Orlando Furioso," 55).

ll. 7-8. *The full cycle . . . crescent sphere :* Keats is here compared to a crescent moon, on account of his youth.

If he had lived to complete his " full cycle " of years, his spirit would, like the full moon, have attained maturity; and his enemies would have fled before him.

l. 16. *The Pythian . . . one arrow . . . :* Lord Byron and his attack on his critics in " English Bards and Scotch Reviewers." His next poem, " Childe Harold," was well reviewed. Pythia was the priestess of Apollo at Delphi, and delivered the oracles of the god there.

l. 20. *Ephemeral :* living only for a day.

P. 124, l. 3. *The Pilgrim of Eternity :* Lord Byron, the author of " Childe Harold's Pilgrimage."

l. 7. *Ierne :* Ireland.

l. 8. *The sweetest lyrist :* the Irish lyric poet, Tom Moore, author of " Irish Melodies."

l. 10. *One frail Form :* Shelley himself.

l. 15. *Actaeon-like :* Actaeon, because he saw Diana bathing, was turned into a stag and hunted and killed by his own hounds.

P. 125, l. 1. *Pansies :* for thoughts.

l. 2. *Violets :* for sweetness.

l. 13. *An unknown land :* the ideal world.

l. 14. *New sorrow :* the death of Keats.

l. 19. *What softer voice :* Leigh Hunt.

P. 127, l. 20. *Thou young Dawn :* Morning, already mentioned (P. 118, l. 14).

P. 129, l. 3. *Chatterton : See* note to P. 89, l. 22.

l. 5. *Sidney :* the Elizabethan soldier, statesman, and poet (1554–1586), author of the " Apologie for Poetrie " and " Arcadia." He was killed at the battle of Zutphen.

l. 8. *Lucan :* a Latin poet condemned by Nero, A.D. 65, for taking part in Piso's conspiracy. He died calmly by his own hand, in his twenty-sixth year. He was the author of a long heroic poem, " Pharsalia," which describes the struggle between Caesar and Pompey.

Approved : confirmed as a great spirit.

P. 130, l. 16. *Slope of green access :* Shelley says in the Preface to " Adonais," that Keats was buried " in the romantic and lonely cemetery of the Protestants, under the pyramid which is the tomb of Cestius, and the massy walls and towers, now mouldering and desolate, which formed the circuit of ancient Rome. The cemetery is an open space among the ruins, covered in winter with violets and daisies. It might make one in love with death, to think that one should be buried in so sweet a place."

P. 131, l. 3. *The seal is set:* Shelley's child William was buried here in June 1819.

The Eve of St. Agnes.

John Keats (1795–1821) was born in London and apprenticed to a surgeon. He was a friend of Shelley and Leigh Hunt. His first long poem, " Endymion " (1818), illustrates the strength and weakness of Keats : it excels in rich sensuous descriptions and happy phrases but the story is lost (and remains unfinished) among the wealth of detail. The influence of Spenser is deeply marked. In his next volume, " Lamia, Isabella, and Other Poems " (1820), Keats illustrates the statement that he went to school with the great English poets. " Lamia " is in the style of Dryden, " Hyperion " is a Miltonic fragment, while many of the sonnets are Shakespearean in tone. These poems show a rapid development and his " Letters " prove that he was even more mature in mind than some of the poems might allow us to suspect. He was attaining to something of the literary perfection of his favourite Greece, when he died of consumption in Rome. Keats at his best is master of a Shakespearean felicity of phrase, and his early death robbed England of one of her potentially greatest poets.

St. Agnes : a Christian martyr of the fourth century.

P. 132, l. 23. *Beadsman :* a person employed, or allowed, to pray for others.

Told his rosary : counted over the beads on a string, each representing a prayer.

l. 25. *Censer :* a pan in which incense is burned.

l. 26. *Without a death :* the Beadsman's breath is compared to a soul " taking flight for heaven " : but no death is involved.

P. 133, l. 6. *Purgatorial rails :* enclosing them as if in purgatory.

l. 7. *Dumb orat'ries :* the epithet " dumb " is transferred from the knights and ladies.

l. 13. *His deathbell rung :* cf. the last line of the poem.

l. 26. *Cornice :* the moulding at the junction of wall and ceiling.

P. 134, l. 1. *Argent :* silver.

l. 2. *Tiara :* a lofty ornamental head-dress.

P. 135, l. 7. *Amort :* unconscious of what was going on around her.

l. 8.   *Her lambs unshorn :* St. Agnes (Fr. *agneau*, a lamb) is associated with lambs, the symbol of purity.   Two lambs are taken yearly to the spot outside Rome where she was beheaded.   They are blessed, and shorn, and the wool woven into the archbishop's cloak.

l. 27.   *Beldame :* old woman.

P. 136, l. 15.   *Gossip :* an old woman.

l. 25.   *The holy loom :* on which the nuns spin the wool.   *See* note to P. 135, l. 8 above.

P. 137, l. 3.   *Hold water . . . :* have supernatural powers.

l. 9.   *Mickle :* much.

l. 16.   *Brook :* restrain.   The word properly means " to endure, to bear."

P. 138, l. 12.   *Passing-bell :* death-knell.   *Cf.* the last stanza of the poem.

l. 14.   *Plaining :* complaining.

l. 24.   *Legion'd faeries :* Madeline's dreams.

l. 27.   *. . . Merlin paid . . . debt :* Merlin's father was a Demon.   The life he owed him—his debt—was paid when Vivien brought about his destruction.   He met Vivien on such a stormy night.   *Cf.* Tennyson's "Merlin and Vivien."

P. 139, l. 2.   *Cates :* dainty food.

l. 3.   *Tambour frame :* a frame on which cloth is stretched for embroidering.

l. 17.   *Covert :* cover, hiding-place.
      Amain : exceedingly.

l. 27.   *Fray'd :* frightened.

P. 140, l. 12.   *Knot-grass :* a kind of grass, with numerous knots on the stem.

l. 20.   *Gules :* blood-red (in heraldry).

P. 141, l. 12.   *Poppied :* as if induced by opium, which is obtained from poppies.

l. 16.   *Missal :* prayer-book.
      Swart Paynims : black-skinned pagans.

P. 142, l. 5.   *Morphean :* having the sleep-giving powers of Morpheus, the god of sleep.
      Amulet : charm.

l. 15.   *Tinct :* tinctured, flavoured.

l. 16.   *Argosy :* merchant-ship.

l. 17.   *Fez :* a town in Morocco.

l. 18.   *Samarcand :* in Turkestan, famous for silks.
      Lebanon : in Palestine, frequently mentioned in the Old Testament for its cedars.

l. 25.   *Eremite :* hermit.

P. 143, l. 13. *Provence:* a province in S.E. France, famous in the Middle Ages for its minstrels.

    La belle . . . mercy: the beautiful merciless lady. Keats's own version of the ditty is well known.

l. 17. *Affrayed:* frightened.

l. 24. *Witless:* without sense or intelligence.

P. 144, l. 19. *Flaw-blown:* blown by the gusts of wind.

l. 27. *Unpruned:* untrimmed.

P. 145, l. 16. *Mead:* honey and water fermented and flavoured.

P. 146, l. 16. *Palsy:* paralysis.

l. 17. *Ave:* hail! (Latin): a prayer to the Virgin Mary beginning with this word.

Rubáiyát of Omar Khayyám.

Edward FitzGerald (1809–1883) came of Irish stock. Part of his youth he spent in France; which cultivated his natural turn for languages and translation. He was educated at Trinity College, Cambridge, among a brilliant group, which included Thackeray. Tennyson, later his intimate friend, was also there, but he knew him only by sight. At Cambridge FitzGerald dabbled in pictures, languages, and poetry, without achieving anything of note either as a student or as a poet.

His friend Cowell, Professor of Oriental Languages at Oxford, interested him in Spanish, and especially in Calderon, whose six plays he translated; and in Persian, bringing to his notice the Bodleian manuscript of the Rubáiyát of Omar Khayyám.

FitzGerald's motto, " Abridge, concentrate, distil," applies pre-eminently to his version of Omar; he has there distilled, with the perfect finish of concentration, the essence of Omar's epicurean philosophy and the sense of the transience of all things human, the pleasures of existence, and the resignation with which the stoics and the people of the East accepted good and evil as alike predestined.

Rubáiyát: quatrains, each complete in itself, and generally epigrammatic. The first, second, and fourth lines rhymed, and sometimes also the third. After composition, the quatrains were rearranged alphabetically in accordance with the last letter of the rhyme-word.

Khayyám: a tent-maker. Omar is said to have followed this occupation at one time. Omar Khayyám lived most of his life in Nishapur in the province of Khorasan, in N.E. Persia, and in the reign of Melik Shah, the Seljuk Turk. He died about 1123, having won fame for his great learning in medicine, philosophy, astrology, and mathematics.

P. 147, l. 1. *False morning :* "the 'False dawn,' a transient light on the horizon about an hour before the true dawn ; a well-known phenomenon in the East " (F.). During periods of fasting (which is confined to the day) Mohammedans use this hour to eat a solid meal. Wine-drinkers, also, after a night of revelry, salute the dawn with a cry for more wine.

l. 2. *A Voice :* that of the Sákí, or cupbearer.

l. 3. *The Temple :* the tavern.

l. 9. *The New Year :* " beginning with the spring equinox (March 22), as formerly in England (March 25). 'The sudden approach and rapid advance of the spring' (says a late traveller in Persia) 'are very striking. Before the snow is well off the ground, the trees burst into blossom, and the flowers start from the soil ' " (F.).

l. 11. *The White Hand of Moses :* " Exodus, iv. 6. (And the Lord said furthermore unto him [Moses], Put now thine hand into thy bosom. And he put his hand into his bosom : and when he took it out, behold, his hand was leprous as snow) ; where Moses draws forth his hand—not, according to the Persians, 'leprous as snow', but *white* as our May-blossom in spring perhaps ! " (F.).

l. 12. *Jesus . . . suspires :* " According to the Persians also the healing power of Jesus resided in his breath " (F.).

l. 13. *Iram :* an enchanted garden " planted by King Schedad, and now sunk somewhere in the sands of Arabia " (F.).

l. 14. *Jamshýd's Sev'n-ring'd Cup :* " a ·divining cup, typical of the seven heavens, seven planets, seven seas, etc." (F.). Jamshýd was a mythical heroic King of Persia.

l. 17. *David :* here considered as a musician, author of the Psalms.

l. 18. *Pehleví :* " the old heroic Sanskrit (or learned language) of Persia. Háfiz also speaks of the nightingale's Pehleví, which did not change with the people's " (F.).

l. 20. *That sallow cheek :* " I am not sure if this refers to the red rose looking sickly, or the yellow rose that ought to be red ; red, white, and yellow roses are all common in Persia " (F.).

P. 148, l. 5. *Naishápúr :* a town in the province of Khorasan, in N.E. Persia : the birth-place, and for long the residence, of Omar.

Babylon : an ancient city on the R. Euphrates.

l. 12. *Jamshýd :* his reign is said to have lasted seven hundred years.

Kaikobád : a famous Persian king, the founder of the Kayanian dynasty.

l. 14. *Kaikhosrú :* a famous king in Persian tradition.

l. 15. *Zál :* the father of Rustum.

Rustum : " the Hercules of Persia, whose exploits are among the most celebrated in the Shah-náma " (F.).

l. 16. *Hátim :* " a well-known type of Oriental generosity " (F.).

l. 20. *Mahmúd :* see note to P. 158, l. 13, below.

P. 149, l. 11. *The silken tassel of my Purse :* " that is, the rose's golden centre " (F.).

l. 15. *Aureate :* made of gold.

P. 150, l. 1. *Caravanserai :* a large enclosed court where caravans may halt.

l. 6. *The Courts . . . deep :* Persepolis, which he is supposed to have founded.

l. 7. *Bahrám :* a Persian hero, nicknamed from his strength and speed " the wild ass."

l. 20. *Yesterday's Sev'n thousand Years :* " a thousand years to each planet " (F.). This was the supposed age of the earth in Omar's time.

P. 151, l. 15. *Muezzín :* the man who cries the regular hours of prayer from the roof of a mosque.

P. 152, l. 4. *Came out . . . : i.e.* no wiser.

l. 15. *Forbidden Wine :* wine is forbidden to Mohammedans.

l. 17. *The Seventh Gate :* the entry to the Seventh Heaven, the highest and most full of delights in the Mohammedan Paradise.

l. 18. *Saturn :* " lord of the Seventh Heaven " (F.).

P. 153, l. 3. *Me and Thee :* " that is, some dividual existence or personality apart from the whole " (F.).

l. 18. *Once did live :* the Eastern idea of the transmigration of souls, or that of the identity of life in all things animate and inanimate.

P. 154, ll. 15–16. *Till Heav'n to Earth invert you :* a reference to the Wheel of Heaven, which is the symbol of continual change, and will finally change man to dust.

l. 20.   *Cypress :* a symbol of grace.

P. 155.   l. 5.   *The darker Drink :* death.

l. 14.   *A Sultán :* the soul.

l. 15.   *Ferrásh :* slave.

l. 16.   *Another Guest :* another soul, which will inhabit the body made from the elements of the one now dead.

l. 19.   *The Eternal Sákí :* God.   He is here described as a sákí, or cup-bearer, pouring out souls or lives as the sákí pours out wine.

P. 156, l. 1.   *The Veil :* the curtain that hides the secrets of God ; death.

l. 8.   *Oh, make haste ! :* addressed to the cup-bearer.

l. 10.   *The secret : sc.* of existence and its mystery.

l. 14.   *Alif :* the first letter of the Arabian alphabet : here, something of no apparent importance.

l. 17.   *Whose secret Presence :* the one essence, of which according to pantheistic systems, all things are appearances or manifestations.   It is thus both subject and object, creator and created, actor and spectator.

l. 19.   *Máh :* the Moon.
Máhi : the Fish : a constellation.

P. 157, l. 12.   *Bitter Fruit :* the hopelessness of speculation on the ultimate questions of existence.

l. 16.   *The Daughter of the Vine :* in the East, the grape, permitted to the Moslem, is spoken of as the mother of wine, which he is forbidden.

ll. 17–18.   *For "Is"* . . . *define :* " a laugh at his mathematics perhaps " (F.).

P. 158, l. 1.   *My Computations :* Omar was an astronomer of repute.

l. 4.   *Unborn To-morrow . . . :* Omar recognises only To-day, the present, which he endeavours to enjoy fully.

l. 10.   *The . . . Sects :* " the seventy-two sects into which Islamism so soon split " (F.).   It seems, however, to refer to the number of sects into which, according to Mohammed, the whole world would be divided.

l. 11.   *Alchemist :* one who, in the Middle Ages, studied chemistry, with the aim of finding " the philosopher's stone," which would turn base metals into gold.

ll. 13–14.   *Mahmúd . . . black Horde :* Mahmúd conquered India and compelled the black " misbelievers " to worship Allah, the God of the Mohammedans.

P. 159, l. 17. *I sent my Soul* . . . : on the day of his birth, while his Soul was still in Heaven, he sought to find out what fate was decreed for him.

P. 160, l. 6. *Magic Shadow-shapes* . . . : " a magic-lantern still used in India ; the cylindrical interior being painted with various figures, and so lightly poised and ventilated as to revolve round the candle lighted within " (F.). The sun is the candle and men the figures.

l. 10. *Chequer-board :* chess-board. Chess originated in Persia.

l. 11. *Checks :* check-mates (in chess), or threatens to do so.

l. 17. *The Moving Finger* . . . : *see* Daniel v. 5. The writing is that of Destiny and its import is unalterable.

P. 161, ll. 3–4. *It* . . . *moves :* Omar suggests—an idea common among the Greeks—that the gods themselves are subject to destiny.

ll. 5–8. *Earth's first Clay* . . . *Last Dawn :* the Mohammedan idea that all things are preordained from the beginning.

l. 14. *The flaming shoulders of the Foal :* the sun. Horses were supposed to draw the chariot of the sun through the sky.

l. 15. *Parwín :* the constellation of the Pleiades.
  Mushtarí : the planet Jupiter.

l. 17. *The Vine had struck a fibre :* on the day of Creation, he was predestined to have a taste for wine—as surely as the paths of the sun and the planets were fixed.

l. 18. *The Dervish :* a member of a Mohammedan sect who live austere lives ; here, a hypocritical priest.

l. 19. *A Key :* the particle of love, " caught within the Tavern," which may ensure his admission to Heaven.

P. 162, l. 7. *Unpermitted Pleasure :* wine.

P. 163, l. 2. *Ramazán :* " the fasting month, at the close of which the first glimpse of the new moon (who rules their division of the year) is looked for with the utmost anxiety, and hailed with all acclamation " (F.).

l. 3. *The Potter :* God.

P. 164, l. 2. *Súfi :* a Mohammedan mystic and fanatic.

l. 14. *The little Moon :* the new moon of Shawwal, the month after Ramazán. The fast is now over.—The Mohammedan month is determined by the moon.

l. 16. *The Porter's shoulder-knot a-creaking :* " towards the cellar, perhaps " (F.).

l. 19. *Shrouded in the living Leaf :* in a coffin of the vine.

P. 166, l. 1. *The Fountain :* governed by "one glimpse of":
Heaven, or future life.

l. 17. *Sáki :* the cup-bearer.

l. 21. *Tamán :* "entirely," hence "end."

The Lotos-Eaters.

Alfred, Lord Tennyson (1809–1892) was the son of a
clergyman and born at Somersby, in Lincolnshire.
At Trinity College, Cambridge, he made the acquaintance of Arthur Henry Hallam, on whose death he
wrote "In Memoriam." His early work, "Poems,
chiefly Lyrical" (1830), shows him already a master
of sound and rhythm, in the tradition of Spenser and
Keats. In his later volumes, this power was increased
and combined with a growing vein of serious thought on
the social and religious questions of the day. "The
Princess" (1847) dealt with the position and education
of women, and "In Memoriam" (1850) with religious
problems. Tennyson's poetry at its finest approaches
the poetry of Virgil in perfection of language and
emotional effect, and his acute powers of observation
are reflected in the accuracy of his descriptions and
character-studies. Tennyson is perhaps at his best
in his lyrics, such as those in "The Princess," and in
dramatic monologues, like "Ulysses," or poems like
the ode "To Virgil" or "The Lotos-Eaters," where
an atmosphere has to be created. His limitations—
a straining, at times over-conscious, after effective
expression, a vein of sentimentality, and a limited
power of purely original thought—explain the decline which he has suffered from his first enthusiastic
popularity.

Lotos : a fruit eaten by the tribes of N. Africa, and said
by Homer to induce content and forgetfulness.

P. 167, l. 18. *Clomb :* climbed.

l. 23. *Galingale :* a kind of sedge.

P. 169, l. 10. "*There is no joy but calm*" : one of the sayings
of the Stoics.

l. 11. *The roof and crown of things :* the highest creatures
in the scale of evolution.

P. 170, l. 24. *Dust . . . urn :* the Greeks burned their
dead, and preserved the ashes in a jar or urn.

l. 31. *The island princes :* the wooers of Ulysses' wife,
Penelope, in his native Ithaca.

P. 171, l. 1. *Eat :* eaten.

l. 2. *The ten years' war in Troy :* the war between Troy and the Greek states.

l. 13. *Amaranth :* an unfading celestial flower.

    Moly : the plant given by Hermes to Ulysses to protect him against the enchantments of Circe.

l. 22. *Acanthus :* a prickly plant, now called brank-ursine. Its leaves were of common appearance in Greek sculpture.

P. 172, l. 2. *The wallowing monster :* the whale.

l. 3. *With an equal mind :* with equanimity.

l. 5. *Gods . . . careless of mankind :* the gods of the philosopher Epicurus.

l. 19. *Elysian valleys :* in Greek mythology, the abode of the blessed after death.

l. 20. *Asphodel :* a kind of lily, supposed to cover the Elysian fields.

Ulysses.

    The poem is based on the post-Homeric legend of Ulysses sailing from Circe's island, near Gaeta, westward through the Strait of Gibraltar towards the unknown regions. The legend is best known from Dante's lines in the " Inferno " (Canto xxvi):

    " When I departed from Circe, who beyond a year detained me at Gaeta, ere Æneas thus had named it, neither fondness for my son, nor reverence for my aged father, nor the due love that should have cheered Penelope, could conquer in me the ardour that I had to gain experience of the world, and of human vice and worth ; I put forth on the deep open sea, with but one ship, and with that small company, which had not deserted me. Both the shores I saw as far as Spain, far as Morocco ; and saw Sardinia and the other isles which that sea bathes round. I and my companions were old and tardy, when we came to that narrow pass, where Hercules assigned his landmarks to hinder man from venturing farther ; on the right hand, I left Seville ; on the other, had already left Ceuta. " O brothers ! " I said, " who through a hundred thousand dangers have reached the West, deny not, to this the brief vigil of your senses that remains, experience of the unpeopled world behind the Sun."

P. 173, l. 2. *Barren crags :* the rocky island of Ithaca, Ulysses' home, off the western shores of Greece.

l. 7. *Lees :* dregs.

l. 10. *Hyades :* a group of seven stars that rises in May

and was thought to bring rain. They were, according to Greek legend, seven nymphs who were entrusted by Jupiter with the care of his infant son Dionysus, and were placed among the stars as a reward.

l. 17. *Plains . . . Troy :* the ten years' war between Troy and the Greek states, in which Ulysses had played a leading part.

l. 27. *That eternal silence :* death.

l. 29. *Three suns :* three years.

P. 174, l. 12. *My mariners :* in Homer, all Ulysses' mariners have perished during his wanderings.

l. 20. *Men that strove with Gods :* in the Trojan war, as described by Homer, the Gods took part on both sides.

l. 29. *The gulfs :* the abyss supposed to lie at the edge of the world.

l. 30. *The Happy Isles :* western islands to which the favourites of the gods were conveyed after death.

l. 31. *Achilles :* one of the greatest Greek heroes in the Trojan war.

To Virgil.

Virgil : Virgil, the Roman poet, author of the "Aeneid," the "Georgics," and the "Eclogues," was born near Mantua, in North Italy, and lived in the first century B.C.

P. 175, l. 5. *Ilion :* Troy, in Asia Minor; Book II of the "Aeneid" describes its capture and burning.

l. 7. *Filial faith :* Aeneas, Prince of Troy, is noted for his attachment to his father Anchises.

Dido's pyre : Aeneas, in his wanderings after the capture of Troy, won the love of Dido, Queen of Carthage, but deserted her. She threw herself into the flames of a funeral pyre.

l. 9. *Works and Days :* the chief work of the early Greek poet Hesiod.

ll. 12–13. *Thou . . . herd :* in the "Georgics."

l. 16. *Tityrus :* a shepherd in Virgil's first Eclogue.

l. 18. *The poet-satyr :* Silenus, in the fifth Eclogue.

P. 176, l. 1. *Pollio :* "to whom Virgil addresses his fourth Eclogue, and to whom he ascribes the remarkable advent of the 'golden age,' was the founder of the first public library of Rome" (Dr. Brewer).

l. 3. *The snakeless meadow:* a feature of the "golden age."

l. 7. *Thy sadness :* the well-known Virgilian "lachrymae rerum."

l. 13. *Forum :* a square in ancient Rome, used for markets and public meetings of the people.

l. 14. *Purple :* worn by the Emperors.

l. 18. *Rome of freemen :* Rome became the capital of a free Italy in 1870.

l. 20. *Sunder'd once :* before Roman civilisation came.

P. 177, l. 1. *Mantovano :* Mantuan (*Ital.*).

l. 3. *The stateliest measure :* the metre of the " Aeneid " is the hexameter.

My Last Duchess.

Robert Browning (1812–1889) began his poetic career with " Pauline " (1833), written under the influence of Shelley. " Paracelsus " (1835) followed. His work gradually became more dramatic in intention, with " Strafford " and other dramas, " Dramatic Lyrics " (1842), " Dramatic Romances and Lyrics " (1845) and " Men and Women " (1855). " The Ring and the Book," his longest poem (1868–1869), is perhaps his masterpiece. The main event of an otherwise uneventful life was his elopement in 1846, with Elizabeth Barrett, the poetess, to whom he was devotedly attached until her death, which took place in Florence. Most of his later themes are drawn from Italian sources. Browning's poetry excels in fertility of ideas, in grasp of psychological subtleties, in power of delineating queer abnormal characters, and in dramatic quality, but suffers from obscurity and irregularity of syntax, and lack of poetic—though never of mental—quality.

P. 177, l. 7. *Frà Pandolf :* a fictitious painter.

P. 178, l. 3. *Favour :* a knot of ribbons worn as a pledge of favour.

l. 32. *Neptune :* the god of the sea.

l. 34. *Claus of Innsbruck :* a fictitious sculptor.

Andrea del Sarto.

Andrea del Sarto (1486–1531), a great Florentine painter, was summoned by Francis I of France to assist in decorating his great palace at Fontainebleau. Recalled to Florence by his wife, Lucrezia, he spent on her the money entrusted to him to purchase works of art for the King. She finally deserted him, and he died of the plague.

P. 179, l. 15. *Fiesole :* a small town about three miles north-west of Florence.

l. 16. *Use :* are accustomed to do.

279   K

P. 180, l. 25. *Cartoon :* a design for tapestry, mosaic, etc., drawn on strong paper.

l. 27. *Madonna :* the Virgin Mary.

l. 33. *Legate :* an ambassador of the Pope.

P. 181, l. 10. *Light of God :* inspiration, genius.

l. 13. *Forthright :* straightforward.

l. 19. *Sudden blood :* passion, enthusiasm.

l. 24. *Morello :* a spur of the Apennines, about seven miles north of Florence.

l. 36. *The Urbinate :* the great Italian painter, Rafael (1483–1520), born at Urbino.

P. 182, l. 1. *George Vasari :* an Italian painter and architect, best known for his " Lives of the Painters." He studied under Andrea del Sarto.

l. 5. *It gives way :* his inspiration bursts into expression through the limits of his technical powers.

l. 12. *Out of me :* I have lost these powers.

l. 24. *The Present . . . that ? :* What is the present (gain) compared with the future (fame) ?

l. 25. *Angelo :* Michael Angelo (1475–1564), the greatest of the Florentine, and Italian, sculptors and painters.

l. 31. *What wife had Rafael :* Rafael had married only a short time before.

P. 183, l. 4. *The Paris lords :* French nobles in Florence.

l. 8. *Fontainebleau :* about 40 miles south-east of Paris.

l. 28. *Grange :* a large farm-house and its outbuildings.

l. 31. *The triumph was . . . there :* the love of Lucrezia should have been the crown of his triumph.

l. 36. *The Roman :* Rafael, who did most of his work in Rome.

P. 184, l. 31. *Cue-owl :* an Italian owl named from its cry.

P. 185, l. 2. *That gold of his . . . :* th͏e͏ French King's money, with which he had built the house.

l. 4. *Cousin :* lover.

l. 19. *Subjects :* themes of paintings.

l. 25. *Scudi :* crowns.

Ruff : a frill worn round the neck.

P. 186, ll. 9–10. *Four great walls . . . reed :* Rev. xxi. 15.

l. 11. *Leonard :* Leonardo da Vinci (1452–1519), a great painter, sculptor, architect, and critic of the Renascence in Italy. His best-known paintings are " The Last Supper " and the " Monna Lisa."

Thyrsis.

Matthew Arnold (1822–1888), eldest son of Dr. Arnold, the famous Headmaster of Rugby, was educated at

Winchester, Rugby, and Balliol College, Oxford. After serving four years as private secretary to Lord Lansdowne, he was appointed an Inspector of Schools. During the thirty-five years for which he held this Inspectorate he was sent on various occasions by the Government to inquire into the methods of Continental education, and his reports had considerable influence in England. One of Matthew Arnold's greatest qualities was his desire to regard the culture of the world as a whole, and in criticism to avoid insularity. He was equally accomplished as a critic—his " Essays in Criticism " earned him the title of the English Sainte-Beuve —and as a poet—his best poetry, classic in style and beauty, wears as well as that of any of the Victorian poets.

For ten years he was Professor of Poetry at Oxford. He is buried where he was born, at Laleham, near Staines.

Thyrsis : a shepherd in Theocritus and Virgil. Here, Clough.

P. 186, l. 19. *Sibylla :* Sybella Curr, of the Cross Keys Inn, South Hinksey. Her husband was a servant of Jesus College.

l. 26. *Childsworth :* or Chilswell, just beyond South Hinksey.

P. 187, l. 1. *The Signal-elm :* an elm on the slopes west of the Hinkseys.

Ilsley Downs : about 16 miles south of Oxford.

P. 187, l. 2. *Three lone weirs :* those on the Thames above Bablock Hythe.

l. 15. *While it stood, we said :* cf. " The Scholar Gipsy."

l. 22. *Our shepherd pipes we first assay'd :* Arnold and Clough both wrote much of their early poetry at Oxford.

l. 24. *My pipe is lost :* Arnold had written very little original poetry for ten years.

l. 32. *Silly :* simple.

l. 33. *Some life of men unblest :* Clough's difficulties as Head of University Hall, London.

P. 188, l. 32. *Cut a smoother reed :* write in a more composed and polished manner.

l. 34. *Corydon :* Arnold himself.

P. 189, l. 4. *Bion's fate :* Bion was a pastoral poet of Smyrna in the third century B.C., and author of the epic poem " The Dirge of Adonis." He spent his last years in Sicily, where he was poisoned.

l. 6. *Pluto :* the god of the under-world.

l. 8. *Proserpine :* carried off to the underworld by Pluto, while gathering flowers in the fields of Enna, in Sicily.

l. 10. *Orpheus :* by the power of his music, Orpheus won back his wife Eurydice from the dead, only to lose her

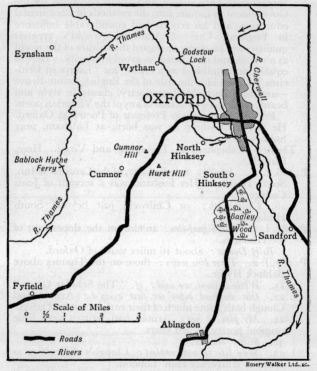

by turning to look at her before they came to the upper world.

l. 12. *Dorian :* belonging to Doris, in Greece, noted for its simplicity and rustic language and manners.

l. 15. *Enna :* an ancient town said to be in the centre of Sicily, among fertile plains. It was near Enna that Pluto was supposed to have carried off Proserpine.

l. 26. *Fyfield tree :* see "The Scholar Gipsy."

l. 27. *Fritillaries :* a small meadow-plant, with white or purple flowers, common around Oxford.

P. 190, l. 2. *Spikes of purple orchises :* these orchises consist each of a spike-like mass of purple flowers. They grow chiefly in marshy places or moorland.

l. 4. *Coronal :* garland, crown.

l. 7. *Prime : i.e.* of the year, spring.

l. 18. *The night . . . :* when he was twenty-four, Arnold had been told by a doctor that he might die at any time of the same heart-disease that had proved fatal to his father and grandfather. He was now approaching the age at which his father died.

l. 22. *Sprent :* sprinkled, streaked.

P. 191, l. 3. *The long-batter'd world :* Arnold's work is, under different forms, a long attack on " the world, the flesh, and the devil," as they were to be found in mid-Victorian England.

l. 11. *Berkshire :* an English shire on the southern bank of the Thames near Oxford.

l. 23. *Arno :* the Italian river on which Florence stands.

l. 26. *Oleander :* the *Rose Bay* or *Rose Laurel,* an evergreen shrub with lance-shaped leathery leaves and beautiful red or white flowers.

l. 31. *Boon :* kind, pleasant.

P. 192, l. 1. *The great Mother :* Demeter, Nature.

l. 9. *Young Daphnis :* " Daphnis, the ideal Sicilian shepherd of Greek pastoral poetry, was said to have followed into Phrygia his mistress Piplea, who had been carried off by robbers, and to have found her in the power of the king of Phrygia, Lityerses. Lityerses used to make strangers try a contest with him in reaping corn, and to put them to death if he overcame them. Hercules arrived in time to save Daphnis, took upon himself the reaping contest with Lityerses, overcame him, and slew him. The Lityerses-song connected with this tradition was . . . one of the early plaintive strains of Greek popular poetry, and used to be sung by the corn-reapers " (A.).

P. 193, l. 1. *Like quest :* the search for truth and certainty in an atmosphere of rapidly changing ideas.

l. 7. *Hurst :* a wooded hill S.W. of Oxford.

l. 10. *A virtue :* strength, power.

The Blessed Damozel.

Dante Gabriel Rossetti (1828–1882), the son of an Italian refugee in England, drew his inspiration, both as artist

and poet, from Italy. In both arts, he returned to
nature as depicted by the early Renascence artists before Raphael, and, with his friends Holman Hunt and
Millais, formed the Pre-Raphaelite Brotherhood to execute his ideals. His painting relies for effect on masses
of contrasted colour ; and his poetic imagery has the
same definiteness of colour and form as his painting.
In spite of this, he succeeds, like Dante, in conveying an
intense mystical and spiritual impression through the
very precision of his images.

"The Blessed Damozel" appeared in "The Germ," a
periodical founded in 1850 by Rossetti and his friends.

Damozel : damsel, maiden of noble blood.

P. 194, l. 6. *Seven :* the Christian mystic number.

l. 7. *Ungirt :* without a girdle—the fashion of nuns.

Clasp : i.e. at the neck.

l. 9. *Mary :* the Virgin Mary, whose servant the damozel
becomes in Heaven.

l. 13. *Herseemed :* it seemed to her.

l. 17. *Albeit :* although.

l. 19. *One :* her lover on earth.

Years of years : years, each consisting of 365 years
instead of 365 days.

l. 25. *Rampart :* Heaven was conceived as a castle in the
Middle Ages.

P. 195, l. 26. *The stars sang : i.e.* at the creation of the
world. See Job xxxviii. 7.

Spheres : orbits, circular paths.

P. 196, l. 6. *Stair :* probably that of a church.

l. 11. *Two prayers . . . :* "If two of you shall agree on
earth as touching anything that they shall ask, it shall
be done for them."—St. Matt. xviii. 19.

l. 16. *Deep wells of light :* "And he showed me a pure
river of water of life, clear as crystal, proceeding out of
the throne of God."—Rev. xxii. 1.

l. 19. *Shrine :* the innermost sanctuary of Heaven.

l. 20. *Occult :* hidden, especially from the uninitiated.

l. 21. *Lamps :* Rev. iv. 5.

l. 24. *A little cloud :* Rev. v. 8. It was believed that
prayers persisted in Heaven in the form of incense,
which, when the prayers were granted, became perfume
smoke and "melted."

l. 26. *Mystic tree :* the heavenly tree of life, described in
Rev. xxii. 2.

l. 27. *The Dove :* the Holy Ghost.

P. 197, l. 17. *With bound locks :* with hair tied up, not loose.
l. 22. *Born : i.e.* into Heaven.
P. 198, l. 2. *Cithern, citole :* obsolete stringed instruments, like a guitar.

Choruses from " Atalanta in Calydon."

Algernon Charles Swinburne (1837–1909) was born in London, and educated at Eton and Balliol College, Oxford. With " Atalanta in Calydon " (1865) he achieved poetic fame. His poetry shows a matchless command of rhythm and sound, and much of it was inspired by sympathy with the cause of political liberty abroad.

"Atalanta in Calydon," from which these choruses are taken, is a drama in the Greek manner, an "attempt to do something original in English which might in some degree reproduce for English readers the likeness of a Greek tragedy."

P. 198, l. 22. *Mother of months :* the moon.
l. 26–P. 199, l. 2. *Itylus . . . pain :* Itylus, or rather Itys, the child of Procne, whose husband Tereus, king of Thrace, deserted her for her sister Philomela, deceiving both. Discovering the truth, they killed Itys and served up his flesh to Tereus. To save them from the anger of Tereus, the gods changed them, Procne into a swallow, Philomela into a nightingale.
l. 33. *Satyr :* a god of the woods, part man, part goat, and given to all kinds of pleasure.
P. 200, l. 1. *Pan :* chief of the satyrs.
Bacchus : the god of wine.
l. 4. *Mænad, Bassarid :* female followers and frenzied worshippers of Bacchus. They are represented as crowned with vine-leaves.
l. 9. *Ivy :* sacred to Bacchus.
Bacchanal : a worshipper of Bacchus.

The Sacrilege.

Thomas Hardy (1840–1928), born in Dorsetshire, and educated at King's College, London, owed much to his apprenticeship as an architect. The Wessex novels are great architecture in the Greek style ; and, including the great tragedies, " Far from the Madding Crowd " (1874), " The Return of the Native " (1878), " Tess of the D'Urbervilles " (1891), and " Jude the Obscure " (1894), and idylls like " Under the Greenwood Tree "

(1872), they surpass in nobility and simple grandeur of design the body of work done by any other modern English novelist. In 1896, Hardy turned definitely to poetry, and published, besides a great number of short poems, early and later, an epic drama. "The Dynasts." Both novels and poems express, in the lives of rustic characters, the sense of impending Fate, tinged with a universal irony and pity—often mistaken for pessimism. The universe and humanity are in the grasp of the " President of the Immortals," the ironical Fate, against whose sport the protagonists nevertheless strive not unworthily.

Sacrilege : breaking into and stealing from a sacred place.

P. 202, l. 2. *Dunkery :* Dunkery Tor or Beacon, on Exmoor.
　　　Exon Moor : Exmoor.

l. 14. *Priddy :* between Bridgwater and Bristol.

P. 203, l. 3. *Sloe :* the blue-black fruit of the blackthorn.

l. 16. *Marlbury Downs :* west of Bristol.

P. 204, l. 2. *Botchery :* bad or clumsy work.

l. 9. *Rafted :* roused, disturbed.

l. 24. *Fay :* lucky spirit.

l. 25. *One more foul :* an evil spirit.

l. 30. *Mendip :* the range of hills south of Bristol.

P. 205, l. 14. *Toneborough :* Taunton.

l. 16. *Stretched :* hanged.

Elegy.

Robert Bridges (1844–1930) was educated at Eton and Corpus Christi College, Oxford, and studied medicine. In 1913 he was appointed Poet Laureate. His works include various plays, critical essays, and " The Testament of Beauty." His interest in the mechanics of his craft and verse experiment is evident in his study, " Milton's Prosody," and in the exquisite workmanship of his own poetry. On its appearance " The Testament of Beauty " was hailed as likely to become a classic in English poetry.

P. 207, l. 26. *Litter :* a stretcher supporting a couch on which a person may be carried.

P. 208, l. 1. *Tabor :* a kind of drum.

l. 3. *Viol :* an older form of the violin or 'cello.

l. 10. *Stoled :* wearing a stole, or band of silk round the shoulders.

l. 14. *Upstaying :* holding up.

P. 209, l. 10. *Forgetful streams :* Lethe, a river in the lower world, from which the shades of the dead drank and obtained forgetfulness of the past.

The Hound of Heaven.

Francis Thompson (1859–1907), after training for medicine at Owen's College, Manchester, abandoned everything for literature. Reduced to the verge of starvation, he was discovered and adopted by Wilfrid and Alice Meynell. His three volumes, " Poems " (1893), " Sister Songs " (1895), and " New Poems " (1897) established his reputation. His greatest poem is " The Hound of Heaven," an inspired version, in the grand style, of the inner religious life of the troubled soul. For the leading idea of the poem see Psalm cxxxix, 1-12, and St. Augustine, *Confessions*, Book x, chapter vi.

P. 209, l. 24. *Titanic :* gigantic, like the Titans, or early gods.

l. 28. *Instancy :* urgency.

P. 210, l. 10. *Margent :* margin.

l. 26. *Savannahs :* great treeless plains.

l. 29. *Plashy :* watery.

P. 211, l. 15. *Our Lady-Mother :* Nature.

P. 212, l. 29. *Lustihead :* lusty-hood, *i.e.* strength.

P. 213, l. 9. *Amaranthine :* unfading.

l. 34. *Bruit :* rumour, report, sound.

P. 214, l. 2. *Shard :* a broken fragment of pottery.

Lepanto.

Gilbert Keith Chesterton (1874–1936) was born in Kensington and studied at St. Paul's School and the Slade School of Art. He gives the impression of abounding energy and spontaneity, and there is usually sound sense beneath the glitter of his paradox. His work is mainly directed against the narrowness of Puritanism, and finds expression through such various channels as the Father Brown detective stories, historical works, novels, poems, and essays. He has written lively studies of his favourite authors, Dickens, Browning, and Chaucer.

Lepanto : the Gulf of Lepanto is on the west coast of Greece. In 1571, a large fleet, combining the naval forces of the Pope, Venice, and Philip II of Spain, and commanded by Philip's half-brother, Don John of Austria, there defeated and destroyed the main fleet of the Turks.

P. 214, l. 27. *Soldan :* Sultan. Selim II became Sultan in 1567.

Byzantium : the former name of Constantinople.

P. 215, l. 1.   *The inmost sea :* Mediterranean.

l. 2.   *Republics :* Venice, Este, Romagna.

l. 3.   *The Lion of the Sea :* Venice.

ll. 4–5.   *The Pope . . . Cross :* Pope Pius V, in 1570, appealed for help against the Turks, and formed the Holy League with Spain and Venice, on 25th May 1571.

l. 6.   *The cold queen of England . . . :* Elizabeth, noted for her vanity, and her reluctance to marry.

l. 7.   *The shadow of the Valois :* the house of Valois governed France from 1328 till 1589. The ruling monarch in 1571 was Charles IX, a youth of twenty. The real power was in the hands of his mother, Catherine de' Medici, who used religion to serve political ends.

l. 9.   *The Golden Horn :* the harbour on which Constantinople or Byzantium is built.

l. 11.   *A crownless prince :* Don John.

l. 12.   *Half-attainted stall :* Don John was a natural son of the Emperor Charles V. His mother's name is uncertain ; she is generally identified as Barbara Blomberg, daughter of a noble family of Ratisbon.

l. 14.   *Troubadour :* a minstrel or lyric poet (originally of Provence).

l. 21.   *Black-purple . . . old-gold :* " The banner of the Holy League was of blue damask ; in its centre was elaborately wrought the image of our crucified Redeemer ; beneath that sacred effigy were linked together the scutcheon of the Pope, displaying three blood-red bars on a silver field, the lion shield of the Republic of St. Mark, and the shield of many quarterings of the chief of the House of Austria, while, lower still, the design ended in the arms of Don John himself." (Sir W. Stirling-Maxwell.)

l. 23.   *Tucket :* a flourish of trumpets.

P. 216, l. 8.   *Mahound :* Mahomet.

l. 10.   *Houri :* a nymph of the Mohammedan paradise.

l. 11.   *His turban :* said to have woven into it all the colours of the rainbow.

l. 15.   *Azrael :* the Angel of Death.

    Ariel : one of the angels cast out of heaven.

    Ammon : the Libyan Jupiter.

ll. 16–19.   *Genii . . . Solomon was King :* one of the Suleymans is said to have built the Pyramids in the Golden Age.

288

P. 217, l. 5.   *Giaour :* one who does not believe in Mahomet.

l. 7.   *The seal of Solomon :* a magic symbol formed of two interlaced triangles, making a six-pointed star.

l. 10.   *The voice . . . four hundred years ago :* a reference to the third Crusade in 1189, in which Richard I of England played a leading part.

l. 11.   *Kismet :* Fate.

l. 12.   *Raymond :* Count of Toulouse.
    Godfrey : of Bouillon, Duke of Lower Lorraine. Both took part in the first Crusade which captured Jerusalem.

l. 18.   *Iberia :* Spain.

l. 20.   *Alcalar :* Alcalá de Henares, an old walled town near Madrid.   It was the birth-place of Cervantes, who joined Don John's expedition.   Don John attended the University there for two years.

l. 21.   *St. Michael . . . Mountain :* see note to P. 12, l. 12.

P. 218, l. 5.   *Texts :* a reference to religious controversies in England and France.

l. 7.   *A narrow dusty room :* a reference to the murder, in the Huguenot wars, of the Duke of Guise (1563).

ll. 17-23.   *King Philip . . . leprous white and grey :* " In his cabinet at Madrid, or in his closet at the Escorial, he would sit day after day from morning to night over his papers, reading, annotating, and dictating, consulting and hesitating ; . . . Under this course of anxiety and labour he early grew pale and gray, lean and gouty ; but he pursued it to the end, even through the long and agonising sickness which at last carried him off."   (Sir W. Stirling-Maxwell.)

l. 17.   *The Fleece :* a Spanish order, the collar of which was of flints and steels and fire, with the badge—the figure of a ram—suspended from it.

P. 219, l. 2.   *Rumour :* noise.

l. 14.   *Plumèd lions :* lions with wings and the heads of men—the emblem of Venice.

P. 220, l. 4.   *Purpling all the ocean . . . :* " For miles around the victorious fleet the waves . . . were reddened with blood, and were strewed with broken planks, masts, spars, and oars, with men's bodies and limbs, with shields, weapons, turbans, chests, barrels, and cabin furniture, the rich scarf of the knight, the splendid robe of the Pasha, the mighty plume of the janissary, the sordid rags of the slave, and all the various spoils of war."   (Sir W. Stirling-Maxwell.)

l. 8. *Blind for . . . liberty :* " from twelve to fifteen thousand Christian captives were released from labour at the Turkish oar." (S.-M.)

l. 13. *Cervantes :* the greatest Spanish writer, author of " Don Quixote," and then in his twenty-fourth year. " On the morning of the battle he lay sick of a fever. Nevertheless, he rose from his bed and sought and obtained the command of twelve soldiers posted near the long-boat, a position exposed to the hottest of the enemies' fire. He remained there until the combat was over, although he had received two wounds. One of these left him marked with an honourable distinction, the only military distinction ever conferred upon him, the loss of ' the movement of his left hand for the honour of the right.' " (S.-M.)

l. 16. *A lean and foolish Knight :* Don Quixote.

Indignation.

Lascelles Abercrombie (1881–1938) received his education, chiefly scientific, at Manchester, but found his natural bent as lecturer in poetry at the University of Liverpool in 1919, and as Professor of English Literature successively at the Universities of Leeds and London. His philosophical intellect, combined with intense emotion, finds expression equally in poetry and in criticism. Of his critical volumes, " The Theory of Poetry," " Romanticism," and " Thomas Hardy " are the best known. His collected poems, which consist chiefly of " dramatic poems," and of odes like " Indignation," have been issued in the Oxford Poets.

P. 221, l. 26. *Fen :* low marshy land.

P. 222, l. 27. *Hosted nights :* nights preserved or sanctified by the " Host "—the consecrated bread of the Eucharist.

l. 31. *Bale :* evil, destruction.

P. 223, l. 7. *Glebe :* piece of land.

l. 25. *Lime :* a sticky substance used for catching birds.

l. 31. *Pales :* enclosure, limits.

P. 225, l. 13. *Laidly :* loathly.

The Song of Honour.

Ralph Hodgson (*b.* 1871) is best known by poems expressing sympathy for animals, and indignation with those who ill-treat them. " The Bull " is one of his most notable longer poems.

P. 226, l. 20. *Babble-wren :* a tropical bird with a loud chattering note.

P. 227, l. 8. *Sons of Light :* angels ; all things in Nature, that unite in praising God.

 Sire : God.

 l. 21. *Beautysprite :* the spirit of Beauty.

P. 228, l. 8. *Fortune Men :* the kings rise above their fortune (*i.e.* the accident of birth which gives them a throne), and prove themselves Men.

P. 230, l. 9. *The Great Compassion :* God.

Theatre of Varieties.

Aldous Huxley (*b.* 1894) has inherited by descent the methods and interests of the families of Huxley and Arnold—literature, criticism, and science. In his literary and social criticism, where he continues the leading trend and ideas of Matthew Arnold and William James, he lays bare the roots of modern diseases. " Do What you Will " and " Vulgarity in Literature " apply the same critical methods to literary men, as " Point Counter Point " does to society in general. " Jesting Pilate " and " Beyond the Mexique Bay " extend the range to many other parts of the world. His poetry— his chief work is " The Cicadas " (1930)—is more often directed to his inner emotional reactions and crises, and shows the influence of the " symbolist " movement.

P. 232, l. 9. *Hanging gardens :* the " Hanging Gardens " of Babylon, in the grounds of Nebuchadnezzar's palace, were one of the wonders of the ancient world. They rose in terraces, each terrace being supported on arches.

 l. 14. *Quick :* alive.

 l. 18. *Tumblers :* acrobats.

P. 233, l. 3. *Ethiop :* negro.

 l. 20. *Bassoon :* a wooden bass instrument.

 l. 22. *Gargoyle :* a grotesque spout, shaped like the head of some animal, to throw water clear of a wall.

 l. 30. *Trapeze :* a suspended bar on which gymnasts perform.

P. 234, l. 9. *Automaton :* a mechanism imitating human actions.

 l. 10. *Viol :* a mediaeval stringed instrument : a large, deep violin.

 Virginals : a keyed musical instrument of the 16th and 17th centuries.

l. 11. *Ombre, loo, mistigri :* card-games.

    Tric-trac : an old variety of backgammon.

    Pushpin : a child's game, in which each player pushes his pin with the object of crossing that of another player.

l. 12. *Lilliburlero :* a famous 17th-century ballad in mockery of the Irish Catholics.

    Falsetto : a pitch of voice higher than the natural register.

l. 14. *Heydiguy :* a country dance.

l. 28. *Picardy . . . roses :* " Roses of Picardy " was a popular sentimental song during the Great War.

l. 30. *God's . . . limelight eyes :* the lights on the stage.

ll. 34–35. *Divine Zenocrate :* a quotation from Marlowe's "Tamburlaine the Great," Part II, Act II, Sc. iv. Zenocrate is here a symbol of the dominating appeal of idealised female beauty.

P. 235, l. 15. *Feat :* neat.

l. 21. *So every spirit . . . :* from Spenser, *Hymne in Honour of Beautie,* ll. 127 *sqq.*

l. 24. *Dight :* dressed.

P. 236, l. 3. *Urim, Thummim :* two crystals said to have been found by Joseph Smith, the originator of Mormonism (cf. Deut. xxxiii. 8) ; here applied as names.

Tristan da Cunha.

Roy Campbell was born in Durban in 1901, sent to Oxford, travelled in France, lived for a time among the fishermen of Marseilles, married and settled down in a fisherman's cabin in Wales, and later went to Spain. His volumes of poetry include " The Flaming Terrapin " (1924) " Adamastor " (1930), " The Georgiad " (1931), and " Flowering Reeds " (1933). His qualities approximate nearest to Byron's. He has the same rebellious and satiric energy, which informs his poetry with vitality and movement, and the same love of the sea, and a much greater force of metaphor and richness of vocabulary.

Tristan da Cunha : a group of three islands in mid-ocean between South Africa and South America.

P. 236, l. 20. *A giant cinder :* the islands are of volcanic origin.

l. 24. *Pivot your . . . shadow :* with the sun's movement.

P. 237, l. 6. *Wandering birds :* his poems.

l. 7. *Pyre :* a pile of wood, on which a dead body is burned.

l. 10. *Antaeus :* " son of Poseidon (the Sea) and Gē (Earth), a mighty giant, whose strength was invincible so long as he remained in contact with his mother earth. Hercules discovered the source of his strength, lifted him from the earth, and crushed him in the air " (Smith's Class. Dict.).

l. 21. *The masthead :* Tristan, the largest island of the group, has a central cone rising 7640 feet.

l. 27. *Seraphs :* the clouds.

P. 238, l. 1. *Memnon :* a king of the Ethiopians. His statue, when struck by the first rays of the rising sun, was said to give forth a sound like the snapping asunder of a chord.

l. 5. *Syren :* a fog-horn.

l. 7. *Nitre :* salt incrustations, resembling saltpetre in appearance.

Spume : foam.

l. 10. *Tocsin :* an alarm-bell.

l. 25. *Nets of seaweed :* the islands are surrounded by a broad belt of seaweed.

QUESTIONS ON THE POEMS

The Pardoner's Tale.

1. Write an appreciation of Chaucer's personification of Death. Mention similar personifications by other poets, and compare them with Chaucer's (*e.g.* " Death the Leveller ").

2. The theme of this tale is rather unnatural—three men setting out to slay Death. How does Chaucer make it seem natural ?

3. Write a note on Chaucer's narrative power. By what devices is it reinforced ?

4. Point out examples of Chaucer's use of dramatic irony.

5. Compare the characterisation in " The Pardoner's Tale" with that of the " Prologue." Which is more mature?

6. Illustrate the working of " poetic justice " throughout this tale. Compare it in this respect with a tragedy, *e.g.* " Macbeth."

7. Read James Bridie's dramatised version of this tale. Compare it with Chaucer's. Which do you prefer ? Dramatise Chaucer's version yourself.

8. Read the account of the Pardoner in the " Prologue." The Pardoner used to introduce this tale into his sermons. Why ?

9. Draw a picture of " Death " or of the three men and their gold.

Lycidas.

1. Write a short summary of the poem to bring out the main topics treated.

2. Dr. Johnson said that there was neither nature nor truth nor art nor pathos in " Lycidas." Discuss.

3. Compare this elegy with " Adonais " and " Thyrsis " as an expression of the sense of personal loss.

4. What characteristics are generally ascribed to the Puritans ? Milton was a Puritan. How far is " Lycidas " typical of Puritanism ?

5. Comment on (*a*) Milton's mingling of classical with Christian mythology, (*b*) the introduction of St. Peter.

6. What light does " Lycidas," written in 1637, throw on the history of the period ?

7. What is meant by " the pastoral convention ? " Compare Milton's use of it with Arnold's in " Thyrsis," and remark on its effectiveness as a convention.

8. What did Milton think of the poet's vocation ? Compare his view with those of other poets, *e.g.* Wordsworth's in " Resolution and Independence."

9. What information does this poem give of Milton's youth and of his friendship with King at Cambridge University ?

Cymon and Iphigenia.

1. Compare Dryden as a story-teller with Chaucer ; and their use of the heroic couplet as a vehicle for narrative.

2. How far does Dryden succeed in making the characters in this story live ?

3. How could you gather from this poem that Dryden was a satirist ? On whom is his satire chiefly expended ?

4. Contrast this poem with " The Eve of St. Agnes."

5. What opinions and devices show that Dryden lived in an age of wit and reason ?

6. Is Dryden's view of Nature natural or artificial. Illustrate by quotations.

7. What is meant by Poetic Diction ? Illustrate from this poem. Point out any other artificial devices used by Dryden.

The Rape of the Lock.

1. What is meant by calling a poem " mock-heroic " ? Show how this poem deserves the name, *e.g.* how it preserves the heroic pretence and how it introduces the " mock" element. Name other mock-heroic poems in English.

2. Collect instances of Pope's use of (*a*) irony, (*b*) innuendo, (*c*) bathos.

3. What can you tell about Pope's personality from " The Rape of the Lock " ?

4. It was said of Pope that " he turned Pegasus into a rocking-horse " : from an examination of " The Rape of the Lock," would you agree or disagree ? Illustrate your answer from particular couplets.

5. What light does " The Rape of the Lock " throw on the social life of the time ?

6. Write a note on the epithets and similes of " The Rape

of the Lock," and compare, if possible, with Virgil or Homer.

7. Write a note on the supernatural machinery. Compare it with the similar machinery in Homer or Virgil, and discuss its effectiveness for mock-heroic purposes.

The Bard.

1. What is an ode? Compare this ode with that by Prof. Abercrombie (p. 220).

2. Compare " Lycidas " and " The Bard " in their use of (a) the grand style, (b) literary allusions and echoes.

3. Comment on Gray's treatment of history.

4. How does the movement of the verse reflect the moods of the Bard?

5. Write a note on the metre and rhyme-scheme of the first three stanzas.

The Deserted Village.

1. Goldsmith's strength lies in his delineation of character. Illustrate from " The Deserted Village " and compare with " The Vicar of Wakefield."

2. " The Deserted Village " is written in the same metre as " The Rape of the Lock." Contrast the treatment of this metre in these poems.

3. What do you learn from this poem directly or indirectly about Goldsmith? Contrast him with Pope.

4. What do you learn from this poem about the social life of the eighteenth century?

5. Write a description or draw a sketch of (a) Auburn in its deserted state, (b) an evening scene there before it was deserted.

6. Distinguish, in " The Deserted Village," the characteristics that belong to the Age of Prose and Reason and to the Romantic Revival respectively.

7. Draw (a) the schoolmaster in school, (b) the parson at home.

On the Receipt of my Mother's Picture.

1. What information regarding Cowper's life and mind may be derived from this poem?

2. Write a short note on the simile of the ship. Mention, or quote, other poems in which man's course in life is compared to a ship at sea, and compare with Cowper's use of the idea.

3. Compare Cowper's use of the heroic couplet with that of, *e.g.*, Pope or Goldsmith.

4. Cowper is described as a forerunner of " The Return to Nature." Does this poem confirm the description or not ?

Peter Grimes.

1. Compare and contrast " Peter Grimes " with " The Deserted Village " as a picture of English village life.

2. Write a note on the " realism " of Crabbe. Compare " Peter Grimes " as a realistic poem with John Masefield's " The Widow in the Bye Street."

3. How is Crabbe akin to Wordsworth ? Compare the two poets as representatives of " The Return to Nature."

4. Contrast the language of Crabbe with that of Keats or Shelley.

5. Compare Crabbe's use of the heroic couplet with Chaucer's, Goldsmith's, and Pope's.

Lines written above Tintern Abbey.

1. What three main stages in Wordsworth's development are described in this poem ? What was his attitude to Nature and Man during each stage ?

2. Wordsworth called poetry " emotion recollected in tranquillity." How does this poem illustrate Wordsworth's practice of " recollection " ? Compare " The Daffodils."

3. What light does this poem shed on Wordsworth's relations with his sister Dorothy ?

4. How does Wordsworth produce the effect of dignity ? (Consider the use of abstract nouns, the simplicity of the imagery, the length of the sentences, and the variation of the caesura.)

Resolution and Independence.

1. Read Lewis Carroll's parody " I met an aged, aged, man." What weaknesses of Wordsworth are caricatured or shown up in this parody ?

2. Comment on the similes used in this poem. From what source are all derived ? Are they effective ?

3. Why was the poet in need of consolation, and how did he derive it from the leech-gatherer ?

4. Write a note on the metre of the poem.

5. Draw a sketch of the leech-gatherer on the moors.

6. Wordsworth says that his purpose was " to imitate, and, as far as possible, to adopt the very language of men." How far has he succeeded in this poem in writing the ordinary speech of men ?

QUESTIONS ON THE POEMS

7. Write a note on Wordsworth's powers of portraying character. Compare his picture of the Leech-Gatherer with Chaucer's personification of Death in "The Pardoner's Tale."

Christabel.

1. Does "Christabel" realise Coleridge's description of it as an "effective realisation" of the "natural-supernatural"; that is, does it treat the supernatural in such a way as to make it appear natural? Compare Coleridge's treatment with Keats's in "La Belle Dame sans Merci," or Scott's in "The Lay of the Last Minstrel."

2. Would "Christabel" have gained by completion? Consider the probable course of the story (p. 265).

3. Compare the interior in "Christabel" with that in Keats's "Eve of St. Agnes."

4. Write a note on the metre, commenting on Coleridge's explanation (p. 265).

5. Write a note on the style of "Christabel," with special reference to its archaisms.

6. What weaknesses of Coleridge as a poet are illustrated by "Kubla Khan" and "Christabel"?

Adonais.

1. Make a short summary of this poem.

2. What information does "Adonais" furnish about Keats?

3. Write a note on Shelley's use of personification.

4. "Ariel." How is this description of Shelley confirmed by "Adonais."

5. Illustrate from "Adonais" Shelley's aversion to the bodily or physical life, and to physical death. Compare with the similar sentiments in "The Sensitive Plant."

6. Compare and contrast this elegy with "Lycidas" or "Thyrsis."

7. Why is Shelley's poetry difficult to understand?

8. What can be learned from "Adonais" about Shelley's (*a*) political ideals, (*b*) views of contemporary poets?

9. Write a note on the stanza-form of "Adonais." Compare its use by Shelley with the use made of it by Keats and Tennyson.

10. Comment on Shelley's vowel-music and his use of liquid consonants (*l, m, n, r*).

11. Contrast the art of Shelley and Keats.

12. Compare the metaphor of the boat (in the last stanza)

with similar passages in Shelley and Tennyson. How did Shelley meet his death ?

13. What is Shelley's consolation for the death of Keats ?

The Eve of St. Agnes.

1. Write a summary of the story of this poem. What is the value of your summary as a criticism ?

2. Quote examples of Keats's delight in richness of (a) sound, (b) colour, (c) taste.

3. Quote expressive phrases describing (a) music, (b) rapturous joy, (c) drunken sleep, (d) the effect of the wind in the corridors.

4. Write a note on the creation of the atmosphere of cold at the beginning of the poem.

5. Write a note on the metre and its suitability to the subject.

6. Write a note on the music of Keats's poetry.

7. Illustrate from this poem the mediaeval aspect of the Romantic Revival. How does Keats convey the impression of remoteness from modern times ? Compare his poetry in this respect with that of Coleridge and Scott.

The Rubáiyát of Omar Khayyám.

1. " It is wisdom that Omar seeks." Discuss.

2. Compare the Epicureanism of Omar with that of " The Lotos-Eaters."

3. Compare the outlook of Omar with that of (a) Ecclesiastes, (b) Shakespeare's sonnets ("Golden Treasury").

4. Write a note on the Eastern imagery of this poem.

5. Compare the allegory of the potter with that found in Browning's " Rabbi Ben Ezra."

The Lotos-Eaters.

1. Trace the influence of Keats in this poem.

2. Study the details of scenery by which Tennyson builds up the languid atmosphere of the opening picture. Write a note on the metre and rhyme-arrangement of these stanzas and their part in the general effect.

3. Write a note on (a) the vowel-music, (b) the metre, of the final strophe.

4. Arnold applied to Tennyson's style the term " tourmenté "—" forced," " striving after effect." How far do you think this term applicable to the style of " The Lotos-Eaters ? "

5. Summarise the mariners' arguments in favour of remaining in the island.

6. Make a list of poems that glorify the inactive, care-free life.

Ulysses.

1. What is the main theme that Tennyson has taken for this poem from Dante (p. 277) ? What has he added or altered ?

2. What is the Homeric conception of Ulysses ? How does it differ from that used in this poem ?

3. Bring out the contrast between Ulysses and Telemachus.

4. Write a note on the management of the blank verse, and the effects produced.

5. Contrast the attitudes of Ulysses and Telemachus with that of the Lotos-Eaters.

6. What do you gather, from the paragraph on Telemachus, as to Tennyson's views on civilisation ? Confirm and expand these by reference to " Locksley Hall " or other poems of Tennyson.

7. With what imagery does Tennyson produce, in this poem, a sense of romance and mystery ?

To Virgil.

1. Write a note on (*a*) the metre, (*b*) the diction, of this poem.

2. How far does Tennyson's estimate of Virgil apply to himself ?

My Last Duchess.

1. What is a " dramatic monologue " ? Compare Browning's use of it with Tennyson's in " Ulysses." Which is more " dramatic " ?

2. Write a short character-sketch of (*a*) the Duchess, (*b*) her husband.

3. Criticise Browning's style.

Andrea del Sarto.

1. " My stress lay on the incidents in the development of a soul : little else is worth study." Illustrate Browning's statement of his aim by reference to " My Last Duchess " and " Andrea del Sarto."

2. Write a short note on Andrea del Sarto, bringing out his qualities and weaknesses, and the main incidents of his career.

3. Write a character-sketch of Lucrezia.

4. Write a note on the art and morality of the Italian Renascence, as seen by Browning. How far is it confirmed by
other works dealing with the same period, *e.g.* " Romola " ?

Thyrsis.

1. Compare " Thyrsis " with " The Scholar Gipsy " in
(*a*) metre and stanza-form, (*b*) treatment of the Oxford
countryside, (*c*) mood.

2. Arnold professes to deal only with the " idyllic " side
of Clough? How far is " Thyrsis " idyllic? Does it succeed
in realising Arnold's intention ?

3. Arnold speaks of poetry having " natural magic."
Point out adjectives and phrases in which he achieves this
magic in his own descriptions of Nature.

4. Illustrate from " Thyrsis " Arnold's knowledge of
flowers.

5. Write a note on Arnold's use of classical mythology.
Compare " Thyrsis " in this respect with " Lycidas."

6. Express briefly Arnold's (*a*) appreciation, (*b*) criticism,
of Clough.

7. Write a note on Arnold's attitude to (*a*) Oxford,
(*b*) " the world " or contemporary life and society, (*c*) old
age and youth. Confirm your conclusions, if possible, from
Arnold's other writings.

The Blessed Damozel.

1. This has been called " a painter's poem." Illustrate.

2. Write a note on Rossetti's cosmogony. Compare it
with that of, *e.g.*, " Paradise Lost."

3. Write a note on (*a*) the similes, (*b*) the use of proper
names, (*c*) the use of colour, (*d*) the archaisms, (*e*) vowel-
music, in " The Blessed Damozel."

4. The conception of " The Blessed Damozel " is essenti-
ally mediaeval. Illustrate from the poem. What light does
this throw on the Pre-Raphaelites ?

Choruses from " Atalanta in Calydon."

1. Comment on the vowel-music and poetical devices
(*e.g.* alliteration) in these poems. Do they injure the sense ?

2. In the first Chorus : (*a*) Write a note on the rhymes
and stanza-form. (*b*) Mention other English poems on
Spring, and compare their treatment of the subject with
Swinburne's.

3. In the second Chorus : (*a*) Write a note on the view
of life here outlined.

QUESTIONS ON THE POEMS

The Sacrilege.

1. What is "melodrama"? Is "The Sacrilege" melodramatic? Compare it as a tragedy of low life with "The Pardoner's Tale" and "Peter Grimes."

2. Write a note on (a) the use of the refrain, (b) the use of local colour, (c) the style, of this poem.

3. Compare this poem with the theme of any of Hardy's tragic novels. What resemblances and what differences do you find?

4. How is "The Sacrilege" akin to the ballad?

Elegy.

1. Compare this with any of the other elegies in this volume.

2. Write a note on the metre and style of this poem, showing how it combines dignified restraint with sincere emotion.

3. Of what other poet or poets do you find echoes in this elegy? Quote to illustrate.

4. Write a note on the use of classical allusion and ceremonial in this poem.

The Hound of Heaven.

1. Thompson deliberately took the style of Shakespeare's later plays as a model, and tried to catch the rhythm of his blank verse. Point out any passages where this is specially evident.

2. Write a note on the metaphors in this poem, showing how they produce the effect of space.

3. Point out the various symbols used in this poem, and state what each symbolises.

4. Write a note on the stanza-form and the versification.

Lepanto.

1. By what devices of metre and language does "Lepanto" produce (a) a martial, (b) an Eastern, effect? Compare the metrical effects with those of the first Chorus from "Atalanta in Calydon," and the Eastern imagery with that in the "Rubáiyát."

2. Write a note on the use of historical allusions. Compare with the use made in "The Bard."

3. Write a note on the character-sketches (the Sultan, Philip II, Cervantes, etc.) in "Lepanto."

4. Make a list of suggestive phrases in "Lepanto."

5. How does the poet appeal to the ear and the eye?

LONGER POEMS OLD AND NEW

Indignation.

1. What is the general theme of this poem? Give particular instances from the poem, and from your own observation.

2. What special aspects of modern civilisation are attacked in " Indignation "? What ideals does the poet wish to see realised?

3. Write a note on the style of this poem, commenting on (*a*) the use of archaic and dialect words, (*b*) the simplicity of diction, (*c*) the metaphors, (*d*) the compression of language.

4. Compare the attitude of this poem to modern life with that of Wordsworth (Sonnets in " The Golden Treasury "), Matthew Arnold, and Aldous Huxley.

The Song of Honour.

1. Explain and justify the title of this poem.

2. Write a note on (*a*) the style, (*b*) the versification, (*c*) the figures of speech, used in this poem.

3. Compare the poet's optimism with that of Wordsworth, Browning, or Tennyson.

4. Write a note on the poet's appreciation of animals and of men.

Theatre of Varieties.

1. Write a paragraph, working out the metaphor of " the hanging gardens."

2. What insight does this poem give into (*a*) popular entertainments, (*b*) popular songs?

3. Why do people go to variety shows, according to Mr. Huxley?

4. What does Mr. Huxley say of note about (*a*) children, (*b*) music, (*c*) mechanical toys?

5. Write a note on the metre of this poem.

Tristan da Cunha.

1. What do you gather from this poem as to (*a*) the appearance of Tristan da Cunha, (*b*) the life and character of the author?

2. Write a paragraph, working out the comparison and contrast of the poet with Tristan da Cunha.

3. Write a note on (*a*) the metre of the poem, (*b*) the metaphors.

4. The poet has been compared with Byron. What justification is there in this poem for the comparison?

PRINTED BY R. & R. CLARK, LIMITED, EDINBURGH

THE SCHOLAR'S LIBRARY

Complete Texts

ESSAYS IN CRITICISM. Second Series. By MATTHEW ARNOLD. Edited by S. R. LITTLEWOOD.

NORTHANGER ABBEY. By JANE AUSTEN. Edited by Mrs. FREDERICK BOAS. Illustrated by HUGH THOMSON.

A TALE OF TWO CITIES. By CHARLES DICKENS. With an Introduction by G. K. CHESTERTON, and Notes by GUY BOAS, M.A. Illustrated.

FAR FROM THE MADDING CROWD. By THOMAS HARDY. Edited by CYRIL ALDRED.

THE MAYOR OF CASTERBRIDGE. By THOMAS HARDY. Edited by Prof. VIVIAN DE SOLA PINTO.

THE RETURN OF THE NATIVE. By THOMAS HARDY. Edited by CYRIL ALDRED. With an Introduction by SYLVIA LYND.

THE TRUMPET-MAJOR. By THOMAS HARDY. Edited by Mrs. F. S. BOAS.

UNDER THE GREENWOOD TREE. By THOMAS HARDY. Edited by ADRIAN ALINGTON.

THE WOODLANDERS. By THOMAS HARDY. Edited by CYRIL ALDRED.

EOTHEN. By A. W. KINGLAKE. Edited by GUY BOAS, M.A.

PARADISE LOST. Books I. and II. By JOHN MILTON. Edited by G. C. IRWIN, M.A., B.L.S. With an Introduction by GUY BOAS, M.A.

PARADISE LOST. Books IX. and X. By JOHN MILTON. Edited by CYRIL ALDRED.

SHORTER POEMS OF JOHN MILTON. Edited by B. A. WRIGHT.

TREASURE ISLAND. By ROBERT LOUIS STEVENSON. Edited by Mrs. FREDERICK BOAS. Illustrated by H. M. BROCK, R.I.

KIDNAPPED. By ROBERT LOUIS STEVENSON. Edited by JAN STRUTHERS. Illustrated by C. E. BROCK, R.I.

GULLIVER'S TRAVELS : THE FIRST THREE VOYAGES. By JONATHAN SWIFT. Edited by F. E. BUDD, B.A., Ph.D.

Selections : Prose

DR. JOHNSON : A SELECTION FROM BOSWELL'S BIOGRAPHY. Edited by M. ALDERTON PINK, M.A.

EIGHT ESSAYISTS. Selected and Edited by A. S. CAIRNCROSS, M.A., D.Litt.

ENGLISH LIFE IN THE EIGHTEENTH CENTURY. Selected and Edited by G. A. Sambrook.

ENGLISH LIFE IN THE NINETEENTH CENTURY. Selected by G. A. Sambrook.

MODERN ESSAYS IN CRITICISM. Selected and Edited by A. S. Cairncross, M.A., D.Litt.

FACT AND FICTION : An Anthology. Selected and Edited by A. S. Cairncross, M.A., D.Litt.

HOMER : The Iliad and the Odyssey. Extracts from the Translations by Lang, Leaf and Myers, and Butcher and Lang. Edited by H. M. King and H. Spooner.

MODERN ENGLISH PROSE. First Series. Selected and Edited by Guy Boas, M.A.

MODERN ENGLISH PROSE. Second Series. Selected and Edited by Guy Boas, M.A.

MODERN ESSAYS. First Series, 1939–1941. Selected and Edited by A. F. Scott, M.A.

MODERN ESSAYS. Second Series, 1941–1943. Selected and Edited by A. F. Scott, M.A.

MODERN AUTOBIOGRAPHY. An Anthology. Edited by Frederick T. Wood, B.A., Ph.D.

MODERN SHORT STORIES. Edited by A. J. Merson, M.A.

MODERN TRAVEL : An Anthology. Selected and Edited by Frederick T. Wood, B.A., Ph.D.

THE DIARY OF SAMUEL PEPYS : Selections. Edited by N. V. Meeres, B.A.

PROSE OF YESTERDAY : Dickens to Galsworthy. Selected and Edited by Guy Boas, M.A.

AN ANTHOLOGY OF WIT. Selected and Edited by Guy Boas, M.A.

QUEST AND CONQUEST : An Anthology of Personal Adventures. Compiled by E. V. Odle.

READINGS FROM THE SCIENTISTS : An Anthology. Selected and Edited by Edward Mason, M.A., M.Ed.

SHORT MODERN PLAYS. First Series. Selected and Edited by Guy Boas, M.A.

SHORT MODERN PLAYS. Second Series. Selected and Edited by S. R. Littlewood.

READINGS FROM RICHARD JEFFERIES : An Anthology of the Countryside. Chosen by R. Hook, M.A.

" THE TIMES " : An Anthology. Selected and Edited by M. Alderton Pink, M.A.

SHORT STORIES BY OSCAR WILDE. Edited by G. C. Andrews, M.A.

AMERICAN PROSE. Selected and Edited by Guy Boas, M.A.

SHORT HISTORICAL PLAYS. By Modern Authors. Selected and Edited by E. R. Wood.

SELECTIONS FROM THE LETTERS OF HORACE WALPOLE. Edited by M. Alderton Pink, M.A.

Selections : Poetry

MODERN POETRY, 1922–1934 : An Anthology. Selected and Edited by Maurice Wollman, M.A.

POEMS OF TWENTY YEARS : An Anthology, 1918–1938. Selected and Edited by Maurice Wollman, M.A.

POEMS OLD AND NEW : An Anthology. Selected and Edited by A. S. Cairncross, M.A., D.Litt.

MORE POEMS OLD AND NEW : An Anthology. Selected and Edited by A. S. Cairncross, M.A., D.Litt., and J. K. Scobbie, M.A.

LONGER POEMS OLD AND NEW. Selected and Edited by A. S. Cairncross, M.A., D.Litt.

POEMS FOR YOUTH. Selected and Edited by A. S. Cairncross, M.A., D.Litt.

THE AENEID OF VIRGIL. Translated by John Dryden. Selections. Edited by Bruce Pattison, M.A., Ph.D.

Selections : Prose and Poetry

A " PUNCH " ANTHOLOGY. Selected and Edited by Guy Boas, M.A.

STORIES AND POEMS OF THOMAS HARDY. Selected and Edited by N. V. Meeres, B.A.

SELECTIONS FROM SIR W. S. GILBERT. Edited by H. A. Treble, M.A.

COUNTRY LIFE : A Prose and Verse Anthology of Country Life in Great Britain. Selected and Edited by A. F. Scott, M.A.

Shakespeare

ANTONY AND CLEOPATRA. Edited by Guy Boas, M.A.

AS YOU LIKE IT. Edited by Cicely Boas.

CORIOLANUS. Edited by Prof. Vivian de Sola Pinto.

CYMBELINE. Edited by Guy Boas, M.A.

HAMLET. Edited by Adrian Alington.

HENRY IV. Parts I. and II. Edited by M. Alderton Pink, M.A.

HENRY V. Edited by Dorothy Margaret Stuart and E. V. Davenport.

HENRY VIII. Edited by M. St. Clare Byrne. With an Introduction by Guy Boas, M.A.

JULIUS CÆSAR. Edited by F. Allen, M.A.

KING JOHN. Edited by N. V. Meeres.

KING LEAR. Edited by F. E. Budd, B.A., Ph.D.

LOVE'S LABOUR'S LOST. Edited by F. E. Budd, B.A., Ph.D.

MACBETH. Edited by M. Alderton Pink, M.A.

THE MERCHANT OF VENICE. Edited by P. H. B. Lyon, M.A.

A MIDSUMMER-NIGHT'S DREAM. Edited by Cyril Aldred. With an Introduction by Walter de la Mare.

MUCH ADO ABOUT NOTHING. Edited by F. E. Budd, B.A., Ph.D.

OTHELLO. Edited by Guy Boas, M.A.

RICHARD II. Edited by Lionel Aldred. With an Introduction by St. John Ervine.

RICHARD III. Edited by Lionel Aldred.

ROMEO AND JULIET. Edited by Guy Boas, M.A.

THE TEMPEST. Edited by Edward Thompson, M.A., Ph.D.

TWELFTH NIGHT. Edited by N. V. Meeres, B.A.

THE WINTER'S TALE. Edited by Guy Boas, M.A.

MACMILLAN AND CO. LTD., LONDON